AUTODESK® 3DS MAX® 2012

ESSENTIALS

AUTODESK OFFICIAL TRAINING GUIDE

Randi L. Derakhshani
Dariush Derakhshani

WILEY

Wiley Publishing, Inc.

Acquisitions Editor: Mariann Barsolo
Development Editor: Dick Margulis
Technical Editor: Jon McFarland
Production Editor: Dassi Zeidel
Copy Editor: Liz Welch
Editorial Manager: Pete Gaughan
Production Manager: Tim Tate
Vice President and Executive Group Publisher: Richard Swadley
Vice President and Publisher: Neil Edde
Book Designer: Happenstance Type-O-Rama
Compositor: Craig W. Johnson, Happenstance Type-O-Rama
Proofreader: Publication Services, Inc.; Paul Sagan, Word One, New York
Indexer: Ted Laux
Project Coordinator, Cover: Katie Crocker
Cover Designer: Ryan Sneed
Cover Image: Randi L. Derakhshani, Dariush Derakhshani

Copyright © 2011 by Wiley Publishing, Inc., Indianapolis, Indiana
Published simultaneously in Canada
ISBN: 978-1-118-01675-6
ISBN: 978-1-118-11779-8 (ebk.)
ISBN: 978-1-118-11780-4 (ebk.)
ISBN: 978-1-118-11781-1 (ebk.)

For general information on our other products and services or to obtain technical support, please contact our Customer Care Department within the U.S. at (877) 762-2974, outside the U.S. at (317) 572-3993 or fax (317) 572-4002.

Wiley also publishes its books in a variety of electronic formats and by print-on-demand. Not all content that is available in standard print versions of this book may appear or be packaged in all book formats. If you have purchased a version of this book that did not include media that is referenced by or accompanies a standard print version, you may request this media by visiting `http://booksupport.wiley.com`. For more information about Wiley products, visit us at `www.wiley.com`.

Library of Congress Cataloging-in-Publication Data is available from the publisher.

10 9 8 7 6 5 4 3 2 1

Dear Reader,

Thank you for choosing *Autodesk 3ds Max 2012 Essentials*. This book is part of a family of premium-quality Sybex books, all of which are written by outstanding authors who combine practical experience with a gift for teaching.

Sybex was founded in 1976. More than 30 years later, we're still committed to producing consistently exceptional books. With each of our titles, we're working hard to set a new standard for the industry. From the paper we print on, to the authors we work with, our goal is to bring you the best books available.

I hope you see all that reflected in these pages. I'd be very interested to hear your comments and get your feedback on how we're doing. Feel free to let me know what you think about this or any other Sybex book by sending me an email at nedde@wiley.com. If you think you've found a technical error in this book, please visit **http://sybex.custhelp.com**. Customer feedback is critical to our efforts at Sybex.

Best regards,

NEIL EDDE
Vice President and Publisher
Sybex, an Imprint of Wiley

To Max Henry

ACKNOWLEDGMENTS

We are thrilled to be a part of *Autodesk 3ds Max 2012 Essentials*, a complete update and style change to our previous *Introducing 3ds Max* series. Education is an all-important goal in life and should always be approached with eagerness and earnestness. We would like to show appreciation to the teachers who inspired us; you always remember the teachers who touched your life, and to them we say thanks. We would also like to thank all our students, who taught us a lot during the course of our many combined academic years. Equally, we want to extend many thanks to the student artists who contributed to this book, many of whom are our own students from The Art Institute of California—Los Angeles.

Having a good computer system is important with this type of work, so a special thank-you goes to Hewlett-Packard for keeping us on the cutting edge of workstation hardware. Special thanks go to Mariann Barsolo, Dick Margulis, Dassi Zeidel, and Liz Welch, our editors at Wiley who have been professional, courteous, and ever-patient. Our appreciation also goes to technical editors Jon McFarland and Jeff Harper, who worked hard to make sure this book is of the utmost quality, in addition to contributing to the writing of a few chapters. We could not have done this revision without their help.

In addition, thanks to Dariush's mother and brother for their love and support, not to mention the life-saving babysitting services.

—Randi L. Derakhshani, Dariush Derakhshani

About the Authors

Randi Lorene Derakhshani is a staff instructor with The Art Institute of California—Los Angeles. She began working with computer graphics in 1992, and was hired by her instructor to work at Sony Pictures Imageworks, where she developed her skills with 3ds Max and Apple Shake, among many other programs. A teacher since 1999, Randi enjoys sharing her wisdom with young talent and watching them develop at The Art Institute. Currently, she teaches a wide range of classes, from Autodesk 3ds Max to compositing with Apple Shake and Adobe After Effects. Juggling her teaching activities with caring for a little boy makes Randi a pretty busy lady.

Dariush Derakhshani is a visual effects supervisor and Supervisor of Games at Zoic Studios in Culver City, CA, and a writer and educator in Los Angeles, as well as Randi's husband. Dariush used Autodesk's AutoCAD software in his architectural days and migrated to using 3D programs shortly after. Dariush started using Alias PowerAnimator version 6 when he enrolled in the University of Southern California (USC) Film School's Animation program, and he has been using Alias/Autodesk animation software for quite a while. He received an M.F.A. in Film, Video, and Computer Animation from the USC Film School in 1997 and holds a BA in architecture and theater from Lehigh University in Pennsylvania. He has worked on feature films, music videos, game cinematics, and countless commercials as a 3D generalist and CG/VFX supervisor. Dariush also serves as an editor and is on the advisory board of *HDRI 3D*, a professional computer graphics (CG) magazine from DMG Publishing.

CONTENTS AT A GLANCE

Introduction   *xv*

CHAPTER 1   The 3ds Max Interface   1

CHAPTER 2   Your First 3ds Max Project   19

CHAPTER 3   Modeling in 3ds Max: Part I   51

CHAPTER 4   Modeling in 3ds Max: Part II   87

CHAPTER 5   Animating a Bouncing Ball   111

CHAPTER 6   Animating a Thrown Knife   129

CHAPTER 7   Character Poly Modeling: Part I   141

CHAPTER 8   Character Poly Modeling: Part II   165

CHAPTER 9   Character Poly Modeling: Part III   185

CHAPTER 10 Introduction to Materials: Red Rocket   201

CHAPTER 11 Textures and UV Workflow: The Soldier   225

CHAPTER 12 Character Studio: Rigging   255

CHAPTER 13 Character Studio: Animating   275

CHAPTER 14 Introduction to Lighting: Red Rocket   289

CHAPTER 15 3ds Max Rendering   311

CHAPTER 16 mental ray and HDRI   341

Index   *371*

CONTENTS

Introduction   *xv*

CHAPTER 1 **The 3ds Max Interface**   **1**

The Workspace 1
  User Interface Elements. 1
  Viewports 4
  ViewCube 5
  Mouse Buttons 6
  Quad Menus 6
  The Caddy Interface 8
  Display of Objects in a Viewport 8
  Viewport Navigation. 10
Transforming Objects Using Gizmos 11
  Move 11
  Rotate 12
  Scale 12
Graphite Modeling Tools Ribbon 13
Command Panel 13
  Object Parameters and Values. 14
  Modifier Stack 14
  Objects and Subobjects 15
Time Slider and Track Bar 15
File Management 16
  Setting a Project. 16
  Version Up! 17
The Essentials and Beyond. 18

CHAPTER 2 **Your First 3ds Max Project**   **19**

Starting to Model a Chest of Drawers 19
  Ready, Set, Reference! 20
  Ready, Set, Model! 21
Modeling the Top 21
I Can See Your Drawers 28
Modeling the Bottom 33

Creating the Knobs. 42

    Editing the Profile 46

    Copying the Knob 47

The Essentials and Beyond. 49

CHAPTER 3   Modeling in 3ds Max: Part I   51

Building the Red Rocket. 51

Creating Planes and Adding Materials. 52

    Creating the Body 55

    Smoothing the Body 61

    Adding Detail to the Rocket Body 62

    Creating the Wheel Well 64

    Creating the Control Panel 69

    Creating the Back Wheel Axle Assembly. 76

    Further Body Work 79

    Hold On to Your Seat 83

The Essentials and Beyond. 85

CHAPTER 4   Modeling in 3ds Max: Part II   87

Creating the Thruster. 87

    Using Lathe for the Thruster Shape 88

    Creating the 3D Object for the Thruster Detail 91

Making the Wheels 96

    Creating the First Wheel 97

    Placing the Wheels. 99

Getting a Handle on Things. 100

    Creating the Path. 101

    Creating the Shape. 102

    Editing the Loft Object 103

    Adding Detail 105

The Essentials and Beyond. 110

CHAPTER 5   Animating a Bouncing Ball   111

Animating the Ball 111

    Copying Keyframes 113

    Using the Track View–Curve Editor 113

    Reading Animation Curves 116

Refining the Animation 118
  Editing Animation Curves. 118
  Finessing the Animation 120
  Squash and Stretch 120
  Setting the Timing. 121
  Moving the Ball Forward 123
  Adding a Roll 124
  Using the XForm Modifier 125
  Animating the XForm Modifier. 126
The Essentials and Beyond. 128

CHAPTER 6   Animating a Thrown Knife   129

Anticipation and Momentum in Knife Throwing 129
  Blocking Out the Animation 129
  Trajectories. 132
  Adding Rotation 133
  Adding Anticipation 135
  Follow-Through 136
  Transferring Momentum to the Target. 137
  Parent and Child Objects 137
The Essentials and Beyond. 139

CHAPTER 7   Character Poly Modeling: Part I   141

Setting Up the Scene 141
  Creating Planes and Adding Materials 142
  Adding the Materials 143
Creating the Soldier 144
  Forming the Torso 144
  Creating the Arms 154
  Creating the Legs. 158
  Fixing Up the Body. 162
The Essentials and Beyond. 164

CHAPTER 8   Character Poly Modeling: Part II   165

Completing the Main Body. 165
Creating the Accessories. 169
Putting On the Boots 176
Creating the Hands. 180
The Essentials and Beyond. 183

CHAPTER 9 **Character Poly Modeling: Part III** 185

Creating the Head. 185
Merging In and Attaching the Head's Accessories 198
The Essentials and Beyond. 200

CHAPTER 10 **Introduction to Materials: Red Rocket** 201

Materials 201
Compact Material Editor 202
Standard. 203
Shaders. 204
Mapping the Rocket 204
The Wheels. 205
Creating a Multi/Sub-Object Material. 205
Selecting Polygons. 206
Loading the MSO Material into the Material Editor. 207
Fine-tuning the Materials 208
Applying a Bump Map 211
Mapping the Fins: Introduction to Mapping Coordinates 211
The Base Material. 212
Adding the Decal 213
Using a UVW Mapping Modifier. 213
Mapping the Body 216
Creating the Material. 218
Flipping the Decal 218
The Control Panel 221
Bring on the Nose, Bring on the Funk 222
The Essentials and Beyond. 224

CHAPTER 11 **Textures and UV Workflow: The Soldier** 225

Mapping the Soldier 225
UV Unwrapping. 226
Pelting the Left Arm UVs. 233
Pelting the Right Arm UVs 235
Unwrapping and Using Pelt for the Head 236
Seaming the Rest of the Body 240
Unfolding the Rest of the Body 242
Applying the Color Map 248
Applying the Bump Map 249
Applying the Specular Map. 253
The Essentials and Beyond. 254

CHAPTER 12   **Character Studio: Rigging**   **255**

Character Studio Workflow 255
    General Workflow. 256
Associating a Biped with the Soldier Model. 258
    Creating and Modifying the Biped. 258
    Adjusting the Torso and Arms. 263
    Adjusting the Neck and Head 264
    Applying the Physique Modifier. 265
    Controlling the View 268
    Tweaking Physique. 270
The Essentials and Beyond. 273

CHAPTER 13   **Character Studio: Animating**   **275**

Character Animation 275
Animating the Soldier 275
    Adding Freeform Animation 277
    Modifying Animation in the Dope Sheet 282
The Essentials and Beyond. 288

CHAPTER 14   **Introduction to Lighting: Red Rocket**   **289**

Three-Point Lighting 289
3ds Max Lights 290
Default Lights 290
Standard Lights 291
    Target Spotlight 291
    Target Direct Light. 293
    Free Spot or Free Direct Light 294
    Omni Light. 296
Lighting the Red Rocket. 297
Selecting a Shadow Type 301
    Shadow Maps 302
    Raytraced Shadows 303
Atmospheres and Effects 303
    Creating a Volumetric Light 304
    Adding Shadows. 305
    Excluding an Object from a Light 306
    Adding a Volumetric Effect 307
    Volume Light Parameters 308
Light Lister 309
The Essentials and Beyond. 310

CHAPTER 15   **3ds Max Rendering**   **311**

Rendering Setup 311
  Common Tab 312
  Choosing a Filename 313
  Rendered Frame Window. 314
  Render Processing 315
  Assign Renderer 315
  Rendering the Bouncing Ball 316
Cameras. 318
  Creating a Camera 318
  Using Cameras 319
  Talk Is Cheap!. 319
  Animating a Camera 321
  Clipping Planes. 321
Safe Frame 322
Raytraced Reflections and Refractions 323
  Raytrace Material. 323
  Tweaking the Render 324
  Raytrace Mapping. 325
  Refractions Using the Raytrace Material. 326
  Refractions Using Raytrace Mapping 329
Rendering the Rocket 331
  Creating the Camera Move 331
  Adding Raytraced Reflections 334
  Turning On the Environment Effects 337
  Outputting the Render. 338
The Essentials and Beyond. 339

CHAPTER 16   **mental ray and HDRI**   **341**

mental ray Renderer 341
  Enabling the mental ray Renderer 341
  mental ray Sampling Quality 342
Final Gather with mental ray. 344
  Final Gather 344
  mental ray Materials 348
  3ds Max Photometric Lights in mental ray Renderings. 352
  3ds Max Daylight System in mental ray Renderings 358
HDRI 363
The Essentials and Beyond. 369

Index   *371*

INTRODUCTION

Welcome to Autodesk 3ds Max 2012 Essentials. The world of computer-generated imagery (CG) is fun and ever-changing. Whether you are new to CG in general or are a CG veteran new to 3ds Max, you'll find this book the perfect primer. It introduces you to Autodesk 3ds Max and shows how you can work with the program to create your art, whether it is animated or static in design.

This book exposes you to all facets of 3ds Max by introducing and plainly explaining its tools and functions to help you understand how the program operates—but it does not stop there. This book also explains the use of the tools and the ever-critical concepts behind the tools. You'll find hands-on examples and tutorials that give you valuable experience with the toolsets. Working through these will develop your skills and the conceptual knowledge that will carry you to further study with confidence. These tutorials expose you to various ways to accomplish tasks with this intricate and comprehensive artistic tool. These chapters will give you the confidence you need to venture deeper into 3ds Max's feature set, either on your own or by using any of 3ds Max's other learning tools and books as a guide.

Learning to use a powerful tool such as 3ds Max can be frustrating. You need to pace yourself. The major complaints CG book readers have are that the pace is too fast and that the steps are too complicated or overwhelming. Addressing those complaints is a tough nut to crack, to be sure. No two readers are the same. However, this book offers the opportunity to run things at your own pace. The exercises and steps may seem confusing at times, but keep in mind that the more you try and the more you fail at some attempts, the more you will learn how to operate 3ds Max. Experience is king when learning the workflow necessary for *any* software program, and with experience comes failure and aggravation. But try and try again. You will find that further attempts will always be easier and more fruitful.

Above all, however, this book aims to inspire you to use 3ds Max as a creative tool to achieve and explore your own artistic vision.

Who Should Read This Book

Anyone who is interested in learning 3ds Max should start with this book.

If you are an educator, you will find a solid foundation on which to build a new course. You can also treat the book as a source of raw materials that you can adapt to fit an existing curriculum. Written in an open-ended style, *Autodesk 3ds Max 2012 Essentials* contains several self-help tutorials for home study, as well as plenty of material to fit into any class.

If you're interested in certification for 3ds Max 2012, this book can be a great resource to help you prepare. See **www.autodesk.com/certification** for more certification information and resources.

What You Will Learn

You will learn how to work in CG with 3ds Max 2012. The important thing to keep in mind, however, is that this book is merely the beginning of your CG education. With the confidence you will gain from the exercises in this book, and the peace of mind you can have by using this book as a reference, you can go on to create your own increasingly complex CG projects.

What You Need

Hardware changes constantly, and it evolves faster than publications can keep up. Having a good, solid machine is important to a production, although simple home computers will be able to run 3ds Max quite well. Any laptop (with discrete graphics; not a netbook) or desktop PC running Windows XP Professional, Windows Vista, or Windows 7 (32- or 64-bit) with at least 2 GB of RAM and an Intel Pentium Core2 Duo/Quad or AMD Phenom or higher processor will work. Of course, having a good video card will help; you can use any hardware-accelerated OpenGL or Direct3D video card. Your computer system should have at least a 2.4-GHz Core2 or i5/i7 processor with 2 GB of RAM, a few GBs of hard drive space available, and a GeForce FX or ATI Radeon video card. Professionals may want to opt for workstation graphics cards, such as the AMD FirePro or the Nvidia Quadro series of cards. The following systems would be good ones to use:

> ► Intel i7, 4 GB of RAM, Quadro FX 2000, 400-GB 7200-RPM hard disk

> ► AMD Phenom II, 4 GB of RAM, ATI FirePro V5700, 400-GB hard disk

You can check the list of system requirements on Autodesk's website at **www.autodesk.com/3dsmax**.

What Is Covered in This Book

Autodesk 3ds Max 2012 Essentials is organized to provide you with a quick and essential experience with 3ds Max software to allow you to begin a fruitful education in the world of computer graphics.

Chapter 1, "The 3ds Max Interface," begins with an introduction to the interface for 3ds Max 2012 to get you up and running quickly.

Chapter 2, "Your First 3ds Max Project," is an introduction to modeling concepts and workflows in general. It shows you how to model using 3ds Max tools with polygonal meshes and modifiers to create a bedroom dresser.

Chapter 3, "Modeling in 3ds Max: Part I," takes your modeling lesson from Chapter 2 a step further by showing you how to model a complex object, a child's toy rocket.

Chapter 4, "Modeling in 3ds Max: Part II," shows you how to use and add to the tools you learned in Chapter 3 to complete the toy rocket model. You will learn how to loft and lathe objects, as well as how to use Booleans.

Chapter 5, "Animating a Bouncing Ball," shows you the basics of 3ds Max animation techniques and workflow using a bouncing ball. You will also learn how to use the Track View - Curve Editor to time, edit, and finesse your animation.

Chapter 6, "Animating a Thrown Knife," rounds out your animation experience by exploring the animation concepts of weight, follow-through, and anticipation when you animate a knife thrown at a target.

Chapter 7, "Character Poly Modeling: Part I," introduces you to the first of three chapters on creating a low polygon mesh character model of a soldier. In this chapter, you begin by blocking out the primary parts of the body.

Chapter 8, "Character Poly Modeling: Part II," continues the soldier model, focusing on using the Editable Poly toolset. You will finish the body and add hands and boots.

Chapter 9, "Character Poly Modeling: Part III," shows you how to finish the model of the special operations soldier started in Chapter 7. You will create the head and merge in elements such as goggles and a face mask and integrate them into the scene.

Chapter 10, "Introduction to Materials: Red Rocket," shows you how to assign textures and materials to your models. You will learn to texture the toy rocket from Chapter 4, as you learn the basics of working with 3ds Max's materials and UVW mapping.

Chapter 11, "Textures and UV Workflow: The Soldier," furthers your understanding of materials and textures and introduces UV workflows in preparing and texturing the soldier.

Chapter 12, "Character Studio: Rigging," covers the basics of Character Studio in creating a biped system and associating the biped rig to the soldier model.

Chapter 13, "Character Studio: Animating," expands on Chapter 12 to show you how to use Character Studio to create and edit a walk cycle using the soldier model.

Chapter 14, "Introduction to Lighting: Red Rocket," begins by showing you how to light a 3D scene with the three-point lighting system. It then shows you how to use the tools to create and edit 3ds Max lights for illumination, shadows, and special lighting effects. You will light the toy rocket to which you added materials in Chapter 10.

Chapter 15, "3ds Max Rendering," explains how to create image files from your 3ds Max scene and how to achieve the best look for your animation by using proper cameras and rendering settings when you render the toy rocket.

Chapter 16, "mental ray and HDRI," shows you how to render with mental ray. Using Final Gather, you will learn how to use indirect lighting as well as get a brief introduction to HDRI lighting.

The companion web page at **www.sybex.com/go/3dsmax2012essentials**, provides all the sample images, movies, and files that you will need to work through the projects in this book. There you will also find a special downloadable chapter in PDF format, Bonus Chapter 1, "Particles," which introduces you to 3ds Max's particle systems and space warps, tools that come in handy when you create a firing machine gun.

The *Essentials* Series

The *Essentials* series from Sybex provides outstanding instruction for readers who are just beginning to develop their professional skills. Every *Essentials* book includes these features:

- ▶ Skill-based instruction with chapters organized around projects rather than abstract concepts or subjects.

- ▶ Suggestions for additional exercises at the end of each chapter, where you can practice and extend your skills.

- ▶ Digital files (via download) so you can work through the project tutorials yourself. Please check the book's web page at **www.sybex.com/ go/3dsmax2012essentials** for these companion downloads.

You can contact the authors through Wiley or on Facebook at **www.facebook .com/3dsMaxEssentials**.

CHAPTER 1

The 3ds Max Interface

This chapter explains the 3ds Max interface and its basic operation. You can use this chapter as a reference as you work through the rest of this book, although the following chapters and their exercises will orient you to the 3ds Max user interface (UI) quickly. It's important to be in front of your computer when you read this chapter, so you can try out techniques as we discuss them in the book.

Topics in this chapter include the following:

▶ **The workspace**

▶ **Transforming objects using gizmos**

▶ **Graphite Modeling Tools ribbon**

▶ **Command panel**

▶ **Time slider and track bar**

▶ **File management**

The Workspace

This section presents a brief rundown of what you need to know about the UI and how to navigate in 3ds Max's 3D workspace.

User Interface Elements

Figure 1.1 shows the 3ds Max UI. At the very top left of the application window is a large button (⑤) called Application; clicking it opens the Application menu, which provides access to many file operations. Also running along the top is the Quick Access toolbar, which provides access to common commands, and the InfoCenter, which offers support for various Autodesk applications.

Some of the most important commands in the Quick Access toolbar are file management commands such as Save File and Open File. If you do something and then wish you hadn't, you can click the Undo Scene Operation icon ( ) or press Ctrl+Z. To redo a command or action that you just undid, click the Redo Scene Operation button ( ) or press Ctrl+Y.

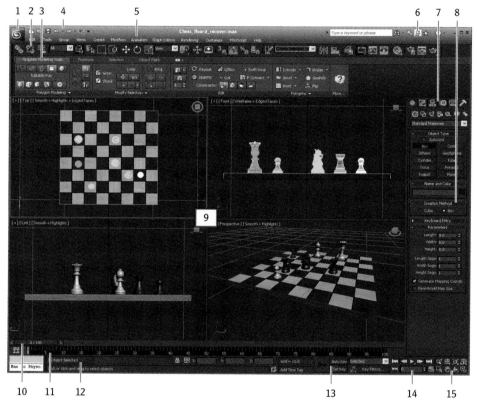

FIGURE 1.1 3DS Max interface elements

1	Application button	Opens Application menu that provides file management commands.
2	Main toolbar	Provides quick access to tools and dialog boxes for many of the most common tasks.
3	Graphite Modeling Tools ribbon	Provides access to a wide range of tools to make building and editing models in 3ds Max fast and easy.

4	Quick Access toolbar	Provides some of the most commonly used file management commands, as well as Undo and Redo.
5	Menu bar	Provides access to commands grouped by category.
6	InfoCenter	Provides access to information about 3ds Max and other Autodesk products.
7	Command panel tabs	Where all the editing of parameters occurs; provides access to many functions and creation options; divided into tabs that access different panels, such as Creation pane, Modify panel, etc.
8	Rollout	A section of the Command panel that can expand to show a listing of parameters or collapse to just its heading name.
9	Viewports	You can choose different views to display in these four viewports as well as different layouts from the viewport label menus.
10	Time slider	Shows the current frame and allows for changing the current frame by moving (or scrubbing) the time bar.
11	Track bar	Provides a timeline showing the frame numbers; select an object to view its animation keys on the track bar.
12	Prompt line and status bar controls	Prompt and status information about your scene and the active command.
13	Coordinate display area	Allows you to enter transformation values.
14	Animation keying controls	Animation playback controls.
15	Viewport navigation controls	Icons that control the display and navigation of the viewports; icons may change depending on the active viewport.

Just below the Quick Access toolbar is the menu bar, which runs across the top of the UI. The menus give you access to a ton of commands—from basic scene operations, such as Undo under the Edit menu, to advanced tools such as those found under the Modifiers menu. Immediately below the menu bar is the Main toolbar. It contains several icons for functions such as the three Transform tools: Move, Rotate, and Scale (⊕ ○ ▥).

When you first open 3ds Max, the workspace has many UI elements. Each is designed to help you work with your models, access tools, and edit object parameters.

Viewports

You'll be doing most of your work in the viewports. These windows represent 3D space using a system based on Cartesian coordinates. That is a fancy way of saying "space on X, Y, and Z axes."

You can visualize X as left–right, Y as up–down, and Z as in–out (into and out of the screen from the Top viewport). The coordinates are expressed as a set of three numbers such as (0, 3, –7). These coordinates represent a point that is at 0 on the X axis, 3 units up on the Y axis, and 7 units back on the Z axis.

Four-Viewport Layout

3ds Max's viewports are the windows into your scene. By default, there are four main views: front, top, left, and perspective. The first three—front, top, and left—are called orthographic (2D) views. They are also referred to as modeling windows. These windows are good for expressing exact dimensions and size relationships, so they are good tools for sizing up your scene objects and fine-tuning their layout. The General viewport label menu (▣) in the upper-left corner of each viewport provides options for overall viewport display or activation as shown in Figure 1.2. It also gives you access to the Viewport Configuration dialog box.

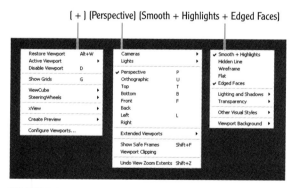

FIGURE 1.2 Viewport label menu

The perspective viewport displays objects in 3D space using perspective. Notice in Figure 1.1 how the distant objects seem to get smaller in the perspective viewport. In actuality, they are the same size, as you can see in the orthographic viewports. The perspective viewport gives you the best representation of what your output will be.

To select a viewport, click in a blank part of the viewport (not on an object). If you do have something selected, it will be deselected when you click in the blank space. You can also right-click anywhere in an inactive viewport to activate it without selecting or deselecting anything. When active, the view will have a mustard yellow highlight around it. If you right-click in an already active viewport, you will get a pop-up context menu called the *quad menu*. You can use the quad menu to access some basic commands for a faster workflow. We will cover this topic in the section "Quad Menus" later in this chapter.

ViewCube

The ViewCube navigation control, shown in Figure 1.3, provides visual feedback of the current orientation of a viewport, lets you adjust the view orientation, and allows you to switch between standard and isometric views.

Home button
resets viewport
to the home view.

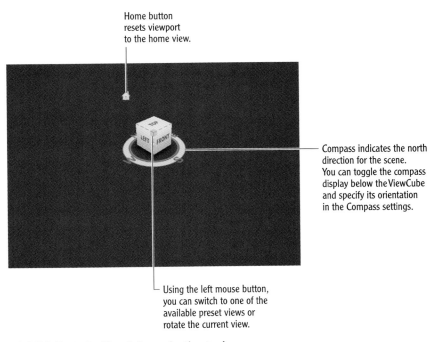

Compass indicates the north
direction for the scene.
You can toggle the compass
display below the ViewCube
and specify its orientation
in the Compass settings.

Using the left mouse button,
you can switch to one of the
available preset views or
rotate the current view.

FIGURE 1.3 ViewCube navigation tool

The ViewCube is displayed by default in the upper-right corner of the active viewport, superimposed over the scene in an inactive state to show the orientation of the scene. It does not appear in camera or light views. When you position your cursor over the ViewCube, it becomes active. Using the left mouse button, you can switch to one of the available preset views, rotate the current view, or change to the home view of the model. Right-clicking opens a context menu with additional options.

Mouse Buttons

Each of the three buttons on your mouse plays a slightly different role when manipulating viewports in the workspace. When used with modifiers such as the Alt key, they are used to navigate your scene, as shown in Figure 1.4.

Right mouse button opens
the quad menu. Specialized
quad menus become
available when you press
any combination of
Shift, Ctrl, and Alt while
right-clicking in any
standard viewport.

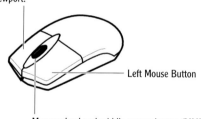

Left Mouse Button

Mouse wheel and middle mouse button (MMB).
Use wheel for zooming. Use MMB to pan,
Alt+MMB for arc rotate, Ctrl+Alt+MMB for
slow zoom.

FIGURE 1.4 Breakdown of the three computer mouse buttons

Quad Menus

When you click the right mouse button anywhere in an active viewport, except on the viewport label, a quad menu is displayed at the location of the mouse cursor (see Figure 1.5). The quad menu can display up to four quadrant areas with various commands without your having to travel back and forth between the viewport and rollouts on the Command panel (the area of the UI to the right—more on this later in the section "Command Panel").

The two right quadrants of the default quad menu display generic commands, which are shared between all objects. The two left quadrants contain context-specific commands, such as mesh tools and light commands. You can also repeat your last quad menu command by clicking the title of the quadrant.

The quad menu contents depend on what is selected. The menus are set up to display only the commands that are available for the current selection; therefore, selecting different types of objects displays different commands in the quadrants. Consequently, if no object is selected, all of the object-specific commands will be hidden. If all of the commands for one quadrant are hidden, the quadrant will not be displayed.

Cascading menus display submenus in the same manner as a right-click menu. The menu item that contains submenus is highlighted when expanded. The submenus are highlighted when you move the mouse cursor over them.

Some of the selections in the quad menu have a small icon next to them. Clicking this icon opens a dialog box where you can set parameters for the command.

To close the menu, right-click anywhere on the screen or move the mouse cursor away from the menu and click the left mouse button. To reselect the last selected command, click in the title of the quadrant of the last menu item. The last menu item selected is highlighted when the quadrant is displayed.

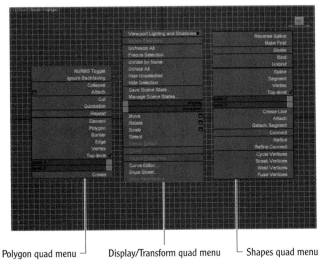

Polygon quad menu — Display/Transform quad menu — Shapes quad menu

FIGURE 1.5 Quad menus

The Caddy Interface

Like the quad menu, the new caddy interface is designed to keep your eyes in the viewports while providing context-sensitive tools. The caddies replace the Settings dialog boxes available in previous versions of 3ds Max. Depending on the tool, clicking the Settings button (identified as a small arrow below the name of the tool) displays the tool-specific caddy directly over the selected objects or subobjects. Figure 1.6 shows the Extrude Polygons caddy. Each tool's caddy is slightly different and may include more than one parameter.

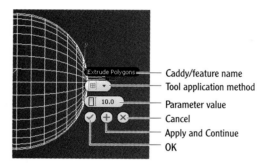

FIGURE 1.6 **The Extrude Polygons caddy**

Pausing your cursor over any of the highlighted features changes the caddy title to reflect the name of that feature. Clicking a feature with a down arrow opens a drop-down menu where you can choose an option. There are three methods for executing the changes in a caddy: OK, Apply And Continue, and Cancel. Clicking OK applies the parameter values set and then closes the caddy. Clicking Apply And Continue applies the parameter values but keeps the caddy open. Clicking Cancel terminates the command.

Display of Objects in a Viewport

Viewports can display your scene objects in a few ways. If you click the viewport's name, you can switch that panel to any other viewport angle or point of view. If you click the viewport display mode, a menu appears to allow you to change the display mode. The display mode names differ depending on the graphics drive mode you selected when starting 3ds Max. This book uses the display modes with Direct3D driver mode selected. If you use the recommended graphics driver mode Nitrous, you will find slightly different names for the viewport display modes.

The most common view modes are Wireframe mode and Smooth + Highlights mode (called Realistic in Nitrous driver mode). Wireframe mode displays the edges of the object. It is the fastest to use because it requires less computation on your video card. The Smooth + Highlights mode is a shaded view where the objects in the scene appear solid (see Figure 1.7).

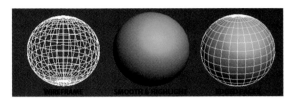

FIGURE 1.7 Viewport rendering options with Direct3D or OpenGL driver modes

Each viewport displays a ground plane grid (as shown in the perspective viewport), called the *Home Grid*. This is the basic 3D-space reference system where the X axis is red, the Y axis is green, and the Z axis is blue. It's defined by three fixed planes on the coordinate axes (X, Y, Z). The center of all three axes is called the origin, where the coordinates are (0, 0, 0). The Home Grid is visible in 3ds Max's default settings when you start the software, but it can be turned off in the right-click viewport menu or by pressing the G key.

Selecting Objects in a Viewport

Click an object to select it in a viewport. If the object is displayed in Wireframe mode, its wireframe turns white while it is selected. If the object is displayed in a Shaded mode, a white bracket appears around the object.

To select multiple objects, hold down the Ctrl key as you click additional objects to add to your selection. If you Alt+click an active object, you will deselect it. You can clear all your active selections by clicking in an empty area of the viewport.

Changing/Maximizing the Viewports

To change the view in any given viewport—for example, to go from a perspective view to a front view—click the current viewport's name. From the menu, select the view you want to have in the selected viewport. You can also use keyboard shortcuts. To switch from one view to another, press the appropriate key on the keyboard, as shown in Table 1.1.

TABLE 1.1 Viewport shortcuts

Viewport	Keyboard shortcut
Top view	T
Bottom view	B
Front view	F
Left view	L
Camera view	C
Orthographic	U
Perspective view	P

If you want to have a larger view of the active viewport than is provided by the default four-viewport layout, click the Maximize Viewport Toggle icon (▣) in the lower-right corner of the 3ds Max window. You can also use the Alt+W keyboard shortcut to toggle between the maximized and four-viewport views.

Viewport Navigation

3ds Max allows you to move around its viewports either by using key/mouse combinations, which are highly preferable, or by using the viewport controls found in the lower-right corner of the 3ds Max UI. An example of navigation icons is shown for the Top viewport in Figure 1.8, though it's best to become familiar with the key/mouse combinations.

FIGURE 1.8 Viewport navigation controls are handy, but the mouse keyboard combinations are much faster to use for navigation in viewports.

Open a new, empty scene in 3ds Max. Experiment with the following controls to get a feel for moving around in 3D space. If you are new to 3D, using these controls may seem odd at first, but it will become easier as you gain experience and should become second nature in no time.

Pan   Panning a viewport slides the view around the screen. Using the middle mouse button (MMB), click in the viewport and drag the mouse pointer to pan the view.

Zoom   Zooming moves your view closer to or farther away from your objects. To zoom, press Ctrl+Alt and MMB+click in your viewport, and then drag the mouse up or down to zoom in or out, respectively. You may also use the scroll wheel to zoom.

Orbit   Orbit will rotate your view around your objects. To orbit, press Alt and MMB+click and drag in the viewport. By default, Max will rotate about the center of the viewport.

Transforming Objects Using Gizmos

Using gizmos is a fast and effective way to transform (move, rotate, and/or scale) your objects with interactive feedback. When you select a transform tool such as Move, a gizmo appears on the selected object. Gizmos let you manipulate objects in your viewports interactively to transform them. Coordinate display boxes at the bottom of the screen display coordinate or angular or percentage information on the position, rotation, and scale of your object as you transform it. The gizmos appear in the viewport on the selected object at their pivot point as soon as you invoke one of the transform tools, as shown in Figure 1.9.

You can select the transform tools by clicking the icons in the Main toolbar's Transform toolset (⬛⭕⬛) or by invoking shortcut keys: W for Move, E for Rotate, and R for Scale. In a new scene, create a sphere by choosing Create ➢ Standard Primitives ➢ Sphere. In a viewport, click and drag to create the sphere object. Follow along as we explain the transform tools next.

Move

Invoke the Move tool by pressing W (or accessing it through the Main toolbar), and your gizmo should look like the top image in Figure 1.9. Dragging the *XYZ* axis handles moves an object on that specific axis. You can also click on the plane handle, the box between two axes, to move the object in that two-axis plane.

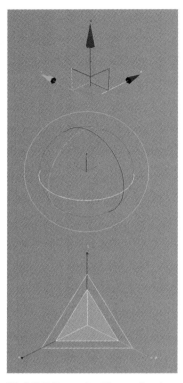

Move Gizmo
Use a colored handle to move
in just that axis.

Rotate Gizmo
Use the colored rings to
rotate about a single axis.
Use the center to rotate
freely.

Scale Gizmo
Drag in the center of the
gizmo to scale uniformly.
To perform non-uniform scaling,
drag on a colored handle.

FIGURE 1.9 Gizmos for the transform tools

Rotate

Invoke the Rotate tool by pressing E, and your gizmo will turn into three circles, as shown in the middle image in Figure 1.9. You can click on one of the colored circles to rotate the object on the axis only, or you can click anywhere between the circles to freely rotate the selected object in all three axes.

Scale

Invoke the Scale tool by pressing the R key, and your gizmo will turn into a triangle, as shown in the bottom of Figure 1.9. Clicking and dragging anywhere inside the yellow triangle will scale the object uniformly on all three axes. By selecting the red, green, or blue handles for the appropriate axis, you can scale along one axis only. You can also scale an object on a plane between two axes by selecting the side of the yellow triangle between two axes.

Graphite Modeling Tools Ribbon

The Graphite Modeling Tools (also called the Graphite Modeling Tools ribbon) is a section of the UI directly under the main toolbar (as you saw earlier in Figure 1.1). The Graphite Modeling Tools ribbon provides you with a wide range of tools to make building and editing models in 3ds Max fast and easy. All the available tools are divided into tabs that are organized by function, and then further divided into panels. For example, the Graphite Modeling Tools tab contains the tools you use most often for polygon modeling and editing, organized into separate panels for easy, convenient access. In the following chapters, you will make copious use of the Graphite Modeling Tools (see Figure 1.10).

FIGURE 1.10 The Graphite Modeling Tools ribbon

The panels found in the Polygon Modeling tab are:

▶ Polygon Modeling panel

▶ Modify Selection panel

▶ Edit panel

▶ Geometry (All) panel

▶ [Subobject] panel

▶ Loops panel

▶ Additional panels

Command Panel

Everything you need to create, manipulate, and animate objects can be found in the Command panel running vertically on the right side of the UI (Figure 1.1). The Command panel is divided into tabs according to function. The function or toolset you need to access will determine which tab you need to click. When you encounter a panel that is longer than your screen, 3ds Max displays a thin vertical scroll bar on the right side. Your cursor also turns into a hand that lets you click and drag the panel up and down.

You will be exposed to more panels as you progress through this book. Table 1.2 is a rundown of the Command panel functions and what they do.

TABLE 1.2 Command panel functions

Icon	Name	Function
⬚	Create panel	Lets you create objects, lights, cameras, etc.
⬚	Modify panel	Lets you apply and edit modifiers to objects
⬚	Hierarchy panel	Lets you adjust the hierarchy for objects and adjust their pivot points
⬚	Motion panel	Lets you access animation tools and functions
⬚	Display panel	Lets you access display options for scene objects
⬚	Utilities panel	Lets you access several functions of 3ds Max, such as motion capture utilities and the Asset Browser

Object Parameters and Values

The Command panel and all its tabs give you access to an object's parameters. Parameters are the values that define a specific attribute of or for that object. For example, when an object is selected in a viewport, its parameters are shown in the Modify panel, where you can adjust them. When you create an object, that object's creation parameters are shown (and editable) in the Create panel.

Modifier Stack

In the Modify panel you'll find the modifier stack (Figure 1.11). This UI element lists all the modifiers that are active on any selected object. Modifiers are actions applied to an object that change it somehow, such as bending or warping. You can stack modifiers on top of each other when creating an object and then go back and edit any of the modifiers in the stack (for the most part) to adjust the object at any point in its creation. You will see this in practice in the following chapters.

FIGURE 1.11
The modifier stack in
the Modify panel

Objects and Subobjects

An object or mesh in 3ds Max is composed of polygons that define the surface. For example, the facets or small rectangles on a sphere are *polygons*, all connected at common edges at the correct angles and in the proper arrangement to make a sphere. The points that generate a polygon are called *vertices*. The lines that connect the points are called *edges*. Polygons, vertices, and edges are examples of subobjects and are all editable so that you can fashion any sort of surface or mesh shape you wish.

To edit these subobjects, you have to convert the object to an editable polygon, which you will learn how to do in the following chapters.

Time Slider and Track Bar

Running across the bottom of the 3ds Max UI are the time slider and the track bar, as shown earlier in Figure 1.1. The time slider allows you to move through any frame in your scene by scrubbing (moving the slider back and forth). You can move through your animation one frame at a time by clicking on the arrows on either side of the time slider or by pressing the < and > keys.

You can also use the time slider to animate objects by setting keyframes. With an object selected, right-click on the time slider to open the Create Key dialog box, which allows you to create transform keyframes for the selected object.

The track bar is directly below the time slider. The track bar is the timeline that displays the timeline format for your scene. More often than not, the track bar is displayed in frames, with the gap between each tick mark representing frames. On the track bar, you can move and edit your animation properties for the selected object. When a keyframe is present, right-click it to open a context menu where you can delete keyframes, edit individual transform values, and filter the track bar display.

The Animation Playback controls in the lower right of the 3ds Max UI ( ) are similar to the ones you would find on a VCR (how old are you?) or DVD player.

File Management

3ds Max provides several subfolders automatically grouped into projects for you. Different kinds of files are saved in categorized folders under the project folder. For example, scene files are saved in a Scenes folder and rendered images are saved in a Render Output folder within the project folder. The projects are set up according to what types of files you are working on, so everything is neat and organized from the get-go. 3ds Max automatically creates this folder structure for you once you create a new project, and its default settings keep the files organized in that manner.

The conventions followed in this book and on the accompanying web page (www.sybex.com/go/3dsmax2012essentials) follow this project-based system so that you can grow accustomed to it and make it a part of your own workflow. It pays to stay organized.

Setting a Project

The exercises in this book are organized into specific projects such as Dresser, the one you will tackle in the next chapter. The Dresser project will be on your hard drive, and the folders for your scene files and rendered images will be in that project layout. Once you copy the appropriate projects to your hard drive, you can tell 3ds Max which project to work on by choosing Application ➤ Manage ➤ Set Project Folder. Doing so will send the current project to that project folder. For example, when you save your scene, 3ds Max will automatically take you to the Scenes folder of the current project.

Designating a specific place on your PC or server for all your project files is important, as is having an established naming convention for its files and folder.

For example, if you are working on a project about a castle, begin by setting a new project called Castle. Choose Application ➢ Manage ➢ Set Project Folder, as shown in Figure 1.12. In the dialog box, click Make New Folder to create a folder named **Castle** on your hard drive. 3ds Max will automatically create the project and its folders.

FIGURE 1.12 Choosing Set Project Folder

Once you save a scene, one of your scene filenames should look like this: Castle_GateModel_v05.max. This tells you right away it's a scene from your Castle project and that it is a model of the gate. The version number tells you that it's the fifth iteration of the model and possibly the most recent version. Following a naming convention will save you oodles of time and aggravation.

Version Up!

After you've spent a significant amount of time working on your scene, you will want to *version up*. This means you save your file using the same name, but you increase the version number by 1. Saving often and using version numbers are useful for keeping track of your progress and protecting yourself from mistakes and from losing your work.

To version up, you can save by selecting Application ➢ Save As and manually changing the version number appended to the end of the filename. 3ds Max also lets you do this automatically by using an increment feature in the Save As dialog box. Name your scene file and click the Increment button (the + icon) to the right of the filename text. Clicking the Increment button appends the filename with 01, then 02, then 03, and so on as you keep saving your work using Save As and the Increment button.

THE ESSENTIALS AND BEYOND

In this chapter you learned about the interface and how to navigate 3d space in 3ds Max. As you continue with the following chapters, you will gain experience and confidence with the UI, and many of the features that seem daunting to you now will become second nature.

ADDITIONAL EXERCISES

▶ From the Create panel, choose Standard Primitives and create each one of the primitives. Pay attention to each object's parameters to get familiar with what each object is capable of.

▶ Explore the viewport labels for rendering types and changing viewports.

▶ Convert each primitive to an editable polygon and, using the selection tools, practice selecting and deselecting vertices, edges, and polygons.

CHAPTER 2

Your First 3ds Max Project

Modeling in 3D programs is akin to sculpting or carpentry; you create objects out of shapes and forms. Even a complex model is just an amalgam of simpler parts. The successful modeler can dissect a form down to its components and translate them into surfaces and meshes.

3ds Max's modeling tools are incredibly strong for polygonal modeling. The focus of the modeling in this book is polygonal modeling because the majority of 3ds Max models are created with polygons. In addition to mechanical models, you will model an organic low polygon count model—a soldier fit for a game—and use that model to animate a character with Character Studio.

In this chapter, you will learn modeling concepts and how to use 3ds Max modeling toolsets. You will also tackle a model to get a sense of a workflow using 3ds Max.

Topics in this chapter include the following:

▶ **Starting to model a chest of drawers**

▶ **Modeling the top**

▶ **I can see your drawers**

▶ **Modeling the bottom**

▶ **Creating the knobs**

Starting to Model a Chest of Drawers

Begin by modeling a chest of drawers (or dresser) to develop your modeling muscles. This exercise introduces you to primitives and polygons. You will be modeling by editing the polygon component, called *editable-poly* modeling. Why buy a chest of drawers when you can just make one in 3ds Max? Be sure you make it large enough for all your socks.

Ready, Set, Reference!

You're so close to modeling something! You'll want to get some sort of reference for what you're modeling. Study the photo in Figure 2.1 for a look at the desired result.

There are plenty of reference photos to help you build different parts of the chest. You may want to flip through the pictures on the following pages to get a better idea of what you will be modeling.

Of course, if this were your chest of drawers, you could have captured tons of pictures already, right?

FIGURE 2.1 Model this chest of drawers.

Ready, Set, Model!

Create a project called Dresser, or download the Dresser project, Dresser.zip, from the companion web page directly to your hard drive.

Modeling the Top

To begin modeling the chest of drawers, follow these steps:

1. Begin with a new scene (choose Application ≻ New ≻ New All, and then click OK in the New Scene dialog box).

2. Select the Perspective viewport, which is set to Smooth + Highlights display mode by default. Enable Edged Faces mode in the viewport by moving the cursor to Viewport Labels in the upper left and clicking Smooth + Highlights. This opens a drop-down menu. Choose Edged Faces. This shows the wireframe edges of the object. (Or use the keyboard shortcut F4 to toggle Edged Faces on or off.)

3. In the Command panel, choose the Create tab ( ), click the Geometry icon, and make sure Standard Primitives is selected. In the Object Type rollout, click Box. You are going to create a box using the Keyboard Entry rollout shown in Figure 2.2. These options allow you to specify the exact size and location to create an object in your scene.

4. Leave the *X*, *Y*, and *Z* values at 0, but enter these values: Length of **15**, Width of **30**, and Height of **40**. Click Create to create a box aligned in the center of the scene with the specified dimensions.

FIGURE 2.2
Keyboard Entry rollout

3ds Max gives you the option of a few display drivers. While nitrous is default, this book uses Direct3D driver set. Some of the screens may be slightly different from yours if you run 3ds Max with the nitrous driver. For example, the viewport display option "Smooth + Highlights" will display as "Realistic" under the nitrous display.

5. With the box still selected, go to the Modify tab (▣). You can see the box's parameters here. You will need to add more height segments, so change the Height Segs parameter to **6**. Your box should look like the one in Figure 2.3.

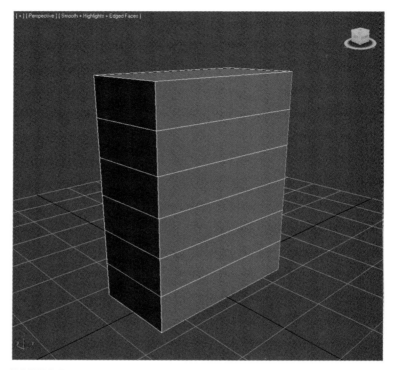

FIGURE 2.3 The box from which a beautiful chest of drawers will emerge

6. To start the process of using the Graphite modeling tools, we will convert the box to an editable poly. Below the main toolbar and in the Graphite Modeling Tools ribbon, click the Polygon Modeling tab. This expands and you see the Convert To Poly button. Click it, as shown in Figure 2.4.

7. Also in the top of the Polygon Modeling tab you see a line of icons (top of Figure 2.5). These are the components, or subobjects, of your object. Click the Polygon icon (▣) or use the keyboard shortcut by pressing 4 to enter the Polygon subobject mode. Now select the polygon on the top of the box. As you can see in the viewport, the polygon is shaded red when it's selected.

FIGURE 2.4
Convert the box to an
editable poly.

8. In the Polygons tab in the Graphite Modeling Tools ribbon, click the
small arrow below the Bevel button, and then click the Bevel Settings
button, which opens the Bevel caddy controls (Figure 2.5). In the following steps, we are going to bevel several times to create the lip on
the crown of the dresser shown in Figure 2.6.

FIGURE 2.5
Bevel caddy controls

FIGURE 2.6 **The lip of the real dresser**

9. In the text boxes of the Bevel caddy, enter the following parameters: Height: **0.5** and Outline: **1.3**. Keep Bevel Type (the top button in the caddy) set to Group. Click Apply And Continue (⊕); 3ds Max applies the specified settings, without closing the caddy, to give you results that should be similar to Figure 2.7.

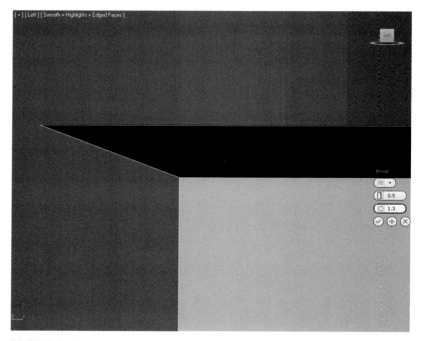

FIGURE 2.7 The first bevel for the crown of the dresser

10. In the still open Bevel caddy, input these parameters: Height: **0.3** and Outline: **0** (as shown in Figure 2.8). Click Apply And Continue.

11. For the last bevel, input the following values: Height: **0.1** and Outline: **-0.03**. Click OK (⊘). Your dresser's top should resemble Figure 2.9.

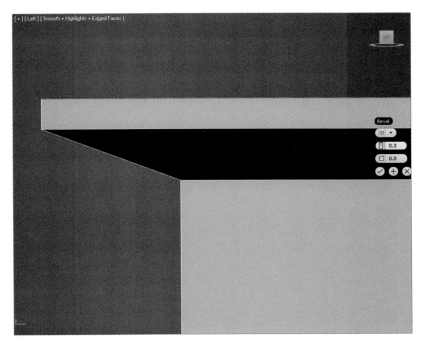

FIGURE 2.8 The second bevel

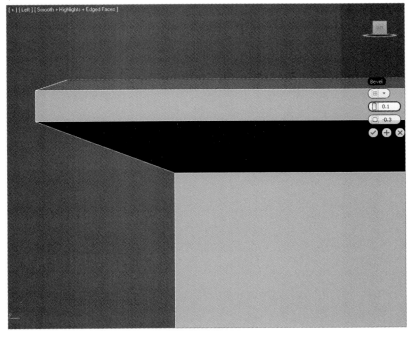

FIGURE 2.9 This shows a rough version of the dresser's crown.

12. Click the Edge icon (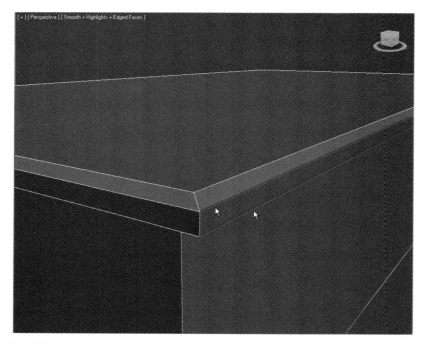) in the Polygon Modeling tab on the Graphite Modeling ribbon or press 2 on your keyboard to enter the Edge subobject mode. Select the two new edges that were created with the bevel, as shown in red in Figure 2.10.

FIGURE 2.10 Select these two edges.

13. Go to the Graphite Modeling Tools ribbon and in the Modify tab click the Loop tool. This selects an edge loop based on your current subobject selection. An edge loop is essentially edges that loop all the way around an object, making it much easier to adjust models.

14. Now with the edges selected (looped) all around the top of the dresser, go to the Edges tab in the Graphite Modeling Tools ribbon. Choose the Chamfer tool and be sure to select the Chamfer Settings drop-down menu using the arrow below the button, as shown in Figure 2.11, to bring up the Chamfer caddy.

15. In the Chamfer caddy, enter the following parameters: Edge Chamfer Amount: **0.1** and Connect Edge Segments: **2**; then click OK. Figure 2.12 shows the result.

FIGURE 2.11
The Edges tab

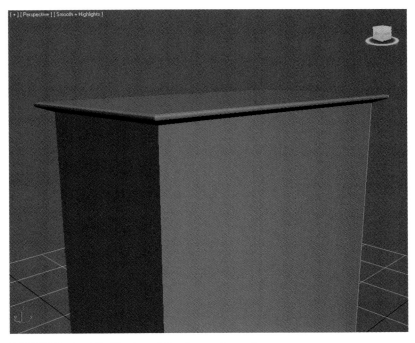

FIGURE 2.12 The top of the dresser is ready.

These values are not necessarily set in stone. You can play around with the settings to get as close to the image as you can or to add your own design flair. Set your project to the Dresser and load the Dresser01.max scene file from the Scenes folder in the Dresser project from the companion web page.

I Can See Your Drawers

In the beginning of this exercise, you created a box with six segments for its height. You can use those segments to create the drawers. This is thinking ahead and planning your model before you start working on an object; using another tool to add segments for the drawers after the box is made is much more laborious.

For simplicity's sake, in this exercise you will not create drawers that can open and shut. If this dresser were to be used in an animation in which the drawers would be opened, you would make them differently. Figure 2.13 shows the drawers and an important detail you need to consider.

— Gap between drawers and dresser main body

FIGURE 2.13 Notice the small gap around the edge of the box. This gap represents the space between the drawer and the main body of the dresser.

To model the drawers, begin with these steps:

1. Go to Polygon mode (press 4), and select the six polygons on the front of the box that represent the drawers. Hold the Ctrl key while selecting the additional polygons to allow you to make multiple polygon selections. You can toggle between shaded and wireframe selected by pressing F2.

2. In the Graphite Modeling Tools ribbon, go to the Polygons tab and click the Inset Settings button to bring up the Inset caddy. Set the Inset Amount to 0.6, as shown in Figure 2.14, and keep the top button's Inset Type set to Group. Click OK.

FIGURE 2.14
Inset settings caddy controls

You can load the Dresser02.max scene file from the Scenes folder in the Dresser project from the companion web page to check your work or to continue here.

3. Keep those newly inset polygons selected (or select them) and go back to the Polygons tab to select the Bevel Settings button to bring up the caddy. Change the Height to −0.5, keep Type set to Group, and click Apply And Continue. The polygons now extrude inward a little bit, as shown in Figure 2.15 (left). Keep those polygons selected and repeat the procedure in step 2 to create another inset with an Inset Amount of 0.6 (see Figure 2.15, right).

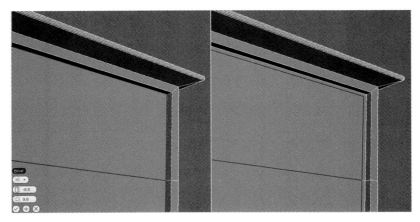

FIGURE 2.15 Using Bevel to perform an extrude and then another 0.6 inset

4. In the original reference picture (Figure 2.1), the top drawer of the dresser is split into two, so you need to create an edge vertically in that top-drawer polygon to create two drawers. Go to Edge mode and select the top and bottom horizontal edges on the top drawer, as shown in red in Figure 2.16.

FIGURE 2.16 Select the upper and lower edges of the top drawer.

5. Go to the Graphite Modeling Tools ribbon and in the Loops tab, click the Connect Settings button to bring up the caddy (Figure 2.17). Set Segments to 1, Pinch to 0, and Slide to 0 (Figure 2.18), and then click OK.

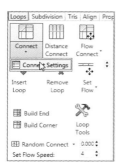

FIGURE 2.17 The Loops tab with an arrow pointing to the Connect tool

FIGURE 2.18
Connect Edges caddy

6. Select the two polygons in the newly created top drawers. Go back to the Polygons tab and click Inset Settings. Set Amount to 0.25. This time you are going to change Inset Type from Group to By Polygon, as shown in Figure 2.19.

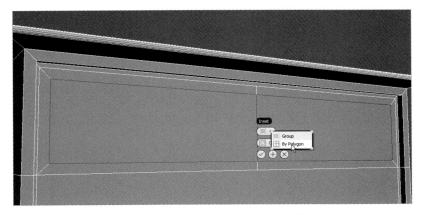

FIGURE 2.19 Inset caddy with settings for the top drawers

This setting insets each polygon individually instead of performing this operation on multiple, contiguous polygons (which is what the Group option does). Click OK to commit the Inset operation and close the caddy. Your polygons should resemble the ones in Figure 2.20.

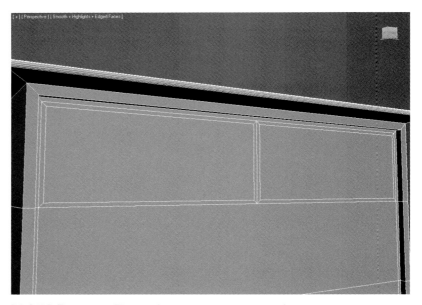

FIGURE 2.20 The top drawers are inset separately.

7. Perform the same inset operation on the remaining drawer polygons on the front of the box. Set the Amount to .25, and set Inset Type to By Polygon. This will inset the five lower, wide drawers, as shown in Figure 2.21.

FIGURE 2.21 The remaining drawers are inset.

8. Select all of the drawer polygons. Go to the Polygons tab and click Extrude Settings. Set Height to 0.7. You don't need it to extrude very much; you just want the drawers to extrude a bit more than the body of the dresser (Figure 2.22).

FIGURE 2.22 The drawers are extruded.

You can load the Dresser03.max scene file from the Scenes folder in the Dresser project from the companion web page to check your work or to skip to this part in the exercise.

Modeling the Bottom

Now it is time to create the bottom of the dresser. This dresser doesn't have legs, but nonetheless has a nice detail at the bottom, as you can see in Figure 2.23. To create this detail, you need to extrude a polygon.

FIGURE 2.23 An angle view of the
dresser's bottom corner

1. Enter polygon mode (press 4). You may already be in Polygon subobject mode if you are continuing with your own file. Select the polygon
on the bottom of the dresser, as shown in red in Figure 2.24.

FIGURE 2.24 Select the polygon at the bottom of the dresser.

2. In the Graphite Modeling Tools ribbon, go to the Polygons tab and click the Extrude Settings button to bring up the caddy. Change Height to **2.5**, as shown in Figure 2.25, and click OK. This will extrude a polygon out from the bottom of the dresser, essentially adding a segment to the box, as shown in Figure 2.26.

FIGURE 2.25
Extrude Polygons caddy

FIGURE 2.26 Extrude the bottom of the dresser.

3. The polygon will still be selected, so click the Inset Settings button to bring up its caddy. Change Amount to **0.6**, and click OK. This creates an inset poly, as shown in Figure 2.27.

4. The poly should still be selected, so click the Extrude Settings button to bring up the caddy, enter a height of –2.0, and click OK. Figure 2.28 shows how the bottom of the dresser has moved up into itself slightly.

To create the detail on the bottom, you need to cut into the newly extruded polygons to create the "legs" in the corners of the dresser that you saw in Figure 2.23. To do this, you will use the ProBoolean tool. This method uses two or more objects to create a new object by performing a Boolean operation.

We need another object to flesh out the shape to cut from the bottom of the dresser. We are going to create this object in the shape of the cutout at the bottom of the dresser (refer to Figure 2.23). It is a very specific shape starting with a simple rectangle.

FIGURE 2.27 The inset polygon

FIGURE 2.28 The dresser's bottom lip

5. In the Command panel, click the Create tab ( ), click the Shapes icon ( ), and click the Rectangle tool, as shown in Figure 2.29.

FIGURE 2.29 Select the Rectangle tool.

6. In a front view, create a rectangle with Length of **3.0** and Width of **26.0** as shown in the top of Figure 2.30. Press W or click the Select And Move Tool ( ), select the rectangle shape, and move it so it is sitting in front of the dresser, as shown in Figure 2.30.

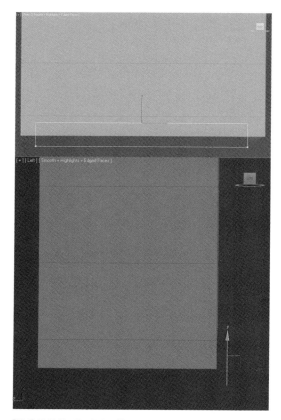

FIGURE 2.30 Move the rectangle into place. The top image shows the Front viewport; the bottom image shows the Left viewport.

7. In the Command panel, select the Modify tab ( ) and in the modifier stack, right-click the Rectangle entry. From the context menu, choose Editable Spline, as shown in Figure 2.31. In the Editable Spline parameters, open the Selection rollout and click the Vertex icon ( ) to enter Vertex subobject mode. An editable spline provides controls for manipulating an object as a spline object and at three subobject levels: Vertex, Segment, and Spline.

8. In the Front viewport, select the two top vertices by clicking and dragging a selection box around them. In the Geometry rollout click the Fillet tool, as shown in Figure 2.32.

9. Click and drag one of the two selected vertices to create a rounded corner. Because both vertices are selected, they will both get the fillet, as shown in Figure 2.33. The amount of the fillet is **0.9**. You can watch the value of the fillet in the Geometry rollout.

FIGURE 2.31 Converting a shape to an editable spline

FIGURE 2.32 Fillet tool

FIGURE 2.33 The two vertices are filleted.

10. With the rectangle shape selected, select the Modify tab. Above the modifier stack is a drop-down menu. From the modifier list choose Extrude, which will then appear in the modifier stack above the existing editable spline object. Use an amount of **30.0** and then move the extrusion so that it penetrates both sides of the dresser.

11. Do the same to the side of the dresser:

    a. Create another rectangle but make it smaller to fit the side of the dresser.

    b. Convert to an editable spline as in step 7.

    c. Select the two top vertices and fillet them.

    d. Add an Extrude modifier and change Amount to **40.0**.

    e. Place that object penetrating through both sides of the dresser, as shown in Figure 2.34.

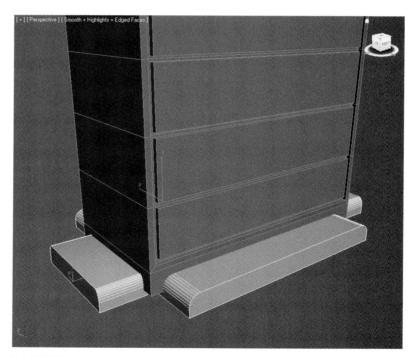

FIGURE 2.34 Objects placed for Boolean

Now for the ProBoolean operation itself. Don't get this confused with the regular Boolean operation, however.

1. To begin, select the object you want to keep—in this case, the dresser object.

2. In the Create Panel, select the Geometry rollout; choose Compound Objects from the drop-down menu, and at the bottom of the Object Type rollout, click the ProBoolean button.

3. In the Pick Boolean rollout, click the Start Picking button (Figure 2.35).

FIGURE 2.35 Click the Start Picking button.

4. Click both extruded rectangles placed at the bottom of the dresser. By default, ProBoolean is always set to Subtraction, so the object's shape will be subtracted from the dresser, as shown in Figure 2.36.

FIGURE 2.36 Finished dresser bottom

5. In the Name text box (shown in the Command panel's Modify tab to the far right of Figure 2.37), change the name of the object to **Dresser**, and pick a nice light color. Go grab yourself a frosty beverage!

The finished dresser body should look like the dresser in Figure 2.1. Remember to save this version of your file. You can load the `Dresser04.max` scene file from the `Scenes` folder in the Dresser project on the companion web page to check your work or to skip to this point in the exercise.

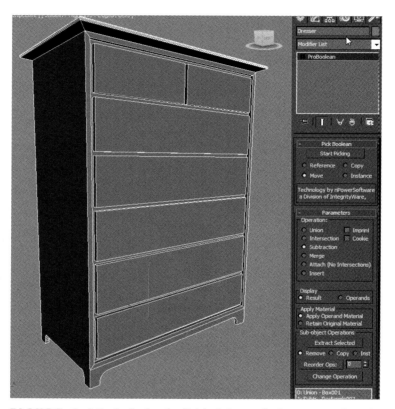

FIGURE 2.37   Assigning the finished dresser body a name and a color

Creating the Knobs

Now that the body of the dresser is done, it's time to add the knobs. We will use splines and a few surface creation tools new to your workflow. Goosebumps, anyone? Take a look at the reference for the knobs in Figure 2.38. You are going to create a profile of the knob and then rotate the profile around its axis to form a surface. This technique is known as *lathe*, not to be mistaken for *latte*, which is a whole different deal and not covered in this book.

FIGURE 2.38 A drawer knob

A spline is a group of vertices and connecting segments that form a line or curve. To create the knob profile, we are going to use the line spline, shaped in the outline of—you guessed it—a knob. The Line tool allows you to create a freeform spline.

You can use your last file from the Dresser exercise, or you can load `Dresser04.max` from the `Scenes` folder of the Dresser project from the companion web page. To build the knobs, follow these steps:

1. Make sure you are in the Left viewport so you can see which side of the dresser the drawers are on, as shown in Figure 2.39. You are going to create a profile of half the knob, as shown in Figure 2.40. Don't worry about creating all the detail in the knob, because detail won't be seen; a simple outline will be fine.

FIGURE 2.39 Left view of the dresser

2. Select Create ➢ Shapes ➢ Line. Use the current default values in the Creation Method rollout.

3. In the Left viewport, click once to lay down a vertex for this line, starting at the bottom of the profile for the knob (Figure 2.41). This is the starting point for the curve. When you are creating a line, every click lays down the next vertex for the line. If you want to create a curve in the line, click once and drag the mouse in any direction to give the vertex a curvature of sorts. This curve vertex creates a curve in that part of the line. You need to follow the rough outline of a knob, so click and drag where there is curvature in the line. Once you have laid down your first vertex, continue to click and drag more vertices for the line clockwise until you create the half-profile knob shape shown earlier in Figure 2.40.

Figure 2.41 shows the profile line with the vertices numbered according to their creation order.

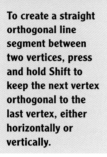

Click once to create a corner vertex for a line, but click and drag to create a Bézier vertex if you want to put a curve into the line.

To create a straight orthogonal line segment between two vertices, press and hold Shift to keep the next vertex orthogonal to the last vertex, either horizontally or vertically.

FIGURE 2.40 The intended profile curve for the knob

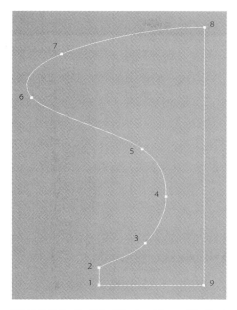

FIGURE 2.41 The knob's profile line's vertices are numbered according to the order in which they were created.

4. Once you lay down your last vertex at the bottom, finish the spline by either right-clicking to release the Line tool or clicking the first vertex you created to close the spline. For this example, it doesn't matter which method you choose. Either an open or closed spline will work; a closed spline is shown in Figure 2.41. Drawing splines entails a bit of a learning curve, so it might be helpful to delete the one you did first and try again for the practice. Once you get something resembling the spline in Figure 2.41, you can edit it. Don't drive yourself crazy; just get the spline as close as you can.

5. With the spline selected, in the Modify Panel's Modifier Stack, choose Line. Click the plus sign (+) to expand the list of subobjects, as shown in Figure 2.42.

FIGURE 2.42
Line subobject modes

Editing the Profile

A line's subobjects are similar to the Editable Spline subobject modes. A spline is made up of three subobjects: a vertex, a segment, and a spline. A *vertex* is a point in space. A *segment* is the line that connects two vertices. To continue with the project, follow these steps:

1. Choose the vertex subobject for the line. Make sure you are still working in the Left viewport. Use the Move tool to click one of the vertices. Use the Move tool to edit the shape to better fit the outline of the knob.

    To catch up to this point and have the profile already created for you, load the Dresser05.max file from the companion web page.

2. The profile line is ready to turn into a 3D object. This is where the modifiers are used. Get out of subobject mode for your line. Choose Modifiers ➢ Patch/Spline Editing ➢ Lathe. When you first put the Lathe modifier on your spline, it probably won't look anything like the knob (see Figure 2.43)—but don't panic; right now the object is turned inside out! Select Y and Max and adjust the parameters to match Figure 2.44.

3. Adjust the Perspective viewport so you can see the top of the knob. You may notice a strange artifact. To correct this, check the Weld Core box under the Parameters rollout for the lathe.

That's it! Check out Figure 2.45 for a look at the lathed knob. By using splines and the Lathe procedure, you can create all sorts of surfaces for your models. In the next section, you will resize the knob, position it, and copy it to fit on the drawers.

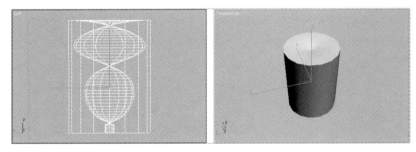

FIGURE 2.43 Eek! That isn't a knob at all.

FIGURE 2.44 The titillating parameters for the Lathe modifier

FIGURE 2.45 The lathe completes the knob.

Now that you have a knob, you may need to adjust it and make it the right size. If you still want to futz with the knob, go back down the stack to the Line to edit your spline. For example, you may want to scale the knob a bit to better fit the drawer (refer to the reference photo in Figure 2.38). Select the Scale tool, and click and drag until the original line is about the right size in your scene. The Lathe modifier will re-create the surface to fit the new size. You can also delete the knob and restart with another line for more practice.

Copying the Knob

In the following steps, you will copy and position the knob for the drawers.

1. Position and rotate the knob to fit on to the front of a top drawer. Change its default color (if you want) and change its name to **Knob**.

2. You'll need a few copies of the original knob, one for each drawer. Choose Edit ➤ Clone to open the Clone Options dialog box (Figure 2.46). You

are going to use the Instance option. An instance is a copy but is still connected to the original. If you edit the original or an instance, all of the instances change (including the original). Click OK to create an instance.

FIGURE 2.46 Using an instance to copy the knob

3. Position the instanced knob in the middle of the other top drawer.

4. Using additional instances of the original knob, place knobs in the middle of all the remaining drawers of your dresser, as shown in Figure 2.47.

FIGURE 2.47 The dresser, knobs and all

As you saw with this exercise, there are plenty of tools for the Editable Poly object. Your model doesn't have to be all of the same type of modeling, either. In this example, we created the dresser with *box modeling* techniques, where you begin with a single box and extrude your way into a model, and with surface creation techniques using splines.

You can compare your work to the scene file Dresser06.max from the Scenes folder of the Dresser project from the companion web page.

THE ESSENTIALS AND BEYOND

In this chapter, you learned how to model with 3ds Max. Through exploring the modeling toolsets and creating a dresser, you saw firsthand how the primary modeling tools in 3ds Max operate.

You learned how to create a primitive box and from that use editable polygons and the Graphite modeling tools, ProBoolean, shapes, editable splines, and the Lathe tool to make a simple dresser.

ADDITIONAL EXERCISES

► Select the Edges around the dresser drawers and use Chamfer to add a bit of roundness to the dresser.

► Model one of the drawers so that you can animate it opening and closing. This can be done by selecting the polygons for one of the drawers and deleting them. Then create a primitive box the size of a drawer.

► Play around with the knobs and create different styles. You can find examples at **www .sybex.com/go/3dsmax2012essentials**.

► Create a similar piece of furniture like a nightstand to match the style of the dresser.

CHAPTER 3

Modeling in 3ds Max: Part I

Building models in 3D is as simple as building them out of clay, wood, stone, or metal. Using 3ds Max to model something may not be as tactile as physically building it, but the same concepts apply: you have to identify how the model is shaped and figure out how to break it down into manageable parts that you can piece together into the final form.

Instead of using traditional tools to hammer or chisel or weld a shape into form, you will use the vertices of the geometry to shape the Computer Generated (CG) model. As you have seen, 3ds Max's polygon toolset is quite robust.

In this chapter, we will tackle a more complex model with a children's red rocket ride-on toy. We will use the Editable Poly toolset to create the toy. We will also examine the use of Boolean operations. Topics in this chapter include the following:

▶ **Building the red rocket**

▶ **Creating planes and adding materials**

Building the Red Rocket

Using reference materials will help you efficiently create your 3D model and achieve a good likeness in your end result. The temptation to just wing it and start building the objects is strong, especially when time is short and you're raring to go. This temptation should always be suppressed in deference to a well-thought-out approach to the task. Sketches, photographs, and drawings can all be used as resources for the modeling process. Not only are references useful for giving you a clear direction in which to head, but you can also use references directly in 3ds Max to help you model. Photos, especially those taken from different sides of the intended model, can be added to a scene as background images to help you shape your model.

Creating Planes and Adding Materials

For the best in modeling reference, bring in photos of your model and use the *crossing boxes* technique, which involves placing the reference images on crossing plane objects or thin boxes in the scene. In this exercise, you'll build a child's rocket ride-on toy, as shown in Figure 3.1.

FIGURE 3.1 You'll build child's red rocket toy like this one.

Before you begin, download the Red Rocket folder from this book's companion web page (**www.sybex.com/go/3dsmax2012essentials**) to your hard drive where you keep your other 3ds Max projects.

1. Set your project folder to the Red Rocket project you just downloaded (Application ➢ Manage ➢ Set Project Folder).

2. Navigate to the place on the hard drive where you saved the book projects.

3. Click Red Rocket, and then click OK.

Now when you want to open a scene file, just choose Application ➢ Open, and you will automatically be in the Red Rocket project's Scenes folder.

To begin the rocket toy, start with a new 3ds Max file:

1. Open a new 3ds Max file by choosing Application ➢ New.

2. Go to the Create panel to create a box, click the Geometry icon ()
   and, under Standard Primitives, click the Box button.

   Instead of creating the box with the click-and-drag method, use the
   Keyboard Entry rollout, as shown in Figure 3.2. Expand the Keyboard
   Entry rollout. Make sure the Perspective viewport is selected. Leave
   the *X*, *Y*, and *Z* parameters all set to 0; this places the box at the origin
   (center) of your scene. Change the parameters to Length 22, Width
   0.01, and Height 12 and click Create:

FIGURE 3.2
The Keyboard Entry rollout
for creating the box

3. When you click Create, 3ds Max creates the image-plane box we'll use
   for the side view. Rename the Box001 object **Side View**.

4. Activate the Top viewport, and using Length 22, Width 12, and
   Height 0.01, create a new box. Rename the box **Top View**.

   Don't forget to click Create! This creates another flat box, which
   you'll use for the Top View image-plane box.

5. Activate the Front viewport and expand the Keyboard Entry rollout.
   Leave the *X*, *Y*, and *Z* parameters all set to 0, and use these parameters: Length 12, Width 12, Height 0.01 Click Create. Rename the box
   Front View. This creates the image-plane box for the front view of the
   rocket toy.

6. Move the Front View box up 6 units in the *Z* axis to raise it so the
   bottom edge is directly on the Home Grid, as shown in Figure 3.3.

Then switch all the viewports to Smooth + Highlights (F3) and Zoom Extents All (Z).

FIGURE 3.3 The Front View box is moved up.

7. In Windows Explorer, navigate to the sceneassets\images folder in the Red Rocket folder that you downloaded to your hard drive. In this folder, you will find three reference JPEG images, one for each of the three image-plane box views you just created in the scene. Select the Top View reference image (called TOP VIEW.jpg), drag it into the Top viewport in 3ds Max, and drop it onto the Top View image-plane box. This automatically places the image onto the box, so the image is viewable in the viewport.

8. Repeat the previous step to place SIDE VIEW.jpg onto the Side View image-plane box in the Left viewport and place FRONT VIEW.jpg onto the Front View image-plane box in the Front viewport. Figure 3.4 shows the image-plane boxes with the reference images applied.

9. If you need to, adjust the placement of the Front View image-plane box so the proportions of the rocket match up. The bottom of the

If the rocket images do not show up in the viewport after you drop them onto the boxes, make sure the viewport is set to Smooth + Highlights and try again.

wheels and the top of the handlebars should line up in all three images. Move the box using the Select And Move tool. Use the Orbit viewport navigation tool to rotate the view so that the image-plane boxes can be viewed from different sides to get them aligned.

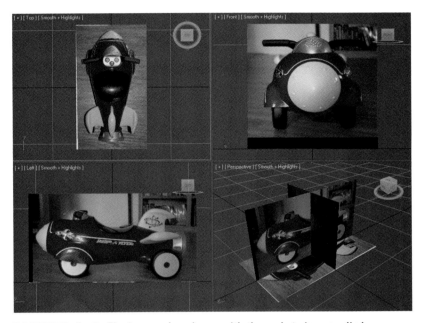

FIGURE 3.4 The image-plane boxes with the rocket views applied

FIXING THE TOP VIEW

If for some reason the image on your Top View object seems to be the reverse of what is shown in the book, rotate the Top View object to line it up the way the images appear in this chapter. Also, you may notice black bars appearing in the images. They are intended to allow the images to better line up with one another.

Creating the Body

To begin the body of the rocket, set your project to Red Rocket and load the scene file Rocket_00.max from the Scenes folder of the Red Rocket project that you downloaded from the web page. In the following steps, you will begin the rocket model:

1. Change the Front viewport to a Back viewport by clicking on the viewport name and choosing Back from the drop-down menu. In the Create panel, click the Geometry icon (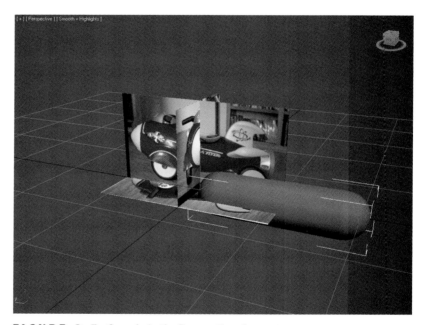) and select Extended Primitives from the drop-down menu. Click to activate the Capsule tool, and then create a Capsule object with Keyboard Entry values set to a radius of 3 and a height of 21. Remember to use the Back viewport so that the capsule is created oriented as shown in Figure 3.5.

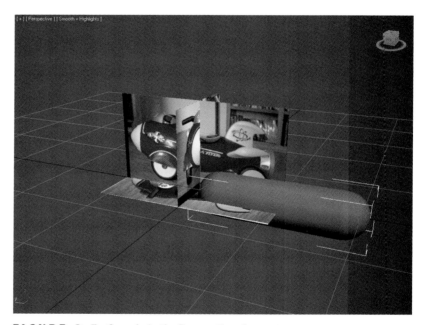

FIGURE 3.5 Capsule in the Perspective viewport

2. Open the Modify panel ( ) to edit the capsule's parameters. Set the capsule's Sides to 8 and Height Segs to 6. Uncheck the Smooth option; we will smooth it out later.

3. Rename the capsule **Rocket Body**. Make Rocket Body see-through by pressing Alt+X in all the viewports. This way, you will be able to see the image-plane boxes through the geometry. Also set the viewports to Edged Faces (F4), which will show the wireframe over the Smooth + Highlights.

4. Using the Select And Move tool, line up the rocket body with the Side, Top, and Front image-plane boxes, matching the rocket body to the front end of the image, as shown in Figure 3.6.

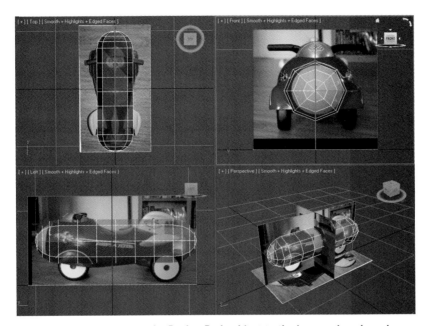

FIGURE 3.6   Line up the Rocket Body object to the image-plane box views.

5. In the Graphite Modeling Tools ribbon, click the Polygon Modeling tab and select Convert To Poly, as shown in Figure 3.7.

FIGURE 3.7
Convert to an editable poly.

6. In the Polygon Modeling tab, click the Vertex subobject mode icon (⋰) or press (1) and select the vertex at the very front tip of the rocket body, as shown in Figure 3.8.

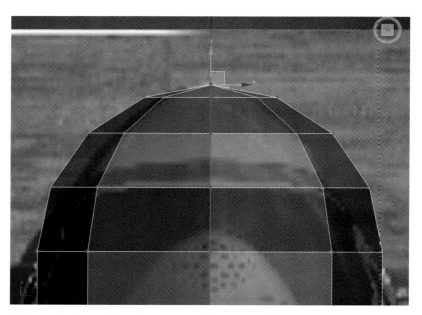

FIGURE 3.8 Select the vertex at the very front tip.

7. In the Polygon Modeling tab, click the Use Soft Selection icon, as shown in Figure 3.9. Look at the end of the Graphite Modeling Tools ribbon tabs; click the Soft tab. Set Falloff to 6.0, as shown in Figure 3.10.

FIGURE 3.9 Click the Use Soft Selection icon in the Polygon Modeling tab.

FIGURE 3.10 Soft tab with Falloff set to 6.0

Soft Selection gives your surface modifications a soft, clay-like feel. When Use Soft Selection is enabled, the effects of move, scale, and rotate edits are the same as usual on selected elements (vertices, edges, or polygons) but are also distributed to adjacent vertices based on a gradual falloff. This causes edits to have a smoothed or softened effect on the model.

8. Now switch to the Scale tool (R). We need to scale along the *XY* axis, which is a nonuniform scale. Do the scale in the Back viewport: center your cursor over the Transform gizmo's *XY* axis, as shown in Figure 3.11, and scale while watching the Top viewport. Scale down to create a more pointed front.

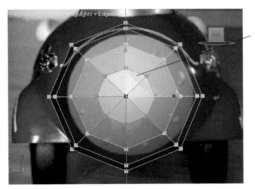

Transform gizmo's *XY* axis

FIGURE 3.11 Center your cursor over the Transform gizmo's *XY* axis (shown as an angled yellow bar).

9. Selecting some of the front vertices in the Top viewport, scale and move the rest of the front to match the front of the rocket in the Top View image-plane box, as shown in Figure 3.12.

10. Using vertices *with or without* Soft Selection and changing the Falloff setting if desired, shape the rest of the body to the shape in the three image-plane boxes. Don't worry about the back end of the rocket body just yet; we'll tackle that in the next step.

11. When you have the general shape of the body of the rocket, go into Polygon mode; select the polygons at the rounded back end of your shape, as shown in Figure 3.13; and delete them by pressing the Delete key on your keyboard.

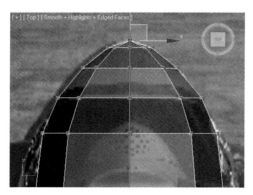

FIGURE 3.12 Select some front vertices and scale and move to match.

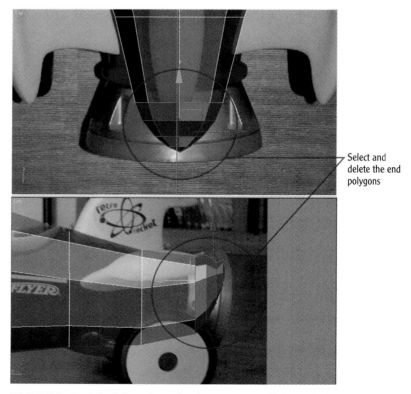

Select and delete the end polygons

FIGURE 3.13 Select the end polygons to cut off the end of the rocket body.

Smoothing the Body

The body looks very rough and chunky right now. To smooth out the rough model, we will use nonuniform rational mesh smooth (NURMS). NURMS is a surface that has been divided into more faces to create a smoother surface while still retaining the object's general shape. You subdivide to add more detail to an object or to smooth out the shape.

The following steps will guide you through the process of smoothing out the rocket body shape:

1. With the rocket body selected, go to the Graphite Modeling Tools ribbon and in the Edit tab click the Use NURMS icon. While in Polygon subobject mode, you will see the orange NURMS cage appear. This cage allows you to continue editing the body's overall shape by selecting the lower-resolution cage's polygons and editing them. This lets you affect its broader form without having to select many more polygons of the smoothed version. Click the Use NURMS icon again to turn it off.

2. Press 4 to enter Polygon subobject mode. With the rocket body selected, select the polygons on the rocket body's right side, as shown in Figure 3.14, and delete them.

3. Go to the top level of the editable poly (press 6); this gets you out of Polygon subobject mode. Open the Modify panel, and from the modifier list, choose the Symmetry modifier. In the Symmetry parameters, choose *X* as the Mirror Axis and uncheck the Flip box. This creates a mirrored copy of that half of the body. Using Symmetry allows you to make changes to the original side of the body and automatically have those changes mirrored to the other side.

   When you go back to editing the mesh, the mirrored half of the rocket disappears. To stop this from occurring, click the Show End Result icon, which is in the line of icons below the modifier stack, shown in Figure 3.15.

FIGURE 3.14 Select the polygons as shown; then delete them.

FIGURE 3.15
Clicking the Show End Result icon

Adding Detail to the Rocket Body

The wheel wells on the front sides of the body are the first details we will add. To create the wheel wells, we need to add some more segments to the main body. To do this, we will use a tool from the Graphite Modeling Tools called Swift Loop. It places edge loops with just a click. As you move the mouse cursor over your object, a real-time preview shows where the loop will be created when you click.

ISOLATE SELECTION

Occasionally, you might need to isolate your model to avoid the distractions of reference image planes and even other meshes in your scene. Here's an easy technique to do this: Right-click your selected model. On the pop-up menu, click Isolate Selection. Suddenly everything but the model is hidden in your scene and you have a floating Exit Isolation Mode icon, which you click when you want your scene back. Isolate Selection can be used on individual objects or several. Just hold down the Ctrl key while selecting multiple objects.

The SwiftLoop tool, as we'll see in the following steps, can be used in any of the subobject modes or in the top level with no subobject mode selected.

1. With the rocket body selected, make sure you are in Editable Poly level. In the Graphite Modeling Tools ribbon, choose the Edit panel and select Swift Loop. Move your cursor over to the rocket to see a preview of where a loop will eventually be placed. When the loop is in the correct place, just click and it will be added. You want to match placement of four new loops with those shown in Figure 3.16.

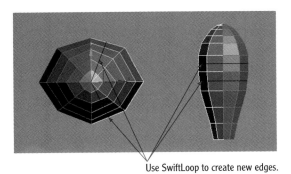

Use SwiftLoop to create new edges.

FIGURE 3.16 Use the Swift Loop tool to add detail to these areas on the rocket body.

Now that the new loops are in, turn off Swift Loop, and you can see there is a little issue. The front-end vertex of the rocket doesn't connect to the newly added Swift Loop edge. All of those edges need to come to a point at the tip, so you will continue the new segment to the tip manually, using the Connect tool, in the next step.

2. Press the 1 key to enter Vertex subobject mode, and turn off Use Soft Selection, if it isn't already off. Select the two vertices shown in Figure 3.17.

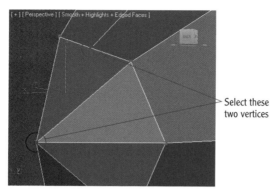

Select these two vertices

FIGURE 3.17 Select these two vertices.

3. Go to the Graphite Modeling Tools ribbon, and in the Loops tab click the Connect tool. This completes the loop.

4. Repeat the same with the vertex on the lower side of the rocket.

Creating the Wheel Well

Now that you have created more detail on the mesh, you can mold the wheel wells, as shown on the rocket in Figure 3.18.

You can continue with your own scene file (just be sure to turn off NURMS smoothing before you continue), or use the scene file Rocket_01.max from the Scenes folder in the Red Rocket project that you downloaded to your hard drive.

Wheel well of the body

FIGURE 3.18 The rocket's wheel wells

Here are the steps to follow:

1. Select the rocket and change to Polygon subobject mode (press 4), and from the Left viewport select the three polygons in the middle of the body, as shown in Figure 3.19.

FIGURE 3.19 Change to the Polygon subobject mode and select these three polygons.

 2. In the Graphite Modeling Tools ribbon in the Polygons tab, click the Extrude Settings button to bring up the caddy. In the Extrude Polygons caddy, set Extrusion Type to Group and Height to 0.8, as shown in Figure 3.20. Click OK.

FIGURE 3.20
Setting the extrusion
parameters in the caddy

3. Now select all the polygons that were created with the extrude operation, shown in Figure 3.21 (on the left). Activate a back view, and exit
Isolate mode if you are still in it. Then, use the Rotate and Move tools
to align the polygons so that they line up with the wheel well in the
Front View image-plane box, as shown in Figure 3.21 (on the right).

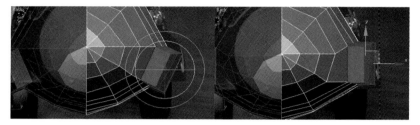

FIGURE 3.21 Use the Rotate and Move tools.

4. Switch to Vertex mode. Use a window selection to select and move the
second row of vertices from the bottom of the rocket body out to the
right and slightly down, as shown in Figure 3.22. This evens out
the bottom part of the body to give it a more rounded look. If we left
those vertices where they were, that part of the body would appear
lopsided. And who wants that?

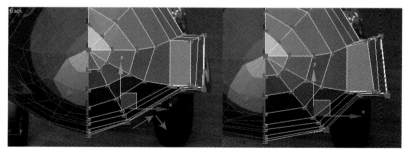

FIGURE 3.22 Round out the bottom of the rocket's body.

5. Let's apply NURMS to the model again to see how the wheel wells
look when smoothed. There are still several things that we need to do
to improve the look of the body. The wheel well polygons need to be
moved down and reshaped to have an arch on the top.

6. Exit subobject mode and select Rocket Body, and in the Graphite
Modeling Tools ribbon, click the Use NURMS button in the Edit tab.
Now, when it is subdivided it looks a bit better. Figure 3.23 shows the
rocket after NURMS has been enabled for the mesh.

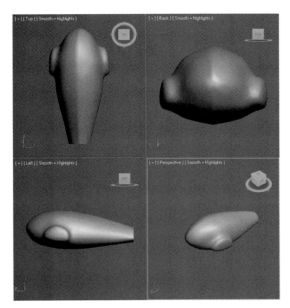

FIGURE 3.23 After Use NURMS is applied, the smoothed rocket looks better (shown here with the rocket in Isolate Selection mode).

Now you need to hollow out the wheel well. Follow these steps.

7. Disable NURMS smoothing by clicking the Use NURMS button again.

8. Enter Polygon subobject mode. Select the polygons at the bottom side of the wheel well, as shown in Figure 3.24. Use Isolate if you need to.

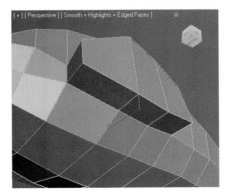

FIGURE 3.24 Select the polygons at the bottom of the wheel well.

9. In the Graphite Modeling Tools ribbon, go to the Polygons tab and click the Bevel Settings button to bring up the caddy. Set Outline to −0.1 and Height to 0.0, and then click Apply And Continue. Reset Outline to 0.0, set Height to −0.7 to push in the area, and then click OK. Finally, delete the inside polygon, as shown in Figure 3.25.

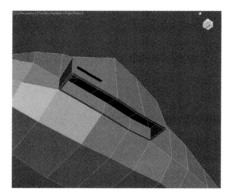

FIGURE 3.25 The wheel well after polygons are deleted. You may see some geometry poking through the side, as shown here.

We don't need to create the inside of the wheel well because we are not going to see it. We extruded into the wheel well in step 3 to make a solid lip at the wheel well, but it only needs to go halfway up.

10. Check to make sure that the new edges don't poke through the mesh, as shown in Figure 3.26. If any do, select the vertices and move them inward.

FIGURE 3.26 The geometry is poking through the outside!

11. Enable NURMS smoothing, and your rocket body should resemble the one in Figure 3.27. Be sure to disable NURMS smoothing before you continue with the rest of the exercise.

12. Save your work.

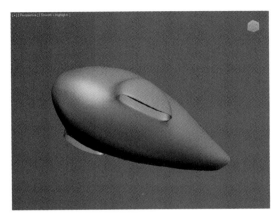

FIGURE 3.27 The smoothed wheel wells look pretty good.

Creating the Control Panel

We'll now create the control panel for the rocket, as shown in Figure 3.28. You can continue with your own scene file or use the scene file Rocket_02.max from the Scenes folder in the Red Rocket project you downloaded from the web page.

FIGURE 3.28 The control panel

1. To create the control panel, you need to add one more segment along the top of the body for extra mesh detail, as you can see in Figure 3.29. Go to the Graphite Modeling Tools ribbon, click the Edit tab, select Swift Loop, and create an edge as shown in Figure 3.29.

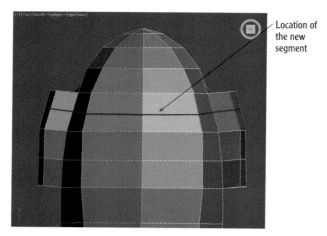

Location of the new segment

FIGURE 3.29 Add an edge loop using Swift Loop to create extra mesh detail for the control panel.

2. Repeat Step 2 to create a segment vertically down the rocket body, from the nose to tail, as shown in Figure 3.30.

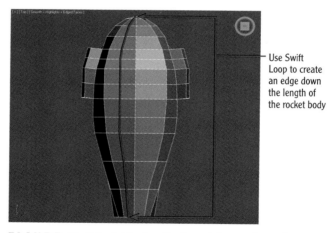

Use Swift Loop to create an edge down the length of the rocket body

FIGURE 3.30 Add a lengthwise cut line to the rocket body.

Now we see the same problem at the tip of the rocket that you saw earlier in this exercise. You need to connect the vertices together as you did earlier. Go back to the steps immediately after Figure 3.16 for a refresher to guide you through connecting two vertices.

3. In the Top viewport, move the vertices to fit the shape of the control panel, as shown in the Top View image-plane box. See Figure 3.31.

4. Switch to Polygon subobject mode and select the control panel polygons shown in Figure 3.32.

5. Go to the Graphite Modeling Tools ribbon and click the Extrude Settings button in the Polygons tab. Extrude the polygons with a Height of 1.0 and with the Extrude Type set to Group, and click OK.

If you look at the top view of the rocket, you will see the new extrusion where it meets the reference half of the rocket body, as shown in Figure 3.33.

The two sides where you extruded should split away from each other. Remember that the two sides are being stitched together to form the whole body using the *Symmetry modifier*, so all we need to do is make sure that all the vertices of the original side are aligned in the middle. For the original rocket half, you'll need to delete the polygons along the middle and move the vertices together. We'll do this in the following steps.

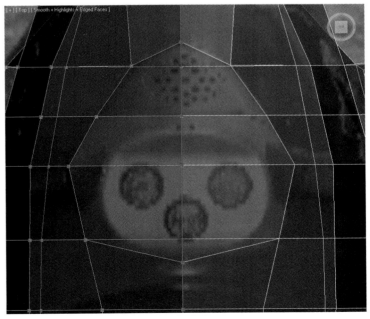

FIGURE 3.31 Shape the new vertices around the control panel in the Top viewport.

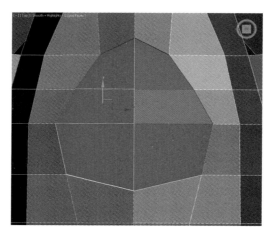

FIGURE 3.32 Select the control panel polygons.

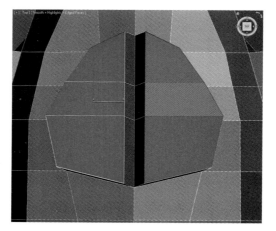

FIGURE 3.33 The top view of the rocket

6. Select the middle inside polygons, as shown in Figure 3.34, and delete them.

7. Switch to Vertex mode and select the vertices on the original side of the model where the control panel halves meet. Move them along the X axis to the middle, where the original and the reference halves meet, as shown in Figure 3.35. The problem is fixed! When the body halves are stitched together later, the body mesh will look seamless.

8. Make sure you are in Vertex mode. Using the Front, Side, and Top viewports, move the vertices of the control panel to line up with the real rocket's control panel in the image-plane boxes, as shown in Figure 3.36.

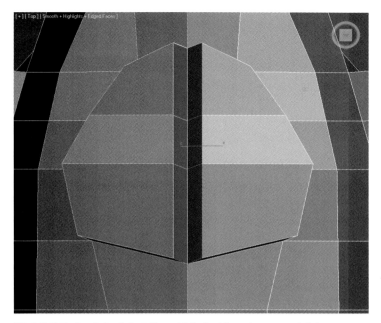

FIGURE 3.34 Select the middle inside polygons and delete.

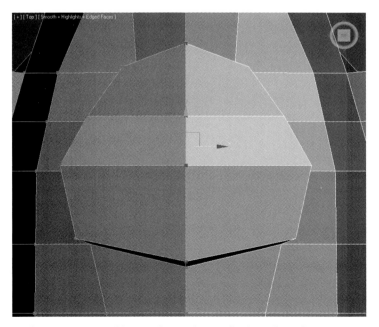

FIGURE 3.35 Line up the vertices to fix the split in the control panel between the two halves of the rocket body.

9. Let's look at this rocket body smoothed. Go to the Edit tab in the Graphite Modeling Tools ribbon and click the Use NURMS button to smooth the model again. It should look like Figure 3.37.

10. Use the cage to further edit the control panel to better fit the real control panel in the reference image-plane boxes.

You will see the Subdivision Surfaces cage as long as you are in a sub-object mode.

FIGURE 3.36 Shape the vertices of the control panel to the outline shown in the image-plane boxes.

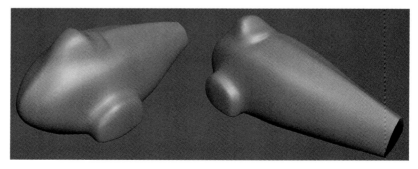

FIGURE 3.37 Use NURMS subdivision.

When you disable NURMS, the polygons for the control panel will seem exaggerated, as shown in Figure 3.38, and will go beyond the outlines of the real control panel in the image-plane boxes.

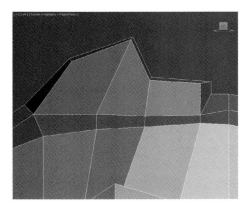

FIGURE 3.38 The polygons appear exaggerated.

That is because the lower-resolution cage model is a rough shape before smoothing is applied to it. Once NURMS is enabled, it smoothes the detail down, shrinking it back from the cage's shape a little. With NURMS smoothing enabled, the control panel looks like Figure 3.39 and fits the real model.

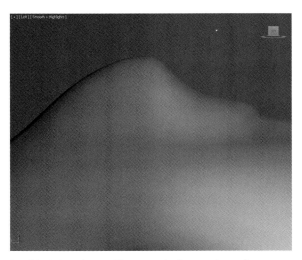

FIGURE 3.39 The smoothed control panel as seen in profile

Creating the Back Wheel Axle Assembly

Let's turn our attention to the back wheels. In the following steps, we will create the back axle assembly shown in Figure 3.40. You can use your own scene file or load the scene file Rocket_03.max from the Scenes folder in the Red Rocket project.

1. If smoothing is on, disable it by clicking the Use NURMS option and switch to Polygon sub-object mode. Change your Top viewport to a Bottom viewport by using (V) on your keyboard in the selected top view, then choose Bottom View from the drop-down menu. Also, select the Rocket and enter Isolate Selection mode.

2. Select the four polygons at the back bottom of the body, shown in Figure 3.41, and extrude them with a Height of 0.6.

FIGURE 3.40 The back wheels

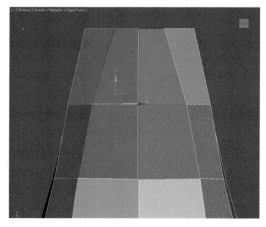

FIGURE 3.41 Select the four polygons at the back bottom of the body.

3. The extruded polygons will split at the middle where the original and mirrored reference halves of the body meet, as they did with the control panel earlier in this exercise. Move the vertices and fix the seam in the center the same way you did for the control panel. Make sure to delete the unneeded inside polygons as you did with the control panel. You can see the result in Figure 3.42.

FIGURE 3.42 The result of the extrude

4. Go into Vertex mode and adjust the extruded polygons of the back axle so that they have the shape of the axle from the Side View image-plane box, as shown in Figure 3.43. Exit Isolate Selection mode so you can see your image plans.

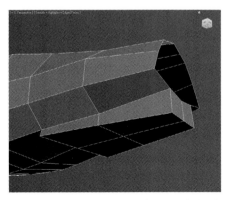

FIGURE 3.43 Adjust the extruded polygons to better fit the shape of the back.

5. Switch to Polygon mode, and select the polygons on the side of the extruded polygons and extrude them with a Height of 0.6, then click OK, as shown in Figure 3.44.

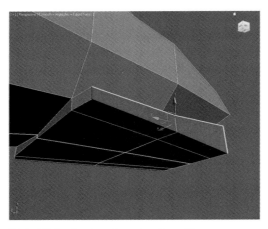

FIGURE 3.44 An extrusion with a Height of 0.6

6. Rearrange the vertices to create a small delta wing coming off the bottom/side of the body, as shown in Figure 3.45.

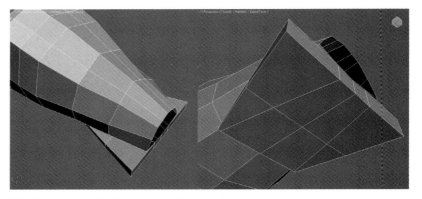

FIGURE 3.45 Create a small delta wing.

7. Turn on NURMS again to see the smoothed results shown in Figure 3.46.

8. While still in Use NURMS, try moving the cage vertices to sculpt the back wheel axle. Save your work.

The body is finished for now. Later we will create the seat and add the small lip that connects the thruster to the back.

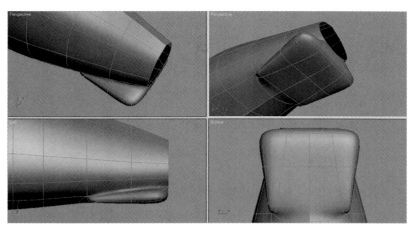

FIGURE 3.46 The rocket body is starting to take shape.

Further Body Work

We need to add some finishing touches to the rocket body. You can continue working with your own scene file or load Rocket_04.max from the Scenes folder in the Red Rocket project.

You should see a seam running along the top middle of the body, as shown in Figure 3.47. To fix this, we need to bring those vertices in toward the center of the body until the seam disappears.

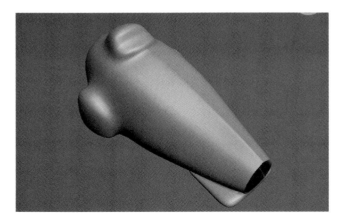

FIGURE 3.47 A seam runs down the middle of the rocket body.

1. Select the rocket, then in the Graphite Modeling Tools ribbon, enter Vertex mode. The mirrored side of the body will disappear because we are lower in the modifier stack. If you want the Symmetry to remain,

click the Show End Result icon ( ), which you will find in the row of icons below the modifier stack.

2. Select Graphite Modeling Tools and click the Edit tab; then turn off Use NURMS. Next, select the vertices that run along the middle. Select and move a few at a time. From the side view, you can see that those vertices stick up farther than the row below; this is what causes the ridge. Make the vertices level with the row of vertices below them by moving them along the *Y* axis, as shown in Figure 3.48.

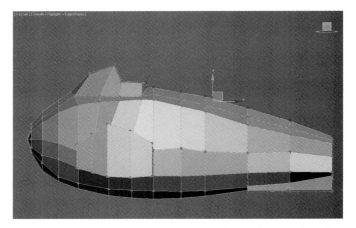

FIGURE 3.48 Make the vertices level with the row of vertices below them.

3. Go to Symmetry up in the modifier stack to view the whole body without the seam. Turn Use NURMS back on to see if the seam is gone, as shown in Figure 3.49.

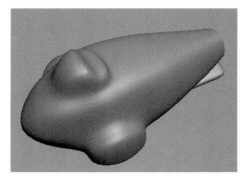

FIGURE 3.49 The seam is gone!

The next detail to manage is a small lip at the back end of the body, as shown in Figure 3.50. We are doing the lip after we complete the body because this detail is easier to create after the body is stitched together.

FIGURE 3.50 The lip between the thruster and the rocket body

1. Turn off Use NURMS if it's currently enabled.

2. Make sure the body is selected (with the Symmetry modifier). Go to the Graphite Modeling Tools ribbon, and in the Polygon Modeling menu click Collapse Stack. This combines the two separate halves of the rocket into one.

3. In the Polygon Modeling menu, click on Border mode ( ) and select the border edges in the back of the body, as shown in Figure 3.51.

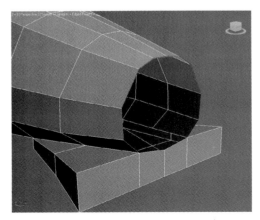

FIGURE 3.51 Select the border edges in the back of the body.

4. Go to the Geometry (All) tab in the Graphite Modeling Tools ribbon and click Cap Poly. This will create a poly where the hole was.

5. Switch to Polygon subobject mode and select the new polygon. Go to the Polygons tab of the Graphite Modeling Tools ribbon and click the Bevel Settings button to open the Bevel caddy. We will do four bevels through the open Bevel caddy. Between each bevel, make sure you click Apply And Continue (⊕), not OK (☑). This applies your bevel but keeps the caddy open for more.

6. Make four bevels with the following values:

Bevel No.	Height	Outline
1	0.05	0.3 (⊕)
2	0.2	0.1 (⊕)
3	0.2	−0.1 (⊕)
4	0.05	−0.3 (☑)

7. Click the Editable Poly entry in the modifier stack. Turn on NURMS to see how the rocket body is looking (see Figure 3.52).

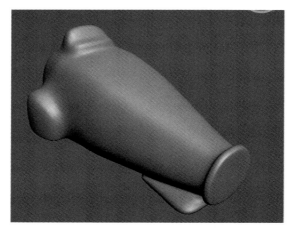

FIGURE 3.52 Thruster detail completed with NURMS

Hold On to Your Seat

What fun would it be to ride a rocket standing up? Speaking from experience, it's not fun. So let's give our rocket model a nice comfy seat. To create the cutout for the seat we will be using ProBoolean. A *Boolean operation* is a geometric operation in 3ds Max that creates a shape from the addition of two shapes, the subtraction of one shape from another, or the common intersection of two shapes.

In theory, we will need to subtract a cylinder shape from the rocket body we have created so far. We'll start by creating the cylinder:

You can continue with your own scene file or load `Rocket_05.max` from the Scenes folder in the Red Rocket project.

1. Using your own scene file or the provided `Rocket_05.max` scene, in the Left viewport create a cylinder with the parameters shown in Figure 3.53.

FIGURE 3.53
The Parameters rollout

2. From the side view, line up the cylinder so it is over the part of the rocket body where the seat would be, as shown in Figure 3.54.

FIGURE 3.54 Line up the cylinder with the seat area.

From the top view, the cylinder should be evenly spaced on both sides of the rocket, as shown in Figure 3.55.

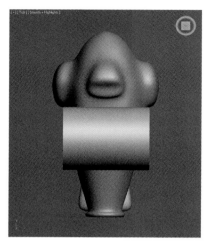

FIGURE 3.55 The top view of the cylinder

3. Select the rocket body, and before performing the Boolean operation, turn on Use NURMS if needed from the Graphite Modeling Tools. Then in the Create tab, click Geometry, Compound Objects, and ProBoolean. Choose Start Picking from the Pick Boolean rollout, and then select the cylinder in a viewport. The cylinder will cut a seat into the rocket body as shown in Figure 3.56.

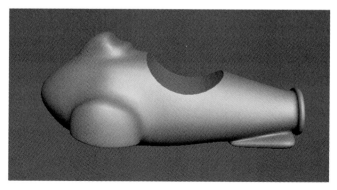

FIGURE 3.56 The rocket body is finished.

Merging Objects into a Scene

Let's try to merge an external model into this scene. Pretend that you have created a fin model for the red rocket in a different scene file. You can import that fin into your current scene with the rocket body instead of creating a whole new fin object in this scene. In 3ds Max, this procedure is called *merging*.

1. Save your work.

2. Click Application ➢ Import ➢ Merge and navigate to the Fin.max file in the Scenes folder in the Red Rocket project.

3. Click Open. The Merge dialog window opens.

4. Select the fin object from the dialog window and click OK. The Fin object will appear in your scene as the top center fin of the rocket.

You can clone and position the fin to create the side fins, or you can load your previous scene file and continue with the Red Rocket exercise.

The Essentials and Beyond

The more you use these tools, the faster they will become an instinctive part of your workflow.

After setting up the scene with background images, you were able to line up model parts and build them to fit the actual object as you worked in the scene. When you built the red rocket, you employed several of the Editable Poly tools and ProBoolean functions you learned about in the previous chapter. You also used the very handy Symmetry modifier to cut your work on the body in half.

If you study the rocket image at the beginning of the chapter, you can see there are many elements that still need to be done. Some will be built in the following chapter. But some of these elements you, as a burgeoning modeler, should attempt on your own.

Additional Exercises

▶ Study the images of the rocket at the start of the chapter. The fins on the back of the rocket are not included in the step-by-step exercises. Try building them on your own. Use reference image planes to guide you, and start with a simple primitive box, convert it to an Editable Polygon, and use Vertex mode to reshape the box into a rough shape of the fin. Apply NURMS and continue to reshape until you have a match to the picture. You can find images of the fins for the rocket at **www.sybex.com/ go/3dsmax2012essentials**.

(Continues)

THE ESSENTIALS AND BEYOND *(Continued)*

▶ Another model you can practice with is the rocket seat. On the rocket we subtracted out a cylindrical shape using ProBoolean, but there should be a smooth rim around the top and edges—using the same techniques as you did on the rocket body and fins.

▶ The control panel on the top of the rocket has some buttons. Study them in the reference, and try to re-create.

If you want to see the finished parts of these models, you can merge the finished models into your rocket body scene by choosing Application ➤ Import ➤ Merge.

CHAPTER 4

Modeling in 3ds Max: Part II

In the previous chapter, you began working on a complex model with a child's red rocket ride-on toy. In this chapter you will complete the model using the Lathe and Bevel modifiers as well as use the Loft compound object to create the toy. You will learn more about splines and shapes. Topics in this chapter include the following:

▶ **Creating the thruster**

▶ **Making the wheels**

▶ **Getting a handle on things**

Creating the Thruster

Before you begin, download the Red Rocket folder from this book's companion web page (**www.sybex.com/go/3dsmax2012essentials**) to your hard drive where you keep your other 3ds Max projects.

The back end of the rocket toy is the round thruster shown in Figure 4.1. You can continue with your own scene file or load Rocket_05.max from the Scenes folder in the Red Rocket project you downloaded from the web page.

FIGURE 4.1 The thruster seen from above and below

You will create the thruster using the Lathe modifier technique, which you used to create the knobs for the dresser model in Chapter 2, "Your First 3ds Max Project." Using Lathe works only when the object to be modeled is round and has the same look and detail all the way around. As you did with the dresser knob you created in Chapter 2, you will use splines—more specifically the Line tool—to fashion the profile of the thruster. The Line tool creates a 2D shape with no depth. The Lathe modifier then creates a 3D object by rotating that shape about one of the three axes (X, Y, or Z).

Using Lathe for the Thruster Shape

You first need to identify the profile and draw it with the Line tool.

1. The profile shape you need to use is laid out in Figure 4.2. In the Create tab, click the Shapes icon. There you will find the Line tool button. Click Line, and in the Top viewport lay out a profile similar in shape to Figure 4.2. The shape will make more sense once you see it lathed.

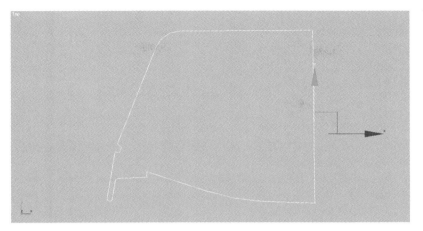

FIGURE 4.2 This shape will be used to lathe the thruster for the rocket.

2. Once you have created the spline or merged the existing one into the scene, select the spline, go to the Modify tab, and add the Lathe modifier to the line.

   Don't worry if you get something like the lathe shown in Figure 4.3, where the profile line is rotating about the axis at the center of the line shape. You need the axis of rotation to be at the inside edge of the profile shape.

You can merge in an existing shape for the thruster's profile. Navigate to the Scenes folder of the Red Rocket project, and open ThrusterProfile .max. Select the Exhaust Profile Line object and click OK.

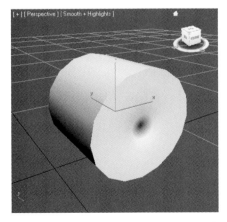

FIGURE 4.3 The lathe is rotating about the wrong axis.

3. Go to the Modify panel and in the modifier stack make sure the Lathe is selected. Under the Parameters rollout, in the Align section click the Min button, as shown in Figure 4.4. This moves the rotation axis for the profile to the inside edge.

FIGURE 4.4
In the Lathe modifier,
click the Min button.

The lathed object should look more like the thruster but will have a big hole in the middle, as shown in Figure 4.5. This is also an axis issue. You need to adjust the lathe's axis of rotation to get rid of the hole.

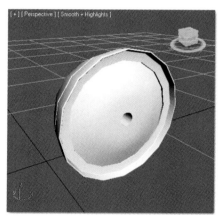

FIGURE 4.5 The lathe is starting to look more like the thruster.

Be cautious with step 4. Don't close the hole; just make it as small as you can. If you cross over the line, the normals flip on the entire object.

4. In the modifier stack, expand the Lathe modifier (click the plus sign to the left of the Lathe entry), and select Axis for the lathe's subobject mode. Go to the Perspective viewport and move the Transform gizmo to the left (or right, depending on your orientation) along the X axis until the hole is closed to the naked eye.

5. Go back to the Lathe parameters and change Segments to 20. This will help the thruster look less faceted than it does right now, but it will look a bit chunky on the edges. Don't be too concerned with that; the thrusters will not be seen close up in this scenario. Use the Segments parameter to make your lathes look only as smooth as needed for your shot.

6. Name your thruster geometry **Thruster**.

7. Move it to the back of the rocket body, according to the reference images.

Creating the 3D Object for the Thruster Detail

To create the indented thruster detail you will use a Boolean operation, so you need the object for the subtraction object. In Figure 4.1, you can see that the top of the indented shape has flat corners, the bottom corners are rounded, and the whole rectangle shape tapers. You will create this detail by using a simple rectangle shape and editing it at a subobject level to fine-tune.

You can continue with your own work or open Rocket_06.max in the Scenes folder of the Red Rocket project to catch up to this point. This scene has the thruster created up to this point in the exercise. If you want to use the one you already created, feel free to just select and delete the thruster. Then merge your thruster into the scene.

1. Let's make the work area a little easier to navigate by hiding some of the rocket parts. You can't use Isolate Selection mode because you want to hide all the objects in the scene. Select all the objects in the scene by zooming out until you have gray all around the model and image planes. Click and drag a selection box around the objects. Right-click over the selected objects to open the context menu and from the list, choose Hide Selection, as shown in Figure 4.6.

2. Go to the Create panel and, under Shapes, select Rectangle. Click and drag in the Top viewport to create a rectangle with Length 0.74 and Width 0.42. Move the rectangle above the thruster geometry you just lathed.

   Oh no…you just hid that! No problem. Just right-click again in your viewport and up comes the context menu. Choose Unhide By Name from the dialog box, as shown in Figure 4.7. Then choose the Thruster from the Unhide Objects dialog box and click the Unhide button at the bottom of the dialog box.

◄

You can merge an already created spline from the scene file Thruster Detail Spline .max in the Scenes folder of the Red Rocket project and skip to step 3.

FIGURE 4.6
Choose Hide Selection
in the context menu.

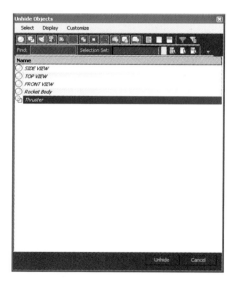

FIGURE 4.7 **Use the Unhide Objects**
dialog box.

3. Now move the rectangle above the thruster geometry you just lathed, as shown in Figure 4.8.

4. Center your cursor over the wireframe of the rectangle and right-click; choose Convert To ➤ Convert To Editable Spline, as shown in Figure 4.9. Converting to an editable spline will give you access to the subobject modes, as you saw in the previous chapter, and it will let you edit the shape for the detail you need in the thruster.

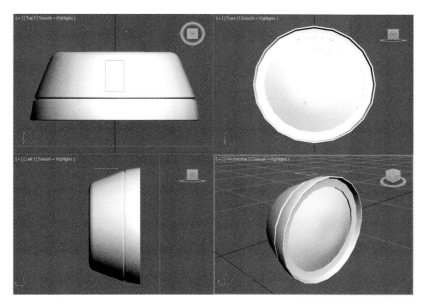

F I G U R E 4 . 8 Move the rectangle above the thruster geometry.

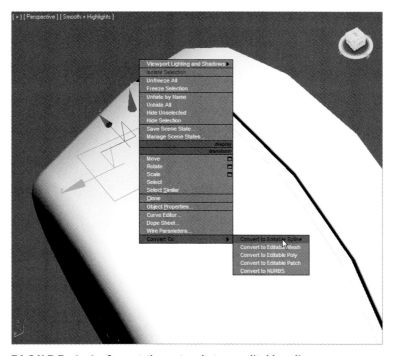

F I G U R E 4 . 9 Convert the rectangle to an editable spline.

Watch carefully to make sure the chamfer and fillet in steps 5 and 6 don't create overlapping vertices. Too much of a good thing can cause trouble.

5. Enter Vertex mode for the rectangle spline and from the Top viewport, select the bottom two vertices. Select the Modify panel and in the Editable Spline parameters open the Geometry rollout and choose Chamfer, enter a value of 0.04, and press Enter. This will give a cutoff angle to the corners of the rectangle.

6. Now select the two top vertices in the Top viewport individually and move them closer together so that the rectangle tapers at that end. Select both of the top vertices and in the Geometry rollout choose Fillet, enter a value of 0.1, and press Enter; doing so will round out the top of the spline, as shown in Figure 4.10.

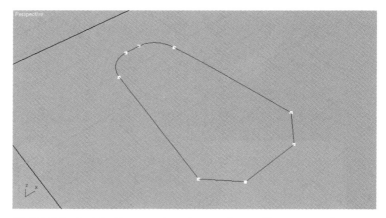

FIGURE 4.10 Enter a value of 0.1 and press Enter to round out the top of the spline.

7. Exit Vertex mode by clicking Editable Spline in the modifier stack.

8. With the spline selected, select the modifier list and choose Extrude. Set Amount to 0.4. You will use this object for the Boolean operation to create the indent into the thruster sides.

9. Line up the thruster detail object with the thruster, as shown in Figure 4.11. Center the object on top of the thruster for best results in the following steps.

   We are going to copy the object and array the indentation around the thruster eight times. To make it easier, move the pivot point of the Boolean object to the center of the thruster; this will enable the object to be copied nicely around the thruster.

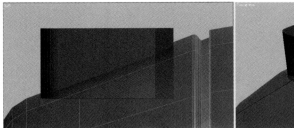

FIGURE 4.11 Center the thruster detail object on the thruster.

10. Select the extruded thruster detail. The pivot of the extruded thruster detail needs to move to the center of the Thruster object. In the Command panel, select the Hierarchy panel ( ) and click the Affect Pivot Only button.

11. In the Main toolbar select the Align icon ( ), and then select the thruster; it does not matter in which viewport. The Align Selection dialog box will appear; leave the dialog box settings at their default values—except for Target Object, which should be set to Center—and click OK.

12. Click Affect Pivot Only again to disable it. Press the A key to turn on Angle Snap, and then select the Rotate tool. While holding down the Shift key, rotate the thruster detail object 45 degrees in either direction around the thruster dish. When you release the mouse button, the Clone Options dialog box should open. Select Copy, enter a value of 7 for Number of Copies, and click OK. This will place seven copies of the object, each at 45 degrees of rotation around the thruster, making a total of eight objects that are 360 degrees around.

13. Next, select the thruster, then choose Create ➢ Geometry ➢ Compound Objects ➢ ProBoolean. Choose Start Picking from the Pick Boolean rollout. Move to the thruster detail objects and click on each one to subtract from the thruster.

    Your thruster should now have the indentations shown in Figure 4.12.

14. Right-click to turn off the Start Picking feature. Then unhide the other parts of the rocket to see how everything looks so far.

You can merge the premade model from the scene file `Thruster Detail .max` in the Scenes folder of the Red Rocket project.

The pivot should be the only thing that moves. If the object moves, Undo (Ctrl+Z) and try the step again.

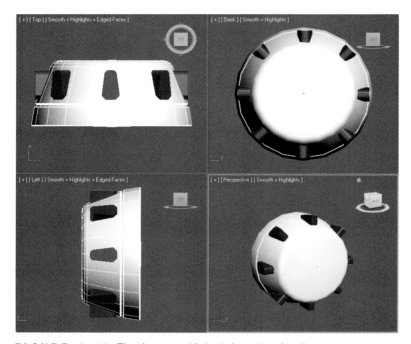

FIGURE 4.12 The thruster with its indentation detail

Making the Wheels

We are in the home stretch. In this section, you will model the wheels shown in Figure 4.13. You can continue with your own scene file or load Rocket_07.max from the Scenes folder in the Red Rocket project.

FIGURE 4.13 The wheels of the rocket are next.

Creating the First Wheel

The wheels are created using the same general technique as the body: Select the polygons of a standard/extended primitive and edit them. This time we are going to use a chamfer cylinder.

1. If the image planes are hidden, unhide the side view image planes. If you are in Isolate Selection mode, exit; then select the side view image plane and enter Isolate Selection again.

2. Choose the Create tab. From the drop-down menu, select Extended Primitives and click ChamferCyl to create a chamfer cylinder.

3. To get the side of the wheel to finish, click and drag in the Left viewport to create the circle of the cylinder, and then release the mouse button. Drag and click the mouse again to set the depth of the cylinder, and finally drag the mouse a third time to set the amount of the chamfer. Click to set the final shape in the Left viewport. Select the Modify panel and set the Chamfer Cylinder parameters as shown in Figure 4.14.

FIGURE 4.14
Set the Chamfer Cylinder parameters as shown.

4. Select the Graphite Modeling Tools ribbon, and in the Polygon Modeling tab click Convert To Poly. Go into Vertex mode and select the vertex on the front in the center, as shown in Figure 4.15.

You can merge the wheels using already created models from the scene file Wheels.max in the Scenes folder of the Red Rocket project.

FIGURE 4.15 Select the vertex on the front in the center.

5. Go to the Graphite Modeling Tools ribbon's Vertices tab and click the Chamfer Settings button. Set Vertex Chamfer Amount to **0.4** and click OK.

6. Switch to Polygon mode and select the new center polygon.

7. Select the Polygons tab and open the Bevel Settings caddy. Set Height to **−0.4** and Outline to **0.0**, and click Apply And Continue to create one bevel. Then set Height to **0.5** and Outline to **−0.12** and click OK to create a second bevel.

8. Now change the viewport so you can see the back of the wheel. The Side View image will be in the way, so exit subobject mode by clicking the Polygon icon in the Graphite Modeling Tools ribbon's Polygon Modeling tab. Select the wheel and enter Isolation mode again. This adds the Side View image to the isolate selection you already have set up.

9. Go back into Vertex mode and select the center vertex. Choose the Vertices tab and click the Chamfer Settings button. Set Vertex Chamfer Amount to **0.2** and click OK.

10. Switch back to Polygon mode and select the new center polygon. In the Polygons tab, extrude the polygon with an Amount of 3.0. You can see the completed wheel in Figure 4.16.

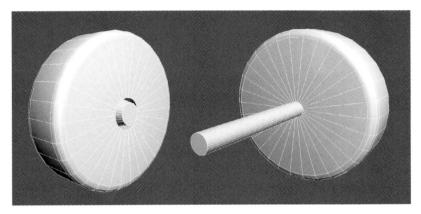

FIGURE 4.16 The completed wheel

Placing the Wheels

One wheel is done! Now exit the Polygon level and make three clones for the front and back wheels. Unhide the rocket body and place the wheels at the wheel wells. Don't worry if the front wheels don't fit perfectly and happen to penetrate the body's geometry. It was hard to tell how big to make the wheel wells until you had the wheels. You will fix that here:

1. Unhide or exit Isolate Selection mode so you can select the rocket body.

2. Enter Vertex mode. Change any viewport to a bottom view. Select the vertices on the inside of the wheel well and move them to make the opening larger so the wheels can fit. Use Soft Selection to make the movement of multiple vertices easier. The finished wheel well is shown in Figure 4.17.

One last thing you can do is give your new wheels proper names; we used Wheel01, Wheel02, Wheel03, and Wheel04.

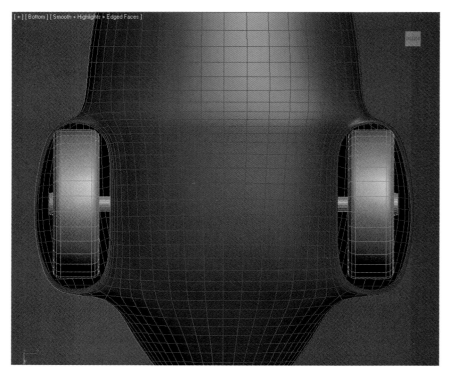

FIGURE 4.17 Make sure the wheels fit into the wheel wells.

Getting a Handle on Things

The red rocket has a set of handlebars just as a bike does. They help keep the driver (usually a child) from face planting every time he or she gets on it. As funny as that may be, a parent can watch it only so many times. This is why most grownups find the handlebars as shown in Figure 4.18 to be the most important part of the rocket. You will model them now.

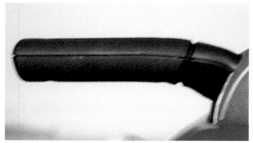

FIGURE 4.18 The handlebars help prevent calamities of the falling kind.

The handlebars will be created using a modeling technique called *lofting,* which creates a shape that is extruded along a path. Each handlebar is a compound object that uses one shape as a profile and another as the path to form a 3D surface or object.

LOFTING

The Loft compound object has many features and only a few restrictions. The Shape object can be complex, consisting of several noncontiguous splines and even nested splines. A new Shape object can be selected at any point along the path, and the cross-section will automatically transition from one shape to the next. Any 2D shape can be used as the Shape object, but only a shape that consists of a single spline can be used as the Path object.

Creating the Path

Take a look at Figure 4.18 and imagine a straight line passing through the middle of one of the handlebars. This is the path you want to create.

You can continue with your own scene file or load Rocket_08.max from the Scenes folder in the Red Rocket project. Select the FRONT VIEW image and enter Isolate Selection mode.

1. Start by choosing the Create panel. Click the Shapes icon and select the Line tool.

2. Switch a viewport to a Back viewport by pressing V in any view and choosing Back from the pop-up list. Against the image of the front view of the rocket, click to place the line's first point where the handlebar ends. Move the cursor to where the handlebar bends, and create another point. Place a final point where the handlebar meets the control panel, as shown in Figure 4.19, and right-click to complete the line. You may need to move the line forward in the Top viewport to get the proper alignment shown in Figure 4.19.

3. Move to the Modify panel and enter Vertex mode for the line. Select the middle vertex, go to the Fillet parameter in the Geometry rollout, and enter 0.1. This will add a smooth corner to the bend.

◄ Merge the scene file Handle Bar Spline.max from the Scenes folder of the Red Rocket project if you don't want to create the path yourself.

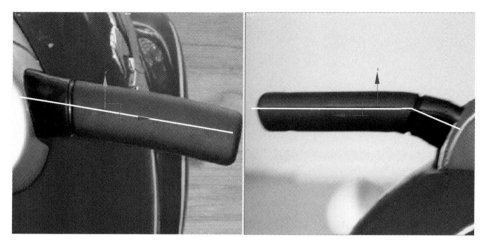

FIGURE 4.19 Completed path for the handlebar loft

Creating the Shape

Now that you have the path for the loft, you need the profile shape, which is a cross-section of the handlebar. This shape is an oval with a flat top, as shown in Figure 4.20.

To create this shape, follow these steps:

1. Exit Vertex mode. Go back to the Create panel and click Shapes, and create a circle shape with a radius of 0.4 in the Left viewport. Convert the circle shape to an editable spline by right-clicking on the circle and choosing Convert To ➢ Editable Spline from the context menu.

2. Go into Vertex mode, select the top vertex, and delete it to flatten the top. Move the new shape so that it sits at the end of the path.
   Next, you will create the Loft object.

3. Exit Vertex mode, then select the path spline for the handlebar and choose the Create panel. Click the Geometry rollout and click Compound Objects ➢ Loft.

4. Because you started the lofting process with the handlebar's path line, you only need to let 3ds Max know which shape to use. In the Creation Method rollout, select Get Shape.

5. Select the handlebar shape in a viewport to use as the loft's shape.

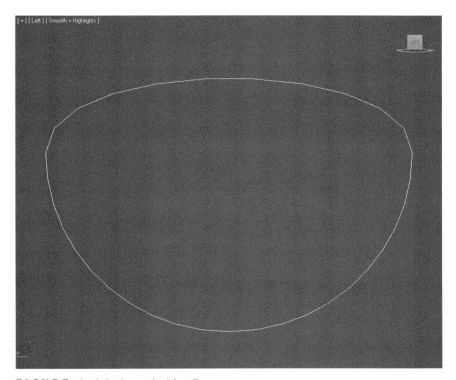

[+] [Left] [Smooth + Highlights]

FIGURE 4.20 An oval with a flat top

Editing the Loft Object

In Figure 4.21, you can see the loft's path and cross-section shape as well as the resulting Loft object. We moved the Loft object next to the path so you can see the result. In your file, the Loft object will be created on top of the path.

In this example the shape is rotated 90 degrees along the path, putting the handle on its side, as you can see in Figure 4.22.

The shape needs to be turned to so that the broad flat side is on the top. To edit the loft, you will go into its subobject mode. The subobjects of a loft are the path and the shape.

1. Select the Loft object and on the Modify tab, expand the Loft object in the modifier stack.

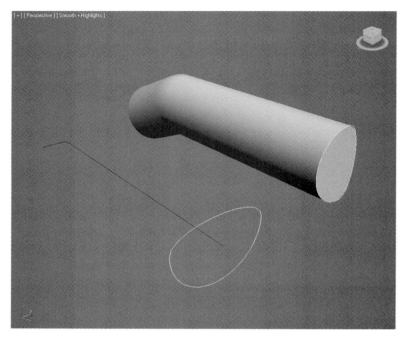

FIGURE 4.21 The loft lives!

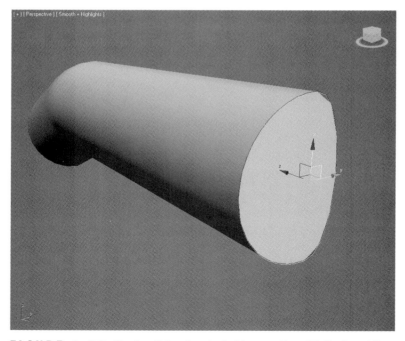

FIGURE 4.22 The handlebar is oriented incorrectly, with the broad flat side facing the rider.

SPLINES FOR THE LOFT

The original splines were instanced when the loft was created, so they are still connected to the loft. This means changes made at the subobject level on the splines will be transferred to the lofted object. If necessary, you can alter the shape of the path line or shape splines and the loft will change accordingly. You cannot, however, move or rotate the path or shape splines to affect the shape of the loft. You must use Move or Rotate at the subobject level of the loft instead.

2. Enter the Shape subobject mode, as shown in Figure 4.23.

FIGURE 4.23
The Shape subobject mode

3. In a viewport, select the loft's shape at the end of the Loft object. The shape will turn red when it is selected, as shown previously in Figure 4.22. The shape spline is the thin, smoother line in this gray-scale figure.

4. Select the Rotate tool and rotate the shape on the loft −90 degrees. The entire loft will be updated.

Adding Detail

The next step is to create the subtle curves and dips of the handlebars. The outside end of the real handlebar is curved. There is a groove toward the middle, and the handle tapers up where it meets the control panel. To look this good, the handlebar you've created needs more than one cross-section. With a Loft compound object in 3ds Max, you can have any number of cross-sections for your loft, and they can be of varying shapes.

To edit a loft for these details, you are going to add more shapes along the path, and then edit those shapes to taste.

1. Go back to the top level of the Loft object in the Modify tab, and open the Skin Parameters rollout. This is where you can manage the steps (subdivisions) in the loft. By default, there is a value of 5 for both Shape Steps and Path Steps. Shape Steps here are fine, but the Path Steps value is too high. To fix this, turn Path Steps down to 1, as shown in Figure 4.24. If there are too many steps in your loft, it will get too heavy and dense to model.

FIGURE 4.24
Reduce the Path
Steps value.

2. Go back to Shape mode and select the shape. Using the Move tool, center the cursor over the *Z* axis wire of the Transform gizmo that is connected to the shape.

3. You need to make copies of the shapes so you can taper down the end of the handlebar. Shift+click and drag the gizmo to move the shape just a bit up the body of the handlebar to make a copy of the loft shape, as shown in Figure 4.25. The loft shape is shown as a dashed red line.

4. In the Copy Shape dialog box, choose Copy and then click OK. Repeat these steps twice to end up with three copies, and place them close to the end of the handle, as shown in Figure 4.26 (left image). Switch to the Scale tool, and scale the outside shape down 30 percent and the middle shape down 10 percent. Leave the last inside shape alone, which should create a nice curved taper at the end of the handlebar, as shown in Figure 4.26 (right image).

> If you prefer, you can merge the scene file Handle Bar.max from the Red Rocket project to check your own work.

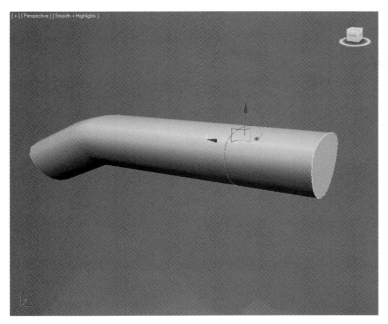

FIGURE 4.25 Make a copy of the loft shape.

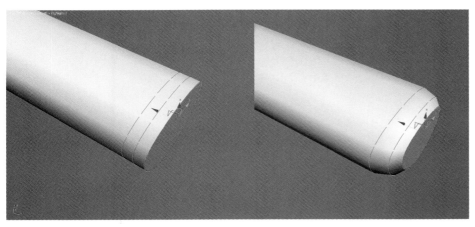

FIGURE 4.26 Place copies of the loft's shape close together (left image). At the end, scale them down to create the handlebar's end (right image).

5. Select the inside shape on the loft, and make four more copies in a row close to where the bar curves down. Select the two inside copies and scale them both down 20 percent. Doing so will create the groove toward the center of the handlebars, as shown in Figure 4.27.

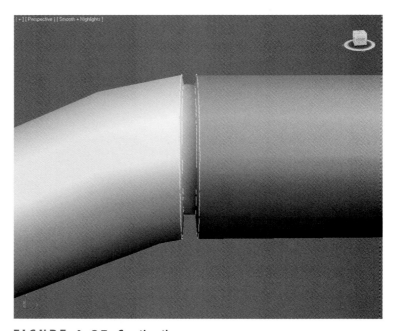

FIGURE 4.27 Creating the groove

6. Select the shape closest to the bend and make a copy. Move it all the way to the other end of the object, away from the tapered tip. This is where it will meet the body of the rocket. Select the Scale tool, and scale this end shape up 50 percent. Exit the loft's subobject mode.

7. If any parts of the rocket are hidden, unhide them and see how the handlebars line up. You will probably agree that there is room for improvement.

8. Instead of rotating the Loft object, rotate the last shape at the end of the loft. Go back to the Shape subobject mode and select the last shape to rotate to line up with the body, as shown in Figure 4.28.

9. Select the handlebar, and in the Main toolbar click the Mirror icon ( ) to mirror a copy of the handle for the other side of the rocket. Place it as needed. Figure 4.29 shows the rocket with its handlebars.

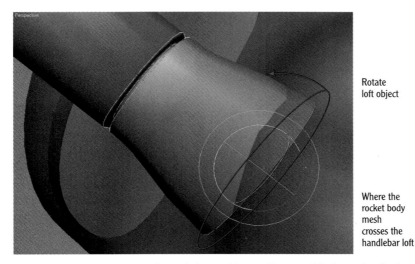

Rotate
loft object

Where the
rocket body
mesh
crosses the
handlebar loft

FIGURE 4.28 Rotate the end shape object to line up with the rocket body.

Most of the parts are built, so this would be a good time to merge in all the other parts you built for the rocket. If you didn't build any of the parts in this chapter and Chapter 3, "Modeling in 3ds Max: Part I," you can merge them in from the Red Rocket/Scenes files. You can select each model and change the color to fit the original, as shown in Figure 4.29.

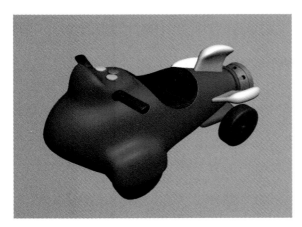

FIGURE 4.29 Final render of the red rocket with all its parts

THE ESSENTIALS AND BEYOND

In this chapter you completed the red rocket. Using the Line tool, you created a profile to lathe. Then, using a rectangle converted to an editable spline, you created the detail, and then using the Boolean operation finished the thruster. You learned how to use Loft, a tool that uses a combination of splines, to create the handlebars. Now that you have completed a complex 3D model using multiple techniques, it is time to apply those techniques to a model of your own. Find an object in which you can clearly see the shapes and primitives.

ADDITIONAL EXERCISES

▶ Start with simple pieces of furniture, such as a dining room chair or coffee table, to practice with editable polygons and the Graphite modeling tools. You can find some examples at **www.sybex.com/go/3dsmax2012essentials.**

▶ Once you feel comfortable, try a softer surface like a comfy couch, bed, or chair, so you can utilize NURMS.

▶ Take some time to explore some of the other tools in the Graphite modeling tools as you create your own models.

CHAPTER 5

Animating a Bouncing Ball

The best way to learn how to animate is to jump right in and start animating. You'll take a good look at 3ds Max's animation tools so you can start editing animation and developing your timing skills.

Topics in this chapter include the following:

▶ **Animating the ball**

▶ **Refining the animation**

A classic exercise for all animators is to create a bouncing ball. It is a straightforward exercise, but there is much you can do with a bouncing ball to show character. Animating a bouncing ball is a good exercise in physics as well as cartoon movement. You'll first create a rubber ball, and then you'll add cartoonish movement to accentuate some principles of the animation. Aspiring animators can use this exercise for years and always find something new to learn about bouncing a ball.

In preparation, download the Bouncing Ball project from the companion web page at **www.sybex.com/go/3dsmax2012essentials** to your hard drive. Set your current project by choosing Application ➢ Manage ➢ Set Project Folder and selecting the Bouncing Ball project that you downloaded.

Animating the Ball

Your first step is to keyframe the positions of the ball. As you learned in Chapter 1, "The 3ds Max Interface," *keyframing* is the process—borrowed from traditional animation—of setting positions and values at particular frames of the animation. The computer interpolates between these keyframes to fill in the other frames to complete a smooth animation.

Open the Animation_Ball_00.max scene file from the Scenes folder of the Bouncing Ball project you downloaded. If you get a warning to "Disable Gamma/LUT," click OK.

Start with the *gross animation*, or the overall movements. This is also called *blocking*. First, move the ball up and down to begin its choreography. Follow these steps to animate the ball:

1. Move the pivot point for the ball from the center of the ball to the bottom of the ball. Select the ball, and then go to the Hierarchy panel (![icon]). Choose Pivot, and under the Adjust Pivot rollout, click the Affect Pivot Only button. Zoom in on the ball in the Front viewport and move the pivot so that it is at the bottom of the ball. Then click the Affect Pivot Only button again to deactivate—but you already knew that.

2. Move the time slider to frame 10. The time slider is at the bottom of the screen below the viewports, as shown in Figure 5.1. The time slider is used to change your position in time, counted in *frames*.

FIGURE 5.1 The time slider allows you to change your position in time and scrub your animation.

SCRUBBING THE TIME SLIDER

You can click and drag the horizontal time slider bar to change the frame in your animation on the fly; this is called **scrubbing**. The bar displays the current frame/end frame. By default, your 3ds Max window may show a start frame of 0 and an end frame of 100.

3. Now, in the lower-right corner of the window, click the Auto Key button, as shown in Figure 5.2. Both the Auto Key button and the time slider turn red. This means that any movement in the objects in your scene will be recorded as animation. How exciting!

4. With the ball selected, move it along the Z axis down to the ground plane, so it is 0 units in Z axis when you release the mouse button in the Transform Type-In box at the bottom of the interface. You can also just enter the value and press Enter.

This exercise has created two keyframes, one at frame 0 for the original position the ball was in, and one at frame 10 for the new position to which you just moved the ball.

FIGURE 5.2
The Auto Key button
records your animations.

Copying Keyframes

Now you want to move the ball up to the same position in the air as it was at
frame 0. Instead of trying to estimate where that was, you can just copy the keyframe at frame 0 to frame 20.

　You can see the keyframes you created in the timeline. They appear as red
boxes in the timeline. Red keys represent Position keyframes, green keys represent Rotation, and blue keys represent Scale. When a keyframe in the timeline is
selected, it turns white. Now we'll copy a keyframe:

1. Select the keyframe at frame 0; it should turn white when it is
   selected. Hold down the Shift key on the keyboard (this is a shortcut
   for the Clone tool), and click and drag the selected keyframe to copy
   it to frame 20. This will create a keyframe with the same animation
   parameters as the keyframe at frame 0, as shown in Figure 5.3.

FIGURE 5.3 Press Shift
and move the keyframe to copy it
to frame 20.

2. Click and drag the time slider to scrub through the keyframes. Turn
   off Auto Key.

Using the Track View–Curve Editor

Right now the ball is going down and then back up. To continue the animation
for the length of the timeline, you could continue to copy and paste keyframes
as you did earlier—but that would be very time-consuming, and you still need
to do your other homework and clean your room. A better way is to loop, or *cycle*,
through the keyframes you already have. An *animation cycle* is a segment of animation that is repeatable in a loop. The end state of the animation matches up to
the beginning state, so there is no hiccup at the loop point.

In 3ds Max, cycling animation is known as *parameter curve out-of-range types*. This is a fancy way to create loops and cycles with your animations and specify how your object will behave outside the range of the keys you have created. This will bring us to the Track View, which is an animator's best friend. You will learn the underlying concepts of the Curve Editor as well as its basic interface throughout this exercise.

The Track View is a function of two animation editors, the Curve Editor and the Dope Sheet. The Curve Editor allows you to work with animation depicted as curves on a graph that sets the value of a parameter against time. The Dope Sheet displays keyframes over time on a horizontal graph, without any curves. This graphical display simplifies the process of adjusting animation timing because you can see all the keys at once in a spreadsheet-like format. The Dope Sheet is similar to traditional animation exposure sheets, or X-sheets.

Navigation inside the Track View – Curve Editor is pretty much the same as navigating in a viewport; the same keyboard/ mouse combinations work for panning and zooming.

You will use the Track View – Curve Editor (or just the Curve Editor for short) to loop your animation in the following steps:

1. With the ball selected, in the menu bar choose Graph Editors ➤ Track View – Curve Editor. In Figure 5.4, the Curve Editor displays the animation curves of the ball so far.

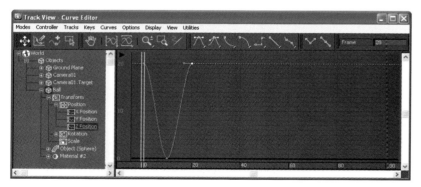

FIGURE 5.4 The Curve Editor shows the animation curves of the ball.

2. A menu bar runs across the top of the Curve Editor. In the Controller menu, select the Out-of-Range Types option, as shown in Figure 5.5.

3. Doing so opens the Param Curve Out-of-Range Types dialog box, shown in Figure 5.6. Select Loop in this dialog box by clicking its thumbnail. The two little boxes beneath it will highlight. Click OK.

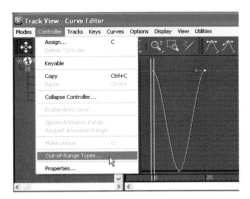

FIGURE 5.5 Selecting Out-of-Range Types

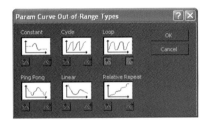

FIGURE 5.6 Choosing to loop your animation

4. Once you set the curve to Loop, the Curve Editor displays your animation, as shown in Figure 5.7. The out-of-range animation is shown as a dashed line. Scrub your animation in a viewport and see how the ball bounces up and down throughout the timeline range.

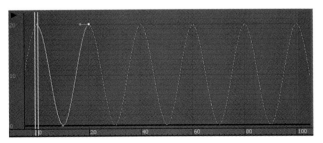

FIGURE 5.7 The Curve Editor now shows the looped animation curve.

Reading Animation Curves

As you can see, the Track View – Curve Editor (from here on called just the Curve Editor) gives you control over the animation in a graph setting. The Curve Editor's graph is a representation of an object's parameter, such as position (values shown vertically) over time (time shown horizontally). Curves allow you to visualize the interpolation of the motion. Once you are used to reading animation curves, you can judge an object's direction, speed, acceleration, and timing at a mere glance.

Here is a quick primer on how to read a curve in the Curve Editor.

In Figure 5.8, an object's Z Position parameter is being animated. At the beginning, the curve quickly begins to move positively (that is, to the right) on the Z axis. The object shoots up and comes to an *ease-in*, where it decelerates to a stop, reaching its top height. The ease-in stop is signified by the curving beginning to flatten out at around frame 70.

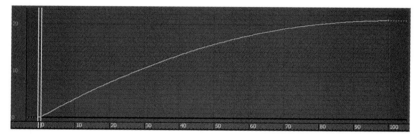

FIGURE 5.8 The object quickly accelerates to an ease-in stop.

In Figure 5.9, the object slowly accelerates in an *ease-out* in the positive Z direction until it hits frame 100, where it suddenly stops.

In Figure 5.10, the object eases in and travels to an ease-out where it decelerates, starting at around frame 69, to where it slowly stops, at frame 100.

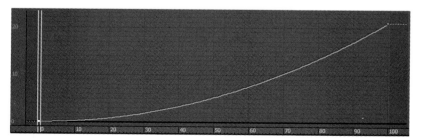

FIGURE 5.9 The object eases out to acceleration and suddenly stops at its fastest velocity.

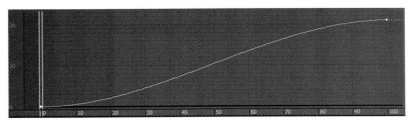

FIGURE 5.10 Ease-out and ease-in

Finally, in Figure 5.11, to showcase another tangent type, step interpolation makes the object jumps from its Z Position in frame 20 to its new position in frame 21.

FIGURE 5.11 Step interpolation makes the object "jump" suddenly from one value to the next.

Figure 5.12 shows the Curve Editor, with its major aspects called out for your information.

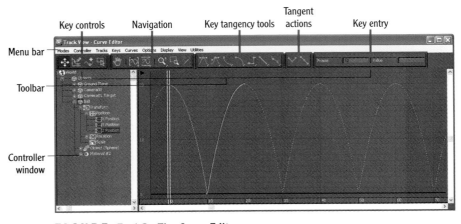

FIGURE 5.12 The Curve Editor

Refining the Animation

Let's play the animation now. In the bottom right of the interface you will see an animation player with the sideways triangle to signify Play. Select the Camera01 viewport and click the play button. The framework of the movement is getting there. Notice how the speed of the ball is consistent. If this were a real ball, it would be dealing with gravity; the ball would speed up as it got closer to the ground and there would be "hang time" when the ball was in the air on its way up as gravity takes over to pull it back down.

   This means you have to edit the movement that happens between the keyframes. This is done by adjusting *how* the keyframes shape the curve itself, using tangents. When you select a keyframe, a handle will appear in the UI, as shown in Figure 5.13.

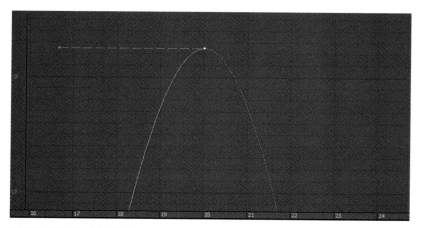

FIGURE 5.13 The keyframe's handle

   This handle adjusts the tangency of the keyframe to change the curvature of the animation curve, which in turn changes the animation. There are various types of tangents, depending on how you want to edit the motion. By default the Auto tangent is applied to all new keyframes. This is not what you want for the ball, although it is a perfect default tangent type to have.

Editing Animation Curves

Let's edit some tangents to better suit your animation. The intent is to speed up the curve as it hits the floor and slow it down as it crests its apex. Instead of opening the Curve Editor through the menu bar, this time you are going to use the shortcut. Close the large Curve Editor dialog box, and then at the bottom-left corner of the interface, click the Open Mini Curve Editor button shown in Figure 5.14.

FIGURE 5.14
Click the Open Mini
Curve Editor button.

The Mini Curve Editor is almost exactly the same as the one you launch through the Main menu. A few tools are not included in the Mini Curve Editor toolbar, but you can find them in the menu bar of the Mini Curve Editor.

To edit the curves, follow these steps:

1. Scroll down the Controller window on the left of the Mini Curve Editor by dragging the Pan tool (the hand cursor) to find the Ball object's position. Click on the Z Position track. This will bring only the curves to the Key Editing window that you want to edit.

2. The Z Position curve is blue, as is almost everything relating to the Z axis. The little gray boxes on the curves are keyframes. Select the keyframe at frame 10. You may need to scrub the time slider out of the way if you are on frame 10. The key will turn white when selected. Remember, if you need to zoom or pan in the Curve Editor's Key Editing window, you can use the same shortcuts you would use to navigate in the viewports. You will change this key's tangency to make the ball fall faster as it hits and bounces off the ground.

3. In the Mini Curve Editor toolbar, change the tangent type for the selected keyframe from the Auto default to Fast by clicking the Set Tangents To Fast icon ( ). When you do this, you will see the animation curve change shape, as shown in Figure 5.15.

4. Select the Camera viewport and play the animation. You can easily correlate how the animation works with the curve's shape as you see the time slider travel through the Mini Curve Editor as the animation plays.

FIGURE 5.15 The effect of the new tangent type

Finessing the Animation

Although the animation has improved, the ball has a distinct lack of weight. It still seems too simple and without any character. In situations such as this, animators can go wild and try several different things as they see fit. Here is where creativity helps hone your animation skills, whether you are new to animation or have been doing it for 50 years.

Animation shows change over time. Good animation conveys the *intent,* the motivation for that change between the frames.

Squash and Stretch

The concept of *squash and stretch* has been an animation staple for as long as there has been animation. It is a way to convey the weight of an object by deforming it to react (usually in an exaggerated way) to gravity, impact, and motion.

You can give your ball a lot of flair by adding squash and stretch to give the object some personality. Follow along with these steps:

1. Press the N key to activate Auto Key. In the Mini Curve Editor, drag the yellow double-line time slider (called the track bar time slider) to frame 10. Click and hold the Scale tool to access the flyout. Choose the Select And Squash tool (■). Center the Scale cursor over the *Z* axis of the Scale Transform gizmo in the Camera viewport. Click and drag down to squash down about 20 percent. Doing so will scale down on the *Z* axis and scale up on the *X* and *Y* axes to compensate, as shown in Figure 5.16.

FIGURE 5.16 Use the Select And Squash tool to squash down the ball on impact.

2. Move to frame 0. Click and drag up to stretch the ball up about 20 per-
    cent (so that the ball's scale in *Z* is about 120). When you scrub through
    the animation, you will see that at frame 0 the ball stretched; then the
    ball squashes and stays squashed for the rest of the time. You'll fix that
    in the next step.

    You need to copy the Scale key from frame 0 to frame 20 first,
    and then apply a loop for the Parameter Curve Out-of-Range Type.
    Because the Mini Curve Editor is open, it obstructs the timeline;
    therefore, you should copy the keys in the Mini Curve Editor.
    You can just as easily do so in the regular Curve Editor in the
    same way.

3. In the Mini Curve Editor, scroll in the Controller window until you
    find the Scale track for the ball. Highlight it to see the keyframes
    and animation curves. Click and hold the Move Keys tool in the Mini
    Curve Editor toolbar to roll out and access the Move Keys Horizontal
    tool ()

4. Click and drag a selection marquee around the two keyframes at
    frame 0 in the Scale track to select them. Hold the Shift key and then
    click and drag the keyframes at frame 0 to frame 20.

5. In the Mini Curve Editor's menu bar, select Controller ➤ Out-of-
    Range Types. Choose Loop, and then click OK. Play the animation.
    The curves are shown in Figure 5.17.

FIGURE 5.17 The final curves

Setting the Timing

Well, you squashed and stretched the ball, but it still doesn't look right. That is
because the ball should not squash before it hits the ground. It needs to return
to 100 percent scale and stay there for a few frames. Immediately before the ball
hits the ground, it can squash into the ground plane to heighten the sense of
impact. The following steps are easier to perform in the regular Curve Editor
rather than in the Mini Curve Editor. So close the Mini Curve Editor by clicking
the Close button on the left side of its toolbar.

Open the Curve Editor to fix the timing, and follow these steps as if they were law:

1. Move the time slider to frame 8; Auto Key should still be active. In the Curve Editor, in the Controller window select the ball's Scale track so that only the scale curves appear in the Editing window. In the Curve Editor's toolbar, click the Insert Keys icon (). Your cursor will change to an arrow with a white circle at its lower right. Click on one of the Scale curves to add a keyframe on all the Scale curves at frame 8. Because scales X and Y are the same value, you will see only two curves instead of three.

2. Because they are selected, the keys will be white. In the Key Entry tools, you will find two text type-in boxes. The box on the left is the frame number, and the box on the right is the selected key's (or keys') value. Because more than one key with a different value is selected, there is no number in that type-in box. Enter **100** (for 100 percent scale) in the right type-in box, and a value of **100** for the scale in X, Y, and Z for the ball at frame 8, as shown in Figure 5.18.

Frame | 12 | Value | 100.000

FIGURE 5.18 Enter a value of 100.

3. Move the time slider to frame 12, and do the same thing in the Curve Editor. These settings are bracketing the squash so that the squash happens only a couple frames before and a couple frames after the ball hits the ground. Press the N key to deactivate Auto Key. Save your work.

Once you play back the animation, the ball will begin to look a lot more like a nice cartoonish one, with a little character. Experiment with changing some of the scale amounts to have the ball squash a little more or less, or stretch it more or less to see how that affects the animation. See if it adds a different personality to the ball. If you can master a bouncing ball and evoke all sorts of emotions with your audience, you will be a great animator indeed.

Moving the Ball Forward

You can load the Animation_Ball_01.max scene file from the Bouncing Ball project on your hard drive (or from the companion web page) to catch up to this point or to check your work.

Now that you have worked out the bounce, it's time to add movement to the ball so that it moves across the screen as it bounces. Layering animation in this fashion, where you settle on one movement before moving on to another, is common. That's not to say you won't need to go back and forth and make adjustments through the whole process, but it's generally nicer to work out one layer of the animation before adding another. The following steps will show you how:

1. Move the time slider to frame 0. Select the ball with the Select And Move tool, and move the ball in the Camera viewport to the left so it is still within the camera's view. That's about −30 units on the *X* axis.

2. Move the time slider to frame 100. Press the N key to activate Auto Key again. Move the ball to the right about 60 units so that the ball's X position value is about 30.

3. Don't play the animation yet; it isn't going to look right. Go to the Curve Editor, scroll down in the Controller window, and select the X Position track for the ball, as shown in Figure 5.19.

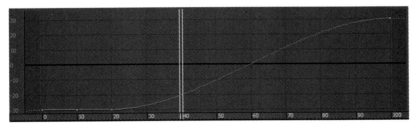

FIGURE 5.19 The X position of the ball does not look right.

When you created the keyframes for the up and down movement of the ball (which was the *Z* axis), 3ds Max automatically created keyframes for the X and Y Position tracks, both with essentially no value. To fix it, keep following these steps.

4. Select the keyframes on the X Position track at frame 10 and frame 20, and delete them by pressing the Delete key on your keyboard.

5. Click the Parameter Curves Out-of-Range Types button, and select Constant. This removes the loop from the X Position track but won't affect the Z Position track for the ball's bounce. Press the N key to deactivate Auto Key. Play the animation. You can use the / (slash) button as a shortcut to play the animation.

6. There is still a little problem. Watch the horizontal movement. The ball is slow at the beginning, speeds up in the middle, and then slows again at the end. It eases out and eases in. This is caused by the default tangent, which automatically adds a slowdown as the object goes in and out of the keyframe. In the Curve Editor, select both keys for the X Position Curve and click the Set Tangents To Linear icon (■) to create a straight line of movement so there is no speed change in the ball's movement left to right.

Figure 5.20 shows the proper curve.

FIGURE 5.20 The X Position curve for the ball's movement now has no ease-out or ease-in.

Adding a Roll

You need to add some rotation, but there are several problems with this. One, you moved the pivot point to the bottom of the ball in the very first step of the exercise. You did that so the squashing would work correctly—that is, it would be at the point of contact with the ground. If you were to rotate the ball with the pivot at the bottom, it would look like Figure 5.21.

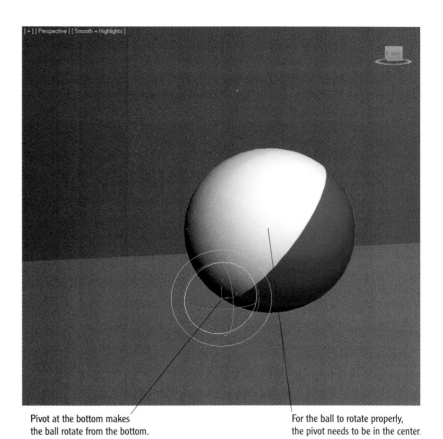

Pivot at the bottom makes
the ball rotate from the bottom.

For the ball to rotate properly,
the pivot needs to be in the center.

FIGURE 5.21 The ball will not rotate properly because the pivot is at the bottom.

Using the XForm Modifier

You need a pivot point at the center of the ball, but you can't just move the existing pivot from the bottom to the middle—it would throw off all the squash and stretch animation. Unfortunately, an object can have only one pivot point. To solve the issue, you are going to use a modifier called *XForm*. This modifier has many uses. You're going to use it to add another pivot to the ball in the following steps:

1. Select the ball. From the menu bar, select Modifiers ≻ Parametric Deformers ≻ XForm. You may also select this option from the modifier list in the Modify tab. XForm will be added to the ball in the modifier stack, and an orange bounding box will appear over the ball in the viewport. XForm has no parameters, but it does have subobjects.

2. Expand the modifier stack by clicking the black box with the plus sign next to XForm. Then click Center. In the next step you will use the Align tool to center the XForm's center point on the ball.

3. Click the Align tool, and then click on the ball. In the resulting dialog box, make sure the check boxes for X, Y, and Z Position are checked, which means those axes are active. Now click Center under Target Object, and then click OK. The XForm's center will move.

Now to be clear, this isn't a *pivot point*. This is the *center point* on the XForm modifier. If you go to the modifier stack and click on the sphere, the pivot point will still be at the bottom.

The XForm modifier allows the ball to rotate without its squashing and stretching getting in the way of the rotation. By separating the rotation animation for the ball's roll into the modifier, the animation on the sphere object is preserved.

Animating the XForm Modifier

To add the ball's roll to the XForm modifier, follow along with these steps:

1. Turn on Auto Key and choose the Select And Rotate tool.

2. In the modifier stack, click on Gizmo for the subobject of XForm. This is a very important step because it tells the modifier to use the XForm's center instead of using the pivot point of the ball.

3. In the Camera viewport, move the time slider to frame 100 and rotate the ball 360 degrees on the *Y* axis (you can use Angle Snap Toggle to make it easier to rotate exactly 360 degrees). Click on the XForm modifier to deactivate the subobject mode. Play the animation.

THE BALL DOESN'T ROTATE 360 DEGREES!

If you rotate the ball in the third step 360 degrees but the ball does not animate, 3ds Max could potentially be interpreting 360 degrees to be 0 degrees in the Curve Editor, thereby creating a flat curve. If this is the case, you can try rotating the ball 359 degrees instead to force the animation to work. You could also manually change the value in the Curve Editor for the keyframe at frame 100 to a value of 360.

The ball should be a rubbery cartoon ball at this point in the animation. Just for practice, let's say you need to go back and edit the keyframes because you rotated in the wrong direction and the ball's rotation is going backward. Fixing this issue requires you to go back into the Curve Editor as follows.

1. Open the Curve Editor (mini or regular) and scroll down in the Controller window until you see the Ball tracks. Below the Ball's Transform track is a new track called Ball/Modified Object.

2. Expand the track by clicking on the plus sign in the circle next to the name. Go to the Gizmo track and select the Y Rotation track. You will see the Function curve in the Key Editing window.

3. You want the keyframe at frame 0 to have the value 0 and the keyframe at frame 100 to be a value of 360. Select both keyframes and change the tangents to Linear, as shown in Figure 5.22.

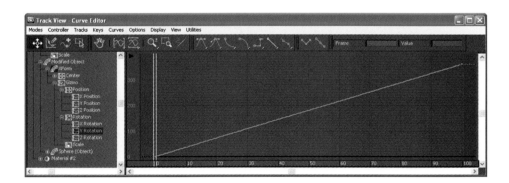

FIGURE 5.22 The XForm's gizmo selected in the Controller window with the rotation of the ball set to Linear Tangents

Close the Curve Editor and play the animation. Play the bounce ball.avi movie file located in the RenderOutput folder of the Bouncing Ball project to see a render of the animation. You can also load the Animation_Ball_02.max scene file from the Bouncing Ball project to check your work.

THE ESSENTIALS AND BEYOND

Working with the bouncing ball gave you quite a bit of experience with the 3ds Max's animation toolset. There are several ways to animate a bouncing ball in 3ds Max. It is definitely a good idea to try this exercise a few times at first, and then to come back to it later—after you have learned other 3ds Max techniques.

Animation can be a lot of fun, but it is also tedious and sometimes aggravating. A lot of time, patience, and practice is required to become good at animation. It all boils down to how the animation makes you think. Is there enough weight to the subjects in the animation? Do the movements make sense? How does nuance enhance the animation? These are all questions you will begin to discover for yourself. This chapter merely introduced you to how to make things move in 3ds Max. It gave you some basic animation techniques to help you develop your eye for motion. Don't stop here. Go back into the chapter and redo some of the exercises.

ADDITIONAL EXERCISES

Try different variations on the same themes, such as:

▶ Bounce the ball on the floor and then off a wall. Try bouncing the ball off a table, onto a chair, and then onto the floor.

▶ Animate three different types of balls bouncing next to one another, such as a bowling ball, a ping pong ball, and a tennis ball. Examples may be found at **www.sybex.com/ go/3dsmax2012essentials.**

Most important, keep working at it!

CHAPTER 6

Animating a Thrown Knife

This chapter is a continuation of the animation work you began in Chapter 5, "Animating a Bouncing Ball," and introduces you to some new animation fundamentals.

Topics in this chapter include the following:

▶ **Anticipation and momentum in knife throwing**

Anticipation and Momentum in Knife Throwing

This exercise will give you more experience animating in 3ds Max. You will edit more in the Curve Editor (yeah!) and be introduced to the concepts of anticipation, momentum, and secondary movement. First, download the Knife project from this book's companion web page. Set your 3ds Max project folder by choosing Application ➤ Manage ➤ Set Project Folder and selecting the Knife project that you downloaded.

Blocking Out the Animation

To begin this exercise, open the `Animation_Knife_00.max` file in the Knife project and follow along here:

1. Move the Time Slider to frame 30 and activate the Auto Key button.

2. Move the knife to the target object, as shown in Figure 6.1.

FIGURE 6.1 Move the knife to the target at frame 30.

3. Move the Time Slider to frame 15, where the knife is halfway between its start and the target, and move the knife slightly up on the *Z* axis so that the knife moves with a slight arc, as shown in Figure 6.2.

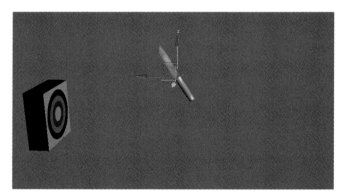

FIGURE 6.2 Move the knife up slightly at frame 15.

4. Click the Time Configuration icon (▦) at the bottom of the UI next to the navigation controls. Figure 6.3 shows the Time Configuration dialog box. In the Animation section, change End Time to 30 from 100 and click OK. The Time Slider will reflect this change immediately.

5. Play your animation, and you should see the knife move with a slight ease-out and ease-in toward the target, with a slight arc up in the middle. The animation of the knife needs to start at frame 0, so open the Curve Editor and scroll down in the Controller window until you see the X, Y, Z Position tracks for the knife. Hold the Ctrl key and select all three tracks to display their curves, as shown in Figure 6.4.

FIGURE 6.3 Change the frame range in the Time Configuration dialog box.

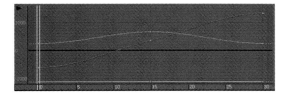

FIGURE 6.4 The initial curves for the knife

6. Drag a selection marquee around the three keys at frame 0. In the Key Controls toolbar, select and hold the Move Keys tool (⊕) to access the flyout icons, and select the Move Keys Horizontal tool in the flyout (⬌). Use this tool to move the keys to frame 10.

7. Doing so compacts the curve, so you need to move the keys at frame 15 to the new middle, frame 20. The finished curve is shown in Figure 6.5.

That's it for the gross animation (or blocking) of the shot. Did you have fun?

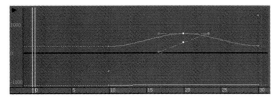

FIGURE 6.5 Finished curves with the position of the knife starting at frame 10.

Trajectories

When it comes to animation, it is very helpful to be able to see the path your object is taking over time, called *trajectories*. Select the knife object, go to the Command panel, click the Motion icon () to open the options shown in Figure 6.6, and then click Trajectories. Your viewports will display a red curve to show you the path of the knife's motion as it arcs toward the target, as shown in Figure 6.7.

FIGURE 6.6
**Turning on Trajectories
for the knife**

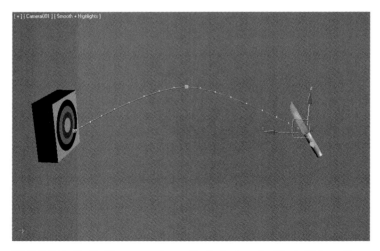

FIGURE 6.7 The curve shows the trajectory for the knife's motion.

The large hollow square points on the trajectory curve represent the keyframes set on the knife so far. Let's adjust the height of the arc using the trajectory curve. Select the Sub-Object button at the top of the Motion Panel.

Keys are your only subobject choice in the pull-down menu to the right of the button. Select the middle keyframe and move it up or down to suit your tastes. Once you settle on a nice arc for the path of the knife, turn off Trajectories mode by clicking the Parameters button in the Motion Panel.

As you can imagine, the Trajectories options can be useful in many situations. It not only gives you a view of your object's path, but it also allows you to edit that path easily and in a visual context, which can be very important.

Adding Rotation

Throwing knives is usually a bad idea, but you can throw something else at a target (the inanimate kind) to see how to animate your knife. You'll find that the object will rotate once or twice before it hits its target. To add rotation to your knife, follow these steps:

1. Move to frame 30, and press the E key for the Select And Rotate tool. Auto Key should still be active. In the Camera001 viewport, rotate on the Y axis 443 degrees.

2. With the knife selected, go into the Curve Editor. Scroll down to find the X, Y, and Z Rotation tracks, and select them. Select the keys at frame 0, then use the Move Keys Horizontal tool to shift the keyframes to frame 10. Press N to deactivate the Auto Key. Figure 6.8 shows the Curve Editor graph for the knife.

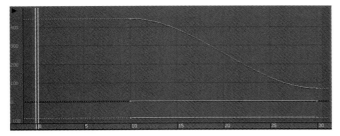

FIGURE 6.8 Curve Editor graph for the knife

3. Play the animation, and you will see that the knife's position and rotation eases in and eases out. A real knife would not ease its rotations or movement. Its speed would be roughly consistent throughout the animation.

4. Go back to the Curve Editor; change Move Keys Horizontal back to Move Keys. Then select the X Position track, select all the keyframes, and switch the tangent to Linear. Now select the Z Position track; you'll need to finesse this one a bit more than the X Position track. You are going to use the handles on the tangents that appear when you select a key. These handles can be adjusted; just center your cursor over the end and click and drag using the Move Keys tool. Figure 6.9 illustrates how you want the Z Position animation curve to look. This will give the trajectory a nice arc and a good rate of travel.

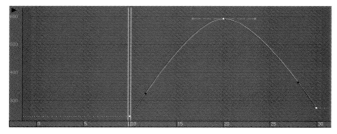

FIGURE 6.9 Adjust the curve for the knife's arc through the air.

5. Now it is time to edit the Rotation keys. In the Curve Editor, scroll to find the *X*, *Y*, and *Z* Rotation tracks. The first thing you can do is add a bit of drama to the knife to make the action more exciting. To this end, you can say that the rotation on the knife is too slow. Select the *X* Rotation track and select its key at frame 30. In the Key Stats, change the value to –290. The higher the value, the faster the knife will rotate. This will add one full revolution to the animation and some more excitement to the action.

6. Adjust the tangent handles to resemble the curve shown in Figure 6.10. The knife will speed up just a bit as it leaves the first rotation keyframe. The speed will be even as it goes into the last keyframe.

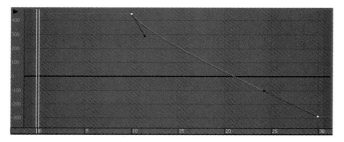

FIGURE 6.10 Match your curve to this one.

With just a little bit of fast rotation as the knife leaves frame 10, you give the animation more spice. The knife should now have a slightly weightier look than before, when it rotated with an ease-in and ease-out.

Adding Anticipation

Now let's animate the knife to move back first to create *anticipation*, as if an invisible hand holding the knife pulled back just before throwing it to get more strength in the throw. This anticipation, although it's a small detail, adds a level of nuance to the animation that enhances the total effect. Follow these steps:

1. Move the Time Slider to frame 0. Go to the Curve Editor, scroll in the Controller window, and select the *X* Rotation track for the knife. In the Curve Editor toolbar, click the Insert Keys icon ( ), bring your cursor to frame 0 of the curve, and click to create a keyframe. Doing so creates a key at frame 0 with the same parameters as the next key, as shown in Figure 6.11.

FIGURE 6.11 Adding a key to the beginning to create anticipation for the knife throw

2. Select the Move Keys tool and select the key at frame 10. In the Key Stats type-in, change the value of that key to 240. If you play back the animation, it will look weird. The knife will cock back really fast and spin a bit. This is due to the big hump between frames 0 and 10.

3. Keep the tangent at frame 0 set to the default, but change the tangent on the key at frame 10 to Linear ( ). Play back the animation. You'll have a slight bit of anticipation, but the spice will be lost and the knife will look less active and too mechanical.

4. To regain the weight you had in the knife, press Ctrl+Z to undo your change to the tangency on frame 10 and set it back to what you had. You may have to undo more than once. Now, select the Move Keys Vertical tool ( ) and select the In tangent handle for keyframe 10. This is the tangent handle on the left of the key.

It's common to try something and rely on Undo to get back to the starting point. You can use Undo several times when you find yourself at a dead end.

5. Press Shift and drag the tangent handle down to create a curve that is similar to the one shown in Figure 6.12. By pressing Shift as you dragged the tangent handle, you broke the continuity between the In and Out handles, so that only the In handle was affected. Play back the animation. It should look much better now.

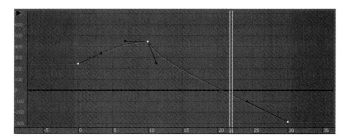

FIGURE 6.13 To create a believable anticipation for the knife throw, set your curve to resemble this one.

Follow-Through

The knife needs more weight. A great way to show that in animation is by adding follow-through; have the knife sink into the target a little bit and push back the target. To add follow-through to your animation, use these steps:

1. You want to sink the knife into the target after it hits. Select the Time Configuration button and change End Time to 45 to add 15 frames to your frame range. Click OK. Doing so will not affect the animation; it will merely append 15 frames to the current frame range.

2. Select the knife and go to frame 30, where it hits the target. In the Curve Editor, select the *X* Position track of the knife. Add a keyframe with the Insert Keys tool at frame 35.

3. Note the value of the key in the type-in boxes at the top right of the Curve Editor (*not* the type-in boxes at the bottom of the main UI). In this case, the value in this scene is about –231. You will want to set the value for this key at frame 35 to about –224 to sink it farther into the target. If your values are different, adjust accordingly so you don't add too much movement. Also make sure the movement flows *into* the target and not back out of the target as if the knife were bouncing out.

4. Keep the tangent for this new key set to Auto. With these relative values, scrub the animation between frames 30 and 35. You should see

the knife's slight move into the target. The end of your curve should look like the curve in Figure 6.13.

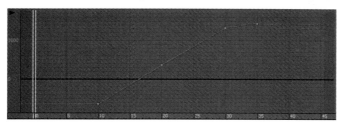

FIGURE 6.13 Your animation should end like this.

5. You still need to add a little bit of follow-through to the rotation of the knife to make it sink into the target better. In the Curve Editor, select the *X* Rotation track to display its curve. Add a key to the curve at frame 35. The value of the key at frame 30 should already be about −652. Set the value of the keyframe at frame 35 to be about −**655**. Keep the tangent set at Auto. If your values are different, adjust accordingly to what works best in your scene.

Be careful about how much the knife sinks into the target. Although it is important to show the weight of the knife, it is also important to show the weight of the target; you do not want the target to look too soft.

Transferring Momentum to the Target

To make the momentum work even better for the knife animation, you will have to push back the target as the knife hits it. The trouble is, if you animate the target moving back, the knife will stay in place, floating in the air. You have to animate the knife *with* the target.

Parent and Child Objects

To animate the knife and target together, the knife has to be linked to the target so that when the target is animated to push back upon impact, the knife will follow precisely since it is stuck in the target. Doing this won't mess up the existing animation of the knife because the knife will be the child in the hierarchy and will retain its own animation separate from the target. Just follow these steps:

1. Go to frame 30, about when the knife impacts. On the far left of the Main toolbar, choose the Select And Link tool (⬚). Select the knife

and drag it to the target as shown in Figure 6.14 (left). Nothing should change until you animate the target object.

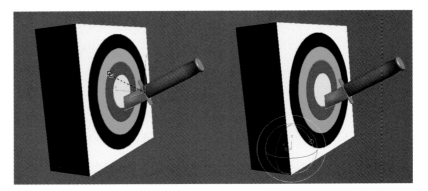

FIGURE 6.14 Link the knife to the target (left), and then rotate the target back slightly (right).

2. Move the Time Slider to frame 34 and press the N key to activate the Auto Key tool. With the Select And Rotate tool, select the target object and rotate it back about 5 degrees, as shown in the second image in Figure 6.14 (right). The pivot of the target has already been placed properly, at the bottom back edge.

3. Go to the Curve Editor, scroll to find the Y Rotation track for the target object, select the keyframe at frame 0, and move it to frame 30. Then hold the Shift key, and click and drag the keyframe (which will make a copy of it) to frame 37.

4. Change the tangent for the key at frame 30 to Fast and leave the other key tangents alone.

5. Add a little wobble to the target to make the animation even more interesting. This can be done easily in the Curve Editor. Use Insert Keys to add keys at frames 40 and 44. Using the Move Keys Vertical tool, give the key at frame 40 a value of about 1.7. Your curve should resemble the one in Figure 6.15.

6. Finally, add a little slide to the target. Using the Select And Move tool, move the Time Slider to frame 37, and move the target just a bit along the X axis. Go to the Curve Editor, scroll to the X position of the target object, select the keyframe at frame 0, and move it to frame 30 so the move starts when the knife hits the target. Change the tangent for frame 30 to Fast and leave the other tangent at Auto.

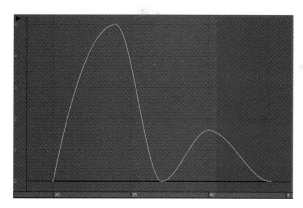

FIGURE 6.15 The target animation curve

Done! Play back your animation. Experiment and change some of the final timings and values of the target's reaction to the impact to see different weights of the knife and target and how the weight looks to the viewer.

You can see a sample render of the scene in the knife_animation.mov QuickTime file in the RenderOutput folder of the Knife project on the companion web page (or copied onto your hard drive). You can also download the Animation_Knife_01.max scene file from the Scenes folder of the Knife project to check your work.

THE ESSENTIALS AND BEYOND

In this, our second chapter on animation, you further expanded your knowledge of creating and editing animation. You learned about hierarchies and how to link objects together to create a hierarchy useful for our knife animation as well as how pivot points are used. You also learned what key animation terms are, such as anticipation, follow-through, and momentum, and how they apply to the animation.

ADDITIONAL EXERCISES

► Try animating simple objects like boxes and just play around with anticipation, follow-through, and momentum.

► Again using simple primitives, create hierarchies and play around with anticipation, follow-through, and momentum.

► Constrain and animate a camera on a path through a nice modeled environment.

► Animate planets around the sun using paths.

CHAPTER 7

Character Poly Modeling: Part I

In games, characters are designed and created cleverly to achieve the best look with the lowest amount of mesh detail to keep the polygon count low. With that in mind, this and the next two chapters introduce you to character modeling, focusing on using the Editable Poly toolset to create a relatively low polygon count soldier model suitable for character animation and for use in a game engine (though that topic is not covered in this book). This chapter begins with the basic form of the character first.

Topics in this chapter include the following:

▶ **Setting up the scene**

▶ **Creating the soldier**

Setting Up the Scene

You can import and use sketches of the character's front and side as background images as you create the character in 3ds Max. Additional sketches of your character from several points of view can be helpful during the modeling process for quick reference to your goal.

HIGH- AND LOW-POLY MODELING

High polygon count models are used when a model's level of detail needs to be impeccable, such as when the model is used in close-ups.

Low polygon count modeling, also called low-poly modeling, refers to a style of modeling that sacrifices some detail in favor of efficient geometry that places a very low load on the system on which it is being created or rendered.

Creating Planes and Adding Materials

Like the toy rocket exercise in Chapter 3, "Modeling in 3ds Max: Part I," this exercise begins by creating crossed boxes and applying reference images to them. Set your project to the Soldier project downloaded to your system:

1. In a new scene, go to the Front viewport and create a plane.

2. In the Parameters rollout of the Command panel, set Length to 635 and Width to 622. The units are in inches, which is the default in 3ds Max. The size of the image planes in units is the same size as the reference images in pixels. Thus, when you apply the image to the plane it will be proportional, maintaining its width and length with no stretching or squeezing of the images.

3. Rename this box Image_Plane_Front.

4. With the plane still selected, go to the Modify tab and in the Parameters rollout set the Length and Width Segs to 1. Then select the Move tool (W) in the Main toolbar and in the transform type-ins at the bottom of the user interface, move the plane to these coordinates: (0.0, 80.169, −5.228).

5. Click in a blank space in the UI, and then press the Z key on your keyboard; it is the shortcut for Zoom Extents All. In the Main toolbar, turn on the Angle Snap toggle (🔲) or press A on your keyboard. Doing so will snap your rotation to every 5 degrees. Select the Rotate tool (E) and hold down Shift on the keyboard; then in the Front viewport rotate the image plane along the *Y* axis 90 degrees. Using Shift activates the Clone tool, as shown in Figure 7.1.

6. In the Clone Options dialog box, under Object select Copy, name it Image_Plane_Side, and click OK.

7. Switch to the Move tool and move the plane to these coordinates: (−311.084, −229.692, −5.228).

FIGURE 7.1 Clone Options dialog box

Adding the Materials

At this point, the reference materials are texture-mapped onto the planes to provide reference inside the scene itself while you model the character. Therefore, it's critical to ensure that the features of the character that appear in both reference images (the front and the side) are at the same height. For instance, the top of the head and the shoulders should be at the same height in both the front and side views to make the modeling process easier.

1. In the Left viewport, press the V key on your keyboard and select Right View from the list. Change the shading in the Right viewport to Smooth + Highlights (F3).

2. Open an Explorer window and navigate to the Soldier/sceneassets/images folder on your hard drive from the Soldier project you downloaded from the book's web page at **www.sybex.com/go/3dsmax2012essentials**. Drag ImagePlane_Front.jpg from the Explorer window to the image plane in the Front viewport.

3. Drag ImagePlane_Side.jpg onto the image plane in the Right viewport. The image planes should have the two images mapped on them, as shown in Figure 7.2.

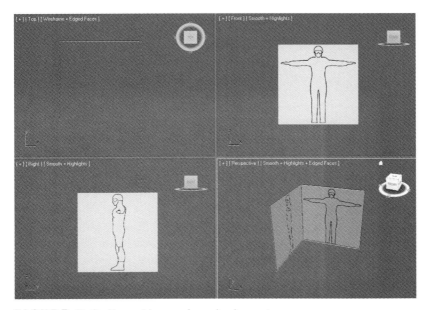

FIGURE 7.2 Mapped image planes in viewports

Creating the Soldier

A good practice is to block out the basic form of the character and focus on the size and crucial shapes of the major elements, and then add detail for the finer features. The following exercises describe the steps required to block out the soldier's major features. Go wild!

Forming the Torso

The basic structure for the torso will begin with a simple box primitive. After converting the box into an editable poly, you will use the Mirror tool on the object so that any manipulations performed on one side are also performed on the other. You will begin forming the basic shape of the torso by moving the editable poly's vertices and extruding its polygons in the following steps.

Continue with the previous exercise's scene file, or open the Soldier_V01.max scene file in the Scenes folder of the Soldier project downloaded from this book's web page.

1. Set each viewport to Smooth + Highlights (F3) with Edged Faces (F4) if it isn't already set that way.

2. Start by creating a box primitive in the Perspective viewport with these parameters: Length: 25, Width: 16, Height: 53, Input Height Segs: 8. Leave the Width and Length Segs at 1, as shown in Figure 7.3. This is a starting point for the detail needed to create the form of the body. Position the box as shown in Figure 7.4. Press Alt+X to make the box see-through. Change the box's name to **Soldier**.

3. In the Graphite Modeling Tools ribbon, click Polygon Modeling ➤ Convert To Poly.

4. Enter the Vertex subobject level. In the Right viewport, position the vertices on the right side of the box to match the side outline of the character on the image plane, as shown in Figure 7.5.

5. In the Graphite Modeling Tools ribbon, click Edit ➤ SwiftLoop. Switch to Edge mode, and then use the Swift Loop tool to create two new edge loops that run vertically from the front of the model to the back, as shown in Figure 7.6. The dashed lines show the loop running in the back and bottom of the model.

FIGURE 7.3 Box parameters

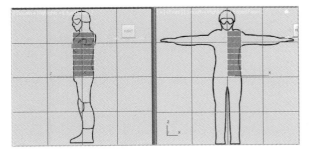

FIGURE 7.4 Box position from the front and side views

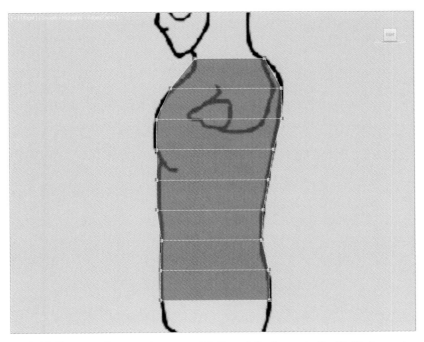

FIGURE 7.5 Move vertices to match the soldier image in the Right viewport.

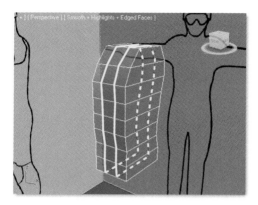

FIGURE 7.6 Create two new edge loops using Swift Loop.

6. Using Swift Loop, create a single new edge on the side of the model running from the left side to the right side, as shown in Figure 7.7. The dashed lines show the loop running across the bottom of the model. Turn off the tool.

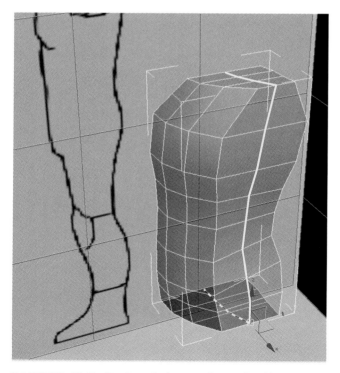

FIGURE 7.7 Create a single new edge on the side of the model using Swift Loop.

7. Now round the side of the torso. You should still be in Edge mode. Select one of the edges running vertically on the side of the torso box (Figure 7.8). In the Graphite Modeling Tools ribbon, select the Modify Selection tab and click Loop to select the loop of edges running along the side of the torso, as shown in Figure 7.8. Move the loop of edges toward the back of the model to begin rounding that edge. Then select the loop of edges to the left of the previous loop with the Loop tool and move them back to form a more rounded front to the torso, as shown in Figure 7.8.

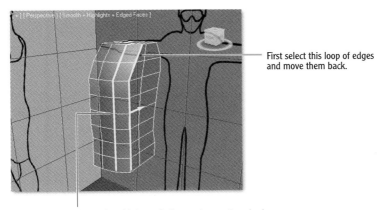

First select this loop of edges and move them back.

Next select this loop of edges and move them back.

F I G U R E   7 . 8   Select and move edges toward the back of the model.

8. Switch to Vertex mode and select the vertex on the left side below the top edge, as shown in Figure 7.9. In the Graphite Modeling Tools ribbon's Vertices tab, select Chamfer Settings by clicking the tool's name under the icon and then clicking Chamfer Settings. Doing so opens the tool caddy shown in Figure 7.10. Use a Vertex Chamfer Amount value of 4.808, and click the green check mark button (OK) in the caddy to commit the action. This is where the arm will be positioned.

9. Switch to Polygon mode, select the new diamond-shaped polygon in the middle, and press Delete to delete the polygon. A hole appears where the arm will be positioned.

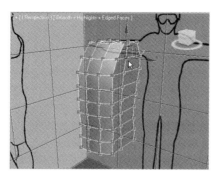

FIGURE 7.9 Select the vertex right above the mouse cursor shown here.

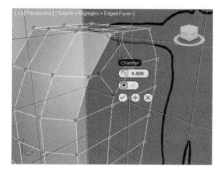

FIGURE 7.10 Use Chamfer to create a new polygon where the arm will be positioned.

10. Switch to Edge mode and select the four diagonal edges of the diamond-shaped hole and the four edges shown in Figure 7.11.

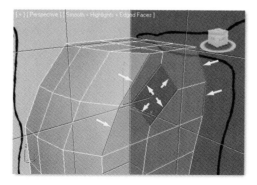

FIGURE 7.11 Select these eight edges.

11. On the Graphite Modeling Tools ribbon, choose Modify Selection ➢ Ring to select the ring of edges running across the top of the chest. Again on the Graphite Modeling Tools ribbon, choose Loops ➢ Flow Connect to create more horizontal divisions for the upper chest. Flow Connect connects selected edges across one or more edge rings and adjusts the new loop position to fit the shape of the surrounding mesh. The newly created edges are illustrated in Figure 7.12. The diamond-shaped hole in the shoulder is now more rounded (the hole is now an octagon) as well, since more edges were created at the hole, too. The dashed lines show the loops running behind the model.

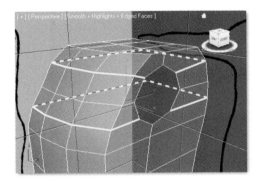

FIGURE 7.12 Use Flow Connect to create two new edges around the model.

12. Select the two horizontal edges under the armhole, as shown in Figure 7.13 (left), and from the Graphite Modeling Tools ribbon choose Modify Selection ➢ Ring to select the horizontal edges running down the side, top, and bottom of the torso. Again from the Graphite Modeling Tools ribbon, select Loops ➢ Flow Connect to create two new loops of edges, as shown on the right in Figure 7.13.

13. The new edge ring does not reach all the way up to the octagon armhole. You will need to cut an edge from the top of the new edges you just made, to the bottom of the armhole. Select the Graphite Modeling Tools ribbon and choose Edit ➢ Cut to enter the Cut tool . Click on the first vertex under the armhole, and then click on the second vertex above at the armhole to create the first new edge. Right-click to commit the edge. You will still be in the Cut tool, so click on the third vertex shown in Figure 7.14 and create the second new edge up to the fourth vertex shown in Figure 7.14. Right-click to commit the second edge.

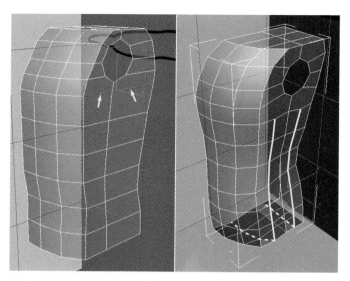

FIGURE 7.13 Select the two horizontal edges under the armhole (left) and use Flow Connect to create more edges (right).

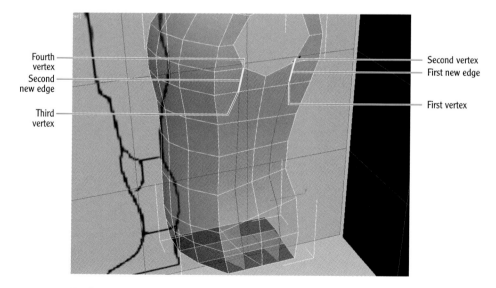

FIGURE 7.14 Use the Cut tool to add two edges to the armhole.

14. The armhole isn't great right now; it will be easier to start from a circular shape rather than the uneven octagon form we have now. Enter Border subobject mode, select the armhole's border, and in the Graphite Modeling Tools ribbon's Geometry (All) tab, click the Cap Poly tool to create an NGon (a polygon with more than four sides) cap to fill the hole.

15. Go to Polygon mode and select the new NGon. Go to the Graphite Modeling Tools ribbon's Polygons tab and click the GeoPoly tool to create a symmetrical polygon from the previous shape, as shown in Figure 7.15. GeoPoly untangles a polygon and organizes the vertices to form a perfect geometric shape. This will make it easier for us when we create the arm later.

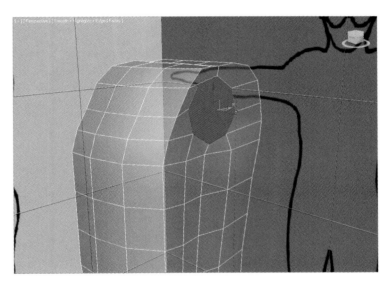

FIGURE 7.15 Use GeoPoly to create a symmetrical shape for the armhole.

16. Select the new NGon cap you created in step 14 and press Delete to delete the NGon. Also select and delete the top and bottom polygons on the model, as shown in Figure 7.16 (left).

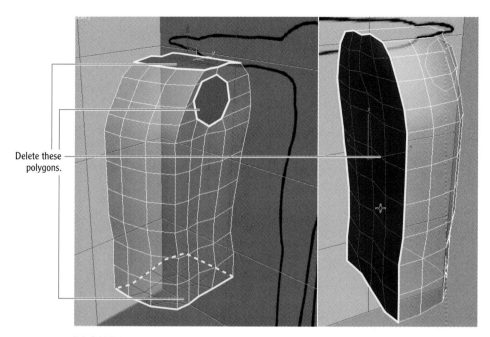

Delete these polygons.

FIGURE 7.16 Delete the NGon as well as the topmost and bottommost polygons of the model.

17. Under the Graphite Modeling Tools ribbon's Polygon Modeling tab, under the subobject mode buttons, turn on Ignore Backfacing ( ). Then select the left-side polygons, as shown in Figure 7.16 (right), and delete them as well. Your torso should now have only a front, side, and back.

18. Now, select the edge loops on the right of the model and move them closer toward the left, and closer to the center of the model, as shown in Figure 7.17. You might want to translate or move them on the *Y* axis as well. Your goal is to round out the character for a more organic feel.

19. Notice how the armhole's circle looks neater in Figure 7.18, but the edges on the right and top are a bit awkward. Enter Vertex mode and move the edges to give the armhole a more rounded feel.

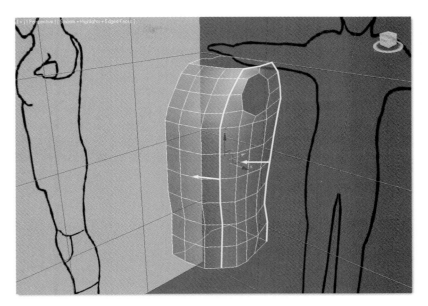

FIGURE 7.17 Select the edge loops and move them to create a more rounded look to the model.

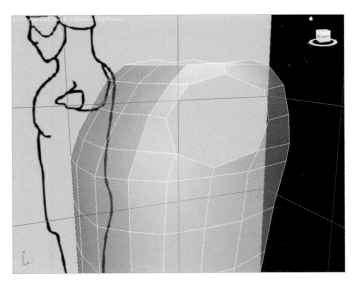

FIGURE 7.18 Adjust the editable poly's vertices to make a cleaner hole for the arm.

20. Go into Edge mode and select the edge running vertically on the right side of the model's back, as shown in Figure 7.19, and move it toward the armhole. This action will make the back rounder.

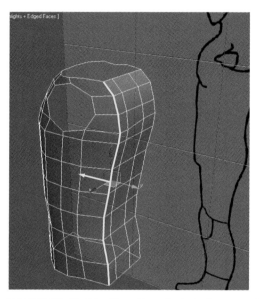

FIGURE 7.19 Move the selected edge toward the front of the torso to round out the back.

Now we are starting to see some shape in the torso. Let's move on to the arms.

Creating the Arms

Continue with the previous exercise's scene file, or open the Soldier_V02.max scene file in the Scenes file of the Soldier project on the book's web page.

1. In Border mode, select the armhole's border, then hold down the Shift key, and with the Move tool, drag out from the body on the *X* axis, extruding polygons as you drag. This method is a form of Border Extrude. This method gives you more control over the extrude process because you can more easily choose the axis along which to extrude. Release the mouse button and view your model in the Front viewport to line up the border to the wrist of the arm in the image plane.

2. From the Graphite Modeling Tools ribbon, select Edit ➢ SwiftLoop to create three edge loops on the arm, evenly spaced over the newly created arm; then turn off the tool.

3. Switch to Vertex mode and move the newly created vertices on the Y axis to fit the form on the image plane. It is okay to select a group of vertices and scale on the Y axis to taper that part of the arm to create the wrist.

4. In Edge mode, select and use Loop selection (on the Graphite Modeling Tools ribbon, choose Modify Selection ➢ Loop) on the horizontal edge running around the body under the arm and move the edges down. Repeat the same process with the loop of edges under the previous loop, as shown in Figure 7.20. This ensures the underarm area geometry is lined up properly, as shown later in Figure 7.22.

5. In Edge mode, select and use Loop (on the Graphite Modeling Tools ribbon, choose Modify Selection ➢ Loop) on the horizontal edge running directly at the underarm and move the loop down, as shown in Figure 7.21.

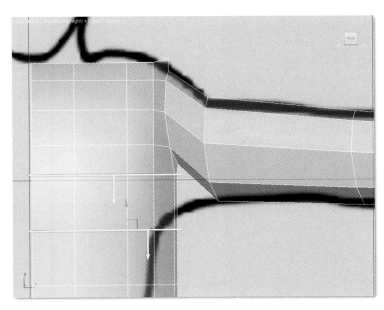

FIGURE 7.20 Move these looped edges down.

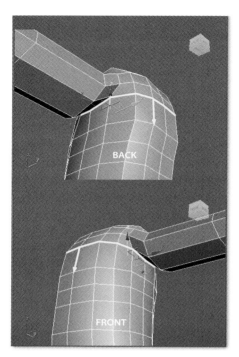

FIGURE 7.21 Select and loop these edges to move them down.

6. In the Front viewport, in Edge mode, select the middle edge on the arm; then from the Graphite Modeling Tools ribbon choose Modify Selection ➢ Loop. Then choose Edges ➢ Chamfer ➢ Chamfer Settings from that ribbon and enter an Edge Chamfer Amount of 2 and a Connect Edge Segments value of 2.

7. Then chamfer the edges to the right and left, using an Edge Chamfer Amount of 3, with a Connect Edge Segments value of 1, as shown in Figure 7.22. Keep the middle edge a bit tighter together. Since this is the area where the elbow bends, it is a good idea to include more detail there for deformations at the elbow. Your model should have the vertical edges you see in Figure 7.22.

8. In Border mode, select the wrist border and, while holding down the Shift key, use the Scale tool to scale the wrist border down on the *Z* and *Y* axes into the center, as shown in Figure 7.23 (left). Using Shift while performing a Scale operation clones the selected objects much

like an extrusion with the Shift+Move method used earlier. In this case, it makes a copy of the border, effectively closing the open end of the wrist.

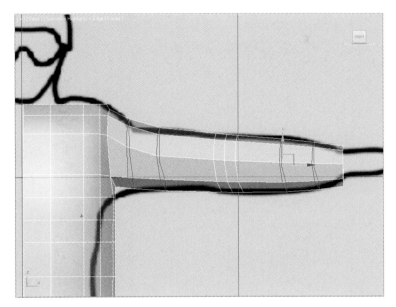

FIGURE 7.22 Chamfer the arm to add more edges for detail.

9. Then switch to Vertex mode, select the vertices of the smaller wrist hole, and select Vertices ➤ Weld ➤ Weld Settings from the Graphite Modeling Tools ribbon to open the Weld Vertices caddy, as shown in Figure 7.23 (middle). Use a Weld Threshold of 3.39, as shown. This creates a completed cap at the end of the arm, as shown in Figure 7.23 (right). We will continue with the hand in a later section.

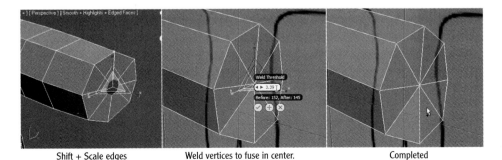

Shift + Scale edges Weld vertices to fuse in center. Completed

FIGURE 7.23 Fuse the wrist edge in toward the center.

Creating the Legs

Continue with the previous exercise's scene file, or open the Soldier_V03.max scene file in the Scenes folder of the Soldier project downloaded from the book's web page.

1. In Edge mode, select the bottommost loop of edges on the model's torso. An easy way to do this is to select one edge and from the Graphite Modeling Tools ribbon, choose Modify Selection and click the Loop button ( ). The Loop tool allows you to select a single edge and then it automatically selects associated edge loops. Now hold Shift+Move (hold down the Shift key while moving with the Move tool, as you did in the previous set of steps) to create a new extrusion all the way down to the groin of the reference illustration. You will extrude and move down on the *Y* axis, as shown in Figure 7.24.

2. We are starting to prepare the model for the legs and groin area. Use the Cut tool (from the Graphite Modeling Tools ribbon, choose Edit ➢ Cut), and cut an edge from about 25 percent to the right from the corner of the bottommost edge of the model, to the top corner on the polygon closest to the groin, as shown in Figure 7.25 (left). Do the same for the polygon at the back of the model in the corresponding corner.

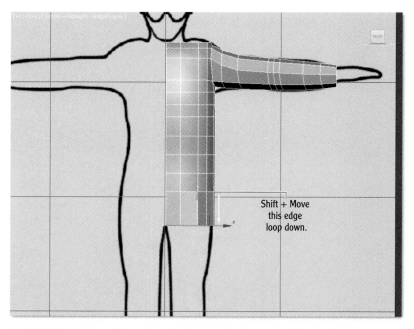

FIGURE 7.24 Select the edge loop at the bottom of the model and Shift+Move down.

Use the Cut tool to cut the edge.

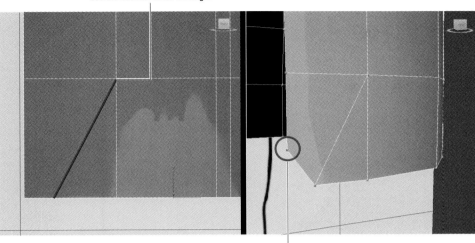

Select this vertex and move it up.

FIGURE 7.25 Cut the polygon and raise the corners.

3. In Vertex mode, select the lowest inside vertices and move them up a bit to create a diagonal edge. Do this for both the front and back of the model, as shown in Figure 7.25 (right).

4. In Edge mode, select both of the new diagonal edges (front and back), then choose Edges ➢ Bridge ➢ Bridge Settings from the Graphite Modeling Tools ribbon. Use four segments to create a bridge, as shown in Figure 7.26. Doing so creates a bridge between the front and back.

   With the bridge in place, the border edge on the bottom of the torso resembles a capital letter *D*, as shown in Figure 7.26. If we extrude the leg down from here, the inner thigh will be flat. For a better starting point to form the leg, we need to cap the hole as we did with the arm previously.

   To begin the upper thigh extrusion, continue with the following steps to cap the D shape.

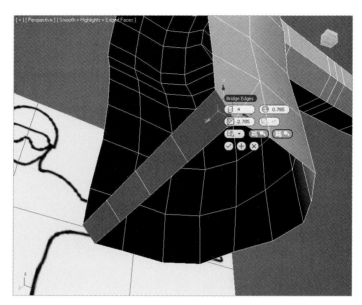

FIGURE 7.26 Bridge between two edges to create the groin area

5. Select the D-shaped border edge and Shift+Move down on the Z axis
to extrude the upper thigh downward to right above the knee pad, as
shown in Figure 7.27 (left). The knee pad's position can be better seen
in the side reference image plane. Don't worry; you will adjust the
shape to fit the thigh later.

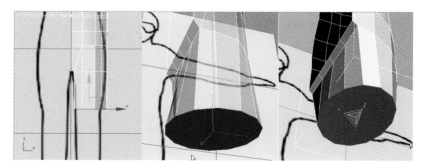

FIGURE 7.27 Creating the upper thigh

6. With the D-shaped border still selected, from the Graphite Modeling
Tools ribbon select Geometry (All) ➢ Cap Poly to cap the end of the
thigh stump. Select the new poly and from the same ribbon choose
Polygons ➢ GeoPoly to make the end of the thigh a more even shape;
see Figure 7.27 (middle).

7. Select the thigh's end polygon and scale on the *X* axis, as shown in Figure 7.27 (right), to create a more oval shape. Then delete the cap so the bottom of the leg is open once again.

8. In the Front viewport, switch to Vertex mode and scale and move the vertices on the leg to match the image plane. Check the Right viewport and shape the thigh as needed. Notice the bottom of the geometry should be located at about the top of the knee pad. Use the Perspective viewport often to make sure some of the vertices are not being accidentally moved.

9. On the inside of the groin area where you created the four-segment bridge in step 4, move the edges to make sure the segments are evenly spaced. This step should be repeated throughout the exercise to keep edges evenly spaced and ensure that the model is organized and clean.

10. Switch to Border mode and select the border opening at the bottom of the leg. Then use the Extrude Border method (hold Shift+Move) to extrude the leg down to the ankle, as shown in Figure 7.28 (left).

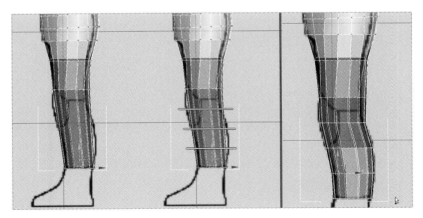

FIGURE 7.28 Extrude down to the ankle, use the Swift Loop tool to create three new loops, and fit the new edges to the image plane.

11. From the Graphite Modeling Tools ribbon, choose Edit ➢ SwiftLoop and create three new horizontal segments around the leg, as shown in Figure 7.28 (middle). Then fit the vertices to the shape of the soldier's leg in the side image plane in the Right viewport, as shown in Figure 7.28 (right). Go into the Front viewport and do the same to shape the leg properly.

12. In Border mode, select the ankle border, as shown in Figure 7.29 (left) and Shift+scale the border down on the *Z* and *Y* axes and in toward the center of the ankle, leaving a small hole; see Figure 7.29 (middle). Then switch to Vertex mode and select the vertices around the resulting small hole, and use Weld (Graphite Modeling Tools ribbon, choose Vertices ➤ Weld) to bring the vertices together, as shown in Figure 7.29 (right). Adjust the Weld Threshold setting as needed to weld these vertices together.

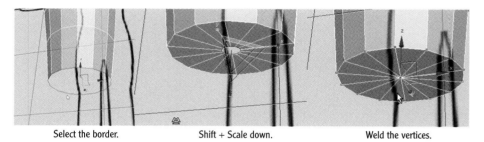

Select the border.   Shift + Scale down.   Weld the vertices.

FIGURE 7.29 Closing the ankle's hole

Fixing Up the Body

Continue with the previous exercise's scene file, or open the Soldier_V04.max scene file in the Scenes folder of the Soldier project from the book's web page.

1. The pelvis looks a bit funky. We need to streamline the mesh by combining some edges together. Select the vertical edges at the waist (select a single vertical edge and from the Graphite Modeling Tools ribbon, choose Modify Selection ➤ Ring); see Figure 7.30.

2. Right-click to bring up the Quad menu. In the upper-left Quad, in the Tools 1 section, choose Collapse. Doing so brings the two horizontal edge loops at the top and bottom of the selected vertical edges together into one edge loop.

3. In the Perspective viewport, use Orbit (use the ViewCube or Alt+MMB) to adjust the view to see under the groin area. In Edge or Vertex mode, move the segments to round out that section, as shown in Figure 7.31.

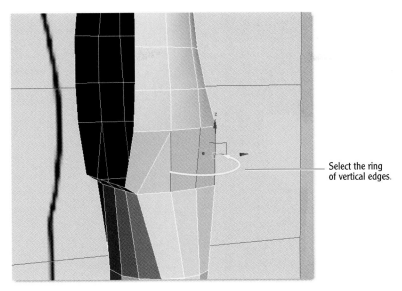

Select the ring
of vertical edges.

FIGURE 7.30 Select waist edges and use Ring to prepare for Collapse.

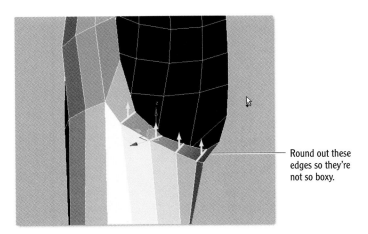

Round out these
edges so they're
not so boxy.

FIGURE 7.31 Round out the edges in the groin area.

4. In the Perspective viewport, use Orbit again around the leg and look for any spikes or pinches that may have occurred in the model. The goal is to split the difference between edges so that they're as close to 50 percent from another edge as possible.

Save your work! Keep in mind that a joint edge, such as the edges that make up the knee or elbow, need to stay where they are. Figure 7.32 shows the leg with good edge spacing. Take a moment to go back through the model and tweak the rest of it until you feel it is right. When modeling for animation, the mesh flow is an important factor.

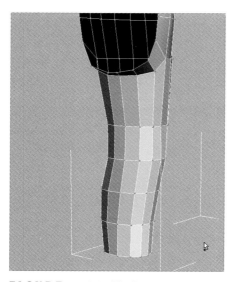

FIGURE 7.32 The leg with good edge spacing

THE ESSENTIALS AND BEYOND

This chapter explored and explained several tools used in modeling, organic or otherwise, to begin the basic form of the soldier character. Reference planes of the soldier design were used at first, and then from a simple box, a torso was formed to match the general shapes shown in the reference images. The arms and legs were extruded and shaped to match as well. As you can see, the more that you model, the easier the process becomes, and the more detailed and finessed your models will turn out.

CHAPTER 8

Character Poly Modeling: Part II

Realistic computer-generated (CG) characters are common in television and films; they appear as stunt doubles, as vast crowds, and as primary characters. Sometimes using a CG character works better than using a real person (using a CG stunt double is safer and sometimes cheaper than using a live stunt person). And weird creatures can be created with better clarity by using CG rather than using puppetry or special makeup effects.

In this chapter you will continue with the model of a special operations soldier model, focusing on using the Editable Poly toolset to create a relatively low polygon count soldier model suitable for character animation and for use in a game engine.

Topics in this chapter include the following:

▶ **Completing the main body**

▶ **Creating the accessories**

▶ **Putting on the boots**

▶ **Creating the hands**

Completing the Main Body

Continue with the previous chapter's exercise scene file, or open the Soldier _V05.max scene file in the Scenes folder of the Soldier project from the book's web page at **www.sybex.com/go/3dsmax2012essentials**.

To create the other half of the model you have so far (Figure 8.1), you are going to use the Mirror tool, which works off your character's current pivot point. You want to mirror on the *X* axis, so the gizmo needs to be in the dead center of your to-be-completed character (at the left side of the half model in the Front viewport); you will take care of that in step 1 of the following exercise.

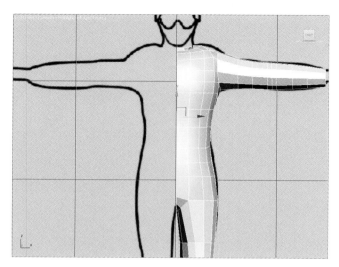

FIGURE 8.1 Move the pivot point to the edge of the geometry.

In Chapter 4, "Modeling in 3ds Max: Part II," when you built the Red Rocket you used a modifier called Symmetry. This mirror technique gives the same results but in a different way. You will mirror the soldier's body in the following steps:

1. In the Front viewport, select the model. Go to the Command panels to the right of the interface; select the Hierarchy tab (▨), and then in the Adjust Pivot rollout, click the Affect Pivot Only button. You want the pivot on the left edge of the model so it's in the center of the torso when it's mirrored. With Affect Pivot Only, use the Move tool to move the gizmo to the left edge of the geometry, as shown in Figure 8.1. If you cannot find the gizmo, click Center To Object under Alignment. Doing so will pop the gizmo to the center of the model.

2. Toggle off Affect Pivot Only. Select all the inside vertices, and on the Graphite Modeling Tools ribbon, choose Align ≻ X. Doing so moves all the vertices to line up along the X axis.

3. In the Main toolbar, click the Mirror button (▨) to open the Mirror dialog box. Select Mirror Axis X and Instance under Clone Selection, as shown in Figure 8.2. Then click OK.

   With the mirror set to Instance, you can make some minor changes to the model before you combine the two sides more permanently. In the next step you will move to the neck area where you will extrude edges on one side and see the mirrored side do the same on the other side.

FIGURE 8.2 Mirror dialog box

4. In Edge mode, select the edges at the top of the right side of the torso geometry, as shown in Figure 8.3 (left image) and Shift+Scale them on the x- and y-axes to extrude the top of the shoulders toward the neck (middle image). The edges all scale in toward the middle of the shoulder area and not the center of the neck at the spine, so switch to Vertex mode and move the vertices to better match the shape shown in Figure 8.3 (right image).

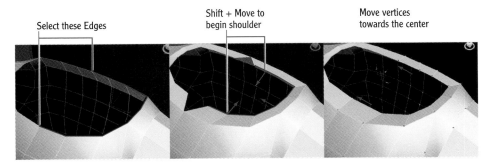

FIGURE 8.3 Drag out the edges around the neck.

5. Go back to Edge mode and select the inner neck edges, and extrude-move them (Shift+Move) to extrude another set of polygons toward the center of the neck, and then move the vertices toward the center of the model.

6. In Edge mode again, select the same inner neck edges again, and extrude-move them down to create a lip downward into the torso (you can see the vertical lip in Figure 8.4). Release the mouse, and then click

again to Shift+Move in toward the center of the model to create a cap at the neck area, as shown in red in Figure 8.4. You can see the original model half is in X-ray mode (Alt+X), whereas the mirrored instanced half mimics what you do to the original part.

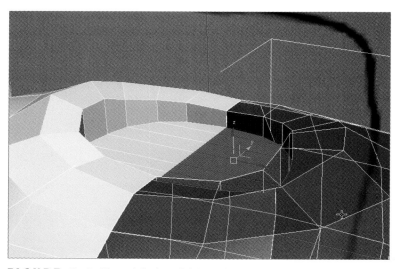

FIGURE 8.4 The original model is in X-ray mode, whereas the mirrored instance is solid.

Now, go through one last time and fix any edge spacing issues or wonky geometry you may have. When you're ready, you are going to combine and weld the two parts of the model together.

To "un-instance" the instanced side of the model, select it and go to the Modify panel. In the toolbar under the modifier stack, click on the Make Unique icon (⍦). Now the two instances are two copies and are no longer mirroring each other.

7. Select the right half, and then from the Graphite Modeling Tools ribbon, select Geometry (All) ≻ Attach. Select the other side of the model; doing so combines both halves.

You are not done, however. The vertices in the center of the model are not welded together yet; they are separate sets of vertices running down the seam where the two halves attach. You need to keep this model solid to prevent the mesh from tearing apart during animation.

8. Enter the Front viewport and switch to Vertex mode. Make sure Ignore Backfacing is off and drag a selection box down the center of the torso

model to select the vertices along the seam of the two halves. From the Graphite Modeling Tools ribbon, select Align and click on the X to align vertices along the X axis.

9. With the vertices selected, from the Graphite Modeling Tools ribbon, select Vertices ➤ Weld ➤ Weld Settings ( ) to open the Weld Vertices caddy. Notice that there is a before-and-after count on the Weld Vertices caddy that pops up in the viewport. Increase the Weld Threshold setting until something visibly changes in the viewport, and then reduce the value slightly to undo the change. Feel free to go into the Perspective viewport to check this. Weld the vertices together by clicking the OK (check mark) button.

Creating the Accessories

Continue with the previous exercise's scene file, or open the Soldier_V06.max scene file in the Scenes folder of the Soldier project from the book's web page. Most of the smaller detail in the model will be added through textures; however, it helps tremendously to add detail, such as pouches and elbow and knee pads, into the actual geometry. This creates a better silhouette for your character. These details are further enhanced with textures in Chapter 10, "Introduction to Materials: Red Rocket."

1. To create the belt, you're going to chamfer and extrude an edge loop that's located closest to the belt line on the model. Choose the edge in the middle of the soldier's waistline and from the Graphite Modeling Tools ribbon, choose Modify Selection ➤ Loop ( ).

2. With the edge loop selected, from the Graphite Modeling Tools ribbon, select Edges ➤ Chamfer ➤ Chamfer Settings. Set Edge Chamfer Amount to 1.5 and click OK.

3. With the two edges from the chamfer still selected, hold Shift and from the Graphite Modeling Tools ribbon, choose Polygon Modeling ➤ Polygon. Doing so selects the polygons associated with the two selected edges. If that doesn't work, hold down the Ctrl key and click on the remaining polygons that need to be selected.

4. Next, from the Graphite Modeling Tools ribbon, choose Polygons ➤ Extrude ➤ Extrude Settings, and make sure you extrude by Local Normal with a Height value of 0.5, as shown in Figure 8.5.

5. Next you're going to block out a pouch on the belt. Delete two sections of the belt on the body's left side, as shown in Figure 8.6.

6. Select the four polygons above and below the deleted area, also shown in Figure 8.6. From the Graphite Modeling Tools ribbon, select Polygons ➤ Extrude ➤ Extrude Settings, set an amount of 0.5, then click (⊕) to apply one extrusion. Then click (✓) for a second extrusion and to exit the caddy. The pouch is now extruded twice for a total extrusion depth of 1″.

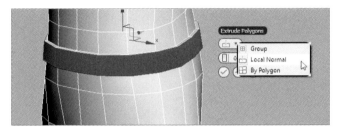

FIGURE 8.5 Extrude polygons for the belt.

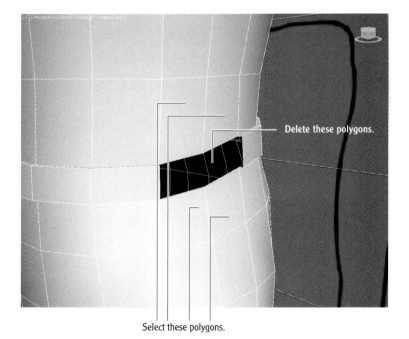

Delete these polygons.

Select these polygons.

FIGURE 8.6 Delete the belt polygons on the left side of the belt. Then select the indicated polygons for the next step.

7. Select the four polygons on top of the bottom half of the pouch and the four polygons on the bottom of the top half of the pouch, as shown in Figure 8.7, and delete them. Figure 8.7 shows the model in See-Through mode. Click Alt+X to see all eight polygons to be selected and deleted.

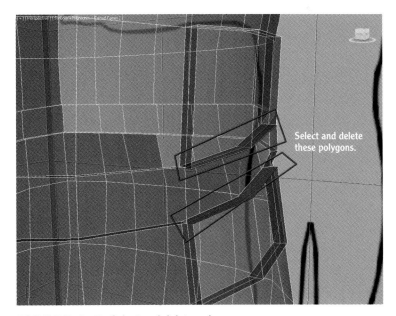

Select and delete these polygons.

FIGURE 8.7 Select and delete polygons.

8. In Edge mode, select the top and bottom edges around the newly deleted areas, and from the Graphite Modeling Tools ribbon, choose the arrow under Edges ➢ Bridge ➢ Bridge, as shown in Figure 8.8, to open the caddy. Accept the default values, shown in Figure 8.9, and click OK.

FIGURE 8.8 Edge Bridge tool

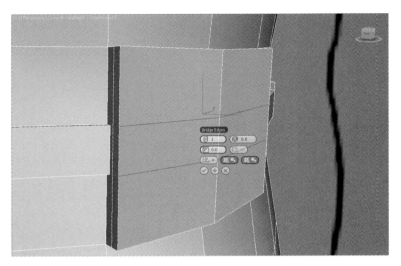

FIGURE 8.9 Bridge caddy settings

The pouch should look like a box; if it doesn't, move vertices around so it does. Once the pouch has the correct shape, move the top level of polygons further out away from the belt to give the pouch more depth.

9. To create some depth to the vest that our character will be wearing, you will want to cut out a level of clothing under the arms. Select two columns and three rows of polygons directly underneath the armpit, as shown in Figure 8.10.

FIGURE 8.10 Select the polygons directly under the armpit.

10. From the Graphite Modeling Tools ribbon, select Polygons ➢ Bevel ➢ Bevel Settings and, in the caddy, use a Height of –0.5 and an Outline of –1.0.

   Adjust any vertices as necessary for an even and smooth look. Do the same for the other side of the model. The final appearance of the area underneath the armpit is shown in Figure 8.11.

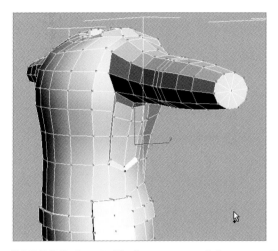

FIGURE 8.11 Final appearance of the area under the arm

11. Next, you're going to add a leg strap to hold a gun holster. From the Graphite Modeling Tools ribbon, choose Edit ➢ SwiftLoop, and add a new horizontal loop of edges below the groin area on both legs. When the loop is created, it is crooked, but you need the new edges to be straight. The Swift Loop tool should still be active when you're doing this. So, after you create the edge, hold Ctrl+Alt and click and drag the edge down, and you will see that it straightens.

12. On the right leg, in Edge mode select one edge of the new edge loop you created in the previous step. From the Graphite Modeling Tools ribbon, select Modify Selection ➢ Loop, then Edges ➢ Chamfer ➢ Chamfer Settings. Enter an edge chamfer amount of **1.5** and click OK.

13. In Polygon mode, select the loop of new polygons by holding Shift and clicking the Polygon icon in the Polygon Modeling panel of the Graphite Modeling Tools ribbon. Then select Polygon ➢ Extrude ➢ Extrude Settings, using a Height value of 0.4.

14. In Polygon mode, select a strip of polygons that goes from the top of the leg strap to the bottom of the belt, and delete them (see Figure 8.12).

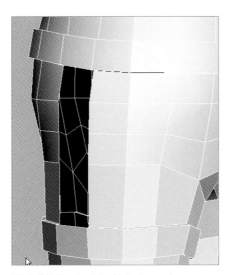

FIGURE 8.12 Deleting polygons

15. Select the edge at the leg strap and at the belt, and use Bridge to create the polygons needed to fill out the strap. The sides of the holster are still open.

16. Select the edges between the new bridged polygons and the model's hip, and then use Bridge again in this area, as shown in Figure 8.13. Be sure to repeat this on the other side of the holster as well.

17. Click the Edge Mode button to get out of subobject mode, and then with the Soldier model still selected, right-click and enter Isolation mode. Now go back into Edge mode, and in the Left viewport, create a plane with these parameters:
　　Length: 20, Width: 7, Length Segs: 4, Width Segs: 1

18. Convert the plane to an editable poly. Position the plane where the holster will be on the soldier. Then in Vertex mode, shape it as shown in Figure 8.14.

19. In the Modify panel, use the modifier list to add a Shell modifier to the plane and give it the following parameters:
　　Inner Amount: 1.2, Outer Amount: 1.2, Segments: 1
　　Now, fit this piece in place on the vertical leg strap you created.

20. Select the body and from the Graphite Modeling Tools ribbon, select Geometry (All) ➢ Attach and click on the gun holster.

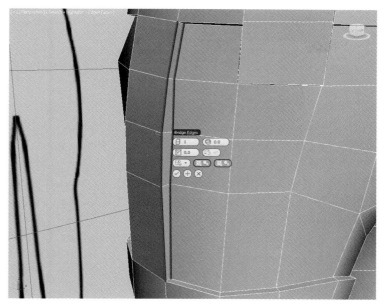

FIGURE 8.13 Use Bridge to fill the gap on the side of the strap.

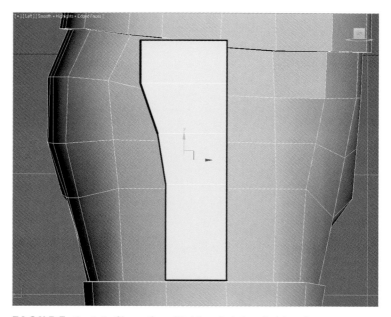

FIGURE 8.14 Shape the editable poly into a holster shape.

Putting On the Boots

Continue with the previous exercise's scene file, or open the Soldier_V07.max scene file in the Scenes folder of the Soldier project from the book's web page. At this point, you are probably feeling comfortable with the tools and interface, so we'll pare down the steps somewhat unless the procedures are new to this chapter.

1. To create the boots, start by creating a cylinder in the Perspective viewport. In the Create panel, select Geometry ➤ Cylinder. Set Radius to 5.0, Height to 8.0, Height Segments to 1, Cap Segments to 1, and Sides to 8, and make sure the Smooth option is checked. Create the cylinder.

2. Select the cylinder and in the Graphite Modeling Tools ribbon, choose Polygon Modeling ➤ Convert To Poly. Then position the cylinder under the left leg to be the top part of the boot.

3. Using the Right viewport, move vertices on the cylinder so the shape mimics the form of the top of the boot in the image plane. Delete the topmost and bottommost polygons that were created with the cylinder.

4. Ignore the two bottom-front edges of the cylinder where the top of the foot would be, and select the bottom U-shaped edges of the cylinder. Extrude-move (Shift+Move) the edges of the back half of the boot top to the bottom of the foot in the image plane, as shown in Figure 8.15.

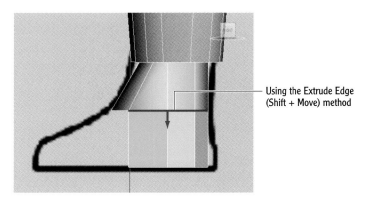

Using the Extrude Edge (Shift + Move) method

FIGURE 8.15 Using Extrude Edge to create another set of polygons for the U-shaped back and side part of the boot

5. Select the two bottom-front edges that you ignored previously, and extrude-move them four times to form the extruded polygons to the image plane, as shown in Figure 8.16. You will need a total of four rows of polygons for the top and front of the foot. As you extrude, you can release the mouse button after one extrusion, and then Shift+Move again for the next extrusion. Repeat for a total of four new strips of polygons, as Figure 8.16 shows. Form the new polygons as needed to fit the top of the foot.

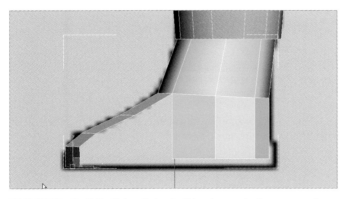

FIGURE 8.16 Using Extrude Edge to create four new polygons that form with the image plane for the top of the foot

6. In Edge mode, select the vertical edges on either side of the gap, as shown in Figure 8.17 (left). Then from the Graphite Modeling Tools ribbon, select Edges ➢ Bridge ➢ Bridge Settings, enter three segments, and bridge the gap. Repeat the same on the opposite side of the foot.

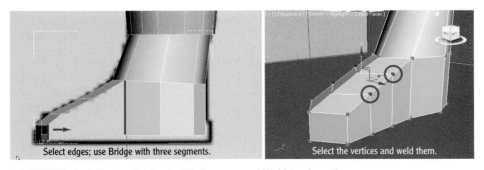

Select edges; use Bridge with three segments.   Select the vertices and weld them.

FIGURE 8.17 Use Bridge to fill the gaps and Weld to close the gaps.

7. Switch to Vertex mode, and from the Graphite Modeling Tools ribbon, choose Vertices ≻ Weld, open the caddy, set Threshold to **2.0**, and click OK, as shown in Figure 8.17 (right).

8. From the Graphite Modeling Tools ribbon, select Edit ≻ SwiftLoop. Create a new horizontal edge loop around the foot from heel to toe on the side of the foot, as Figure 8.18 shows.

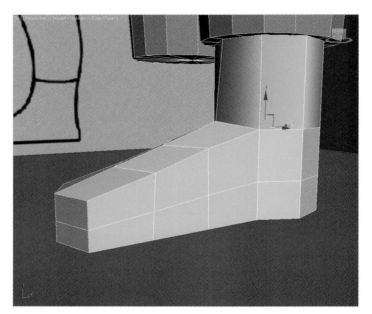

FIGURE 8.18 Use Swift Loop to create a new horizontal edge around the side of the foot.

The eight segments you defined on the original boot cylinder are not enough, so you need to create more segments for the cylinder.

9. In Edge mode, select the middle vertical edge of the foot, and select Loop. From the Graphite Modeling Tools ribbon, select Edges ≻ Chamfer ≻ Chamfer Settings, and enter the caddy parameters: Chamfer Amount: 0.667, Segments: 1. Click OK.

10. Follow the same process to chamfer the very back vertical edge on the boot (running just below the calf) and use the added vertices to round out the heel. The top of the foot is a bit boxy, so scale in the vertices and smooth out the sides as in Figure 8.19.

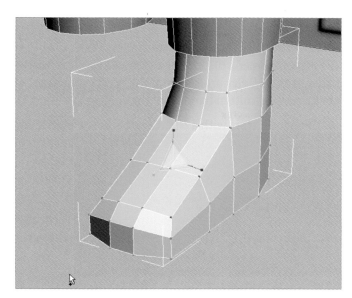

FIGURE 8.19 Smoothing out the sides of the boot

When you are happy with how this looks, center the pivot point to the soldier model and mirror it on the X axis as a copy (not an instance). You can then attach the boots to the rest of the body, as you did with the gun holster. Figure 8.20 shows the two completed boots, now attached to the body.

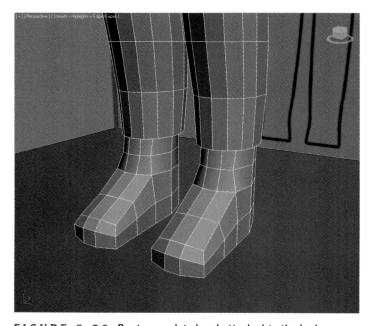

FIGURE 8.20 Boots completed and attached to the body

The soldier is complete—well, at least the model. Now that the head objects are attached to the body, they cannot be selected individually. As a matter of fact, the entire soldier is one object, from the boots to the helmet. You have to select the boots, hands, or any accessories you added to the model by using Element mode from the modifier stack. You will see this approach in action in Chapter 11 as you lay out UVs for the soldier. Figure 9.21 shows the completed model of our special operations soldier with some added accessories, elbow and knee pads, and with the head's accessories.

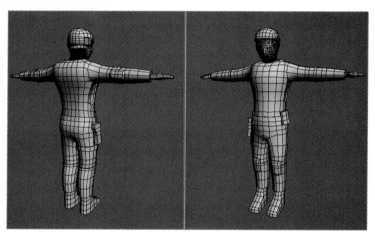

FIGURE 9.21 Completed soldier model

Go grab a beverage; you've earned it!

THE ESSENTIALS AND BEYOND

This chapter explored several tools used in modeling. From a simple box, you formed a torso to match the general shapes shown in the images. The arms and legs were extruded and shaped. Using Mirror required you to model only half of the soldier character at a time. The head modeling came next, and then you merged in already completed accessories from another scene file to add detail to the model's head.

ADDITIONAL EXERCISES

Although we used a fairly low polygon count soldier character in this chapter, this toolset can be utilized for any type of model. Try variations on the same themes, such as:

▶ Design and build another special operations soldier to form a team.

▶ Build different accessories for the soldier, such as a rifle.

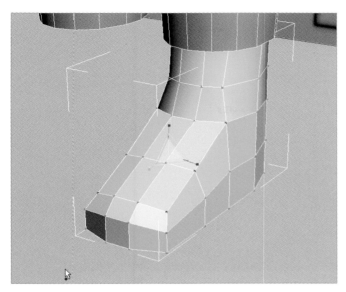

FIGURE 8.19 Smoothing out the sides of the boot

When you are happy with how this looks, center the pivot point to the soldier model and mirror it on the *X* axis as a copy (not an instance). You can then attach the boots to the rest of the body, as you did with the gun holster. Figure 8.20 shows the two completed boots, now attached to the body.

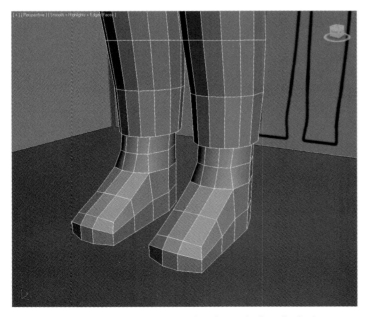

FIGURE 8.20 Boots completed and attached to the body

Creating the Hands

Continue with the previous exercise's scene file, or open the Soldier_V08.max scene file in the Scenes folder of the Soldier project from the book's web page. In this section, you will create simple "mitten hands" for the soldier:

1. To create one of the hands, start with a box. Create a box primitive in the Perspective viewport, and then in the Modify panel, set Length to **7.5**, Width to **16.0**, and Height to **5.0**. All segments should be set to 1. Position the box in your Top viewport over the wrist. Finish positioning it in the Front viewport and convert it to an editable poly.

2. In the Top viewport, use Swift Loop to create two segments vertically and two segments horizontally. Then, in Vertex mode, move the vertices to create a mitten arc, as shown in Figure 8.21.

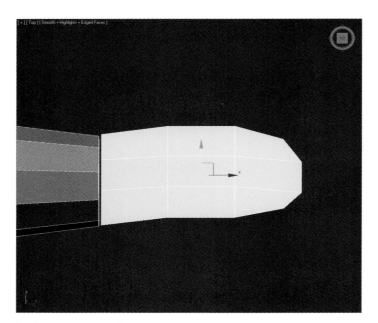

FIGURE 8.21 Reshape vertices to create a mitten shape.

3. With the hand selected, go into Polygon mode and select the polygons on the hand where the wrist and the arm meet; then delete them. The result is a hollow hand.

4. In Edge mode, select the outer edge loop running along the top and bottom of the hand lengthwise. Then from the Graphite Modeling

Tools ribbon, choose Edges ≻ Chamfer ≻ Chamfer Settings, and set Edge Chamfer Amount to **0.7**, as shown in Figure 8.22.

5. Use Swift Loop to create an edge up from the wrist, as shown in Figure 8.23.

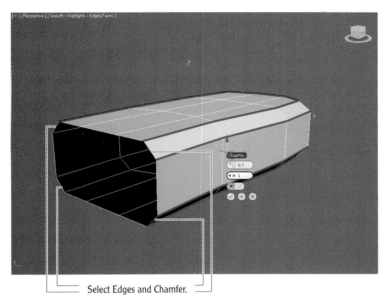

Select Edges and Chamfer.

FIGURE 8.22 Select and chamfer the edge loops running lengthwise along the top and bottom of the hand.

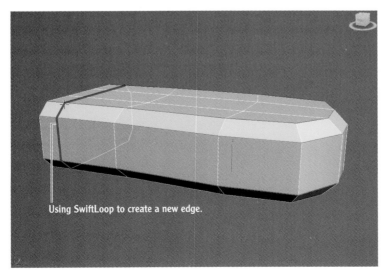

Using SwiftLoop to create a new edge.

FIGURE 8.23 Use Swift Loop to create an edge at the wrist.

6. In Polygon mode, select the three polygons just up from the newly created edge on the side of the hand, where the thumb should be. From the Graphite Modeling Tools ribbon, select Polygons ➢ Extrude ➢ Extrude Settings and use a Height value of 0.8 to start pulling out the thumb. Then move the corner edges in to round out the beginning shape of the thumb.

7. Bevel the polygons at the end of the thumb for the knuckle. From the Graphite Modeling Tools ribbon, select Polygons ➢ Bevel ➢ Bevel Settings. Set Bevel Amount to 3.0 and Outline Amount to –.55, and click OK.

8. Repeat step 7 at the tip of the thumb geometry to create another segment for the thumb from the knuckle to the tip of the thumb. Adjust the polygons, vertices, and edges to get the thumb to look like Figure 8.24.

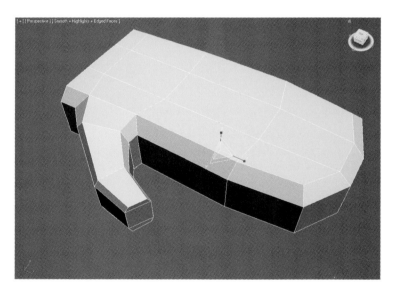

FIGURE 8.24 The thumb with all its joints

9. Select the polygon at the ends of the thumb and fingers. From the Graphite Modeling Tools ribbon, choose Polygon Modeling and click the Soft Selection icon (○). In the Front viewport, move the thumb and fingers down to give them a slight slope.

10. In the Perspective viewport, scale the wrist down to fit within the sleeve if necessary. Center the pivot point to the model's body, and mirror it as a copy for the other side. Place the hands at the wrists and attach them to the rest of the model. The final gloved hand is shown in Figure 8.25.

FIGURE 8.25 The final gloved hand

THE ESSENTIALS AND BEYOND

In this chapter, you completed the main body for the soldier and continued using edge loops and vertices to shape the accessories and various parts of the character model.

ADDITIONAL EXERCISES

▶ Create additional pouches or straps for your model. (Keep in mind that any changes you make to the design of the book's model will make your model differ from the one you use for texturing in Chapter 11, "Textures and UV Workflow: The Soldier.")

▶ With the tools you used to create the belt and pouches, create geometry for knee pads and elbow pads.

(Continues)

THE ESSENTIALS AND BEYOND *(Continued)*

You can see our completed body here:

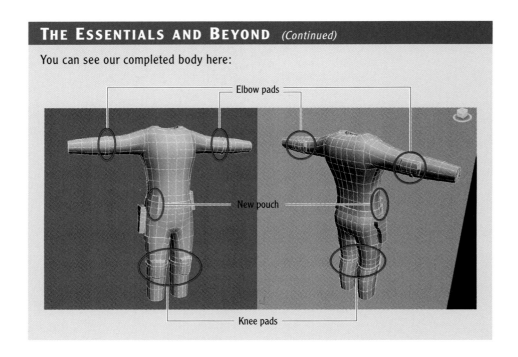

CHAPTER 9

Character Poly Modeling: Part III

In this chapter you will finish the model of the special operations soldier started in Chapter 7, "Character Poly Modeling: Part I," by modeling the head shape and merging in elements for the head (such as goggles and a face mask) and integrating them into the scene. Finishing elements are critical to the veracity of a model's design, and they can be modeled separately for ease and later incorporated into the base model.

Topics in this chapter include the following:

▶ **Creating the head**

▶ **Merging in and attaching the head's accessories**

Creating the Head

Continue with the previous exercise's scene file (from Chapter 8, "Character Poly Modeling: Part II"), or open the Soldier_V09.max scene file in the Scenes folder of the Soldier project from the book's web page at **www.sybex.com/go/3dsmax2012essentials**.

The soldier's head will consist of four parts: a helmet, goggles, a face mask, and a head shape for them to sit on. The easiest way to create and fit these components is to start with the head shape. First, though, you need to adjust the body's neckline so it's a bit better to work with. Right now the neck area is close to a circle shape. You want this to be closer to an oval that follows the contour of the rest of the model.

1. In Polygon mode, select the front of the neckline. Then, from the Graphite Modeling Tools ribbon, choose Polygon Modeling ➢ Use Soft Selection ( ). Then choose the Soft panel and change the Falloff value to 4.000, as shown in Figure 9.1. Move the polygons down on the *Y* axis. Do the same for the back of the model.

These actions will smoothly create a lower neckline, giving more definition to the shoulders as well.

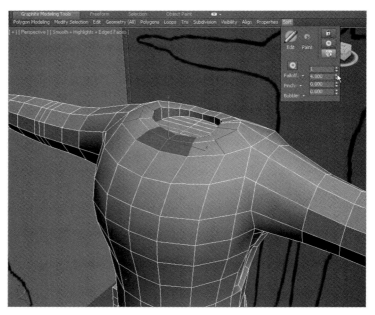

FIGURE 9.1 Soft-select the polygons at the front of the neck and move them down.

2. Create a cylinder with these parameters:

Radius: 5.0

Height: 6.0

Height Segments: 1

Cap Segments: 1

Sides: 12

Convert the cylinder to an editable poly and position the cylinder inside the neckline.

3. You'll model half of each part and then use mirroring to save time. Delete the left half, the top, and the bottom of the cylinder, and move the edges and vertices so the new neck geometry is formed better within the neckline, as shown in Figure 9.2.

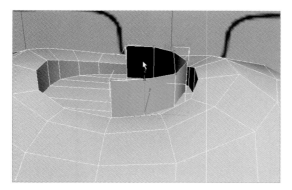

FIGURE 9.2 Delete half of the cylinder and its top and bottom.

4. Select the top edges of the cylinder and extrude-move them (Shift+Move) to create another level of polygons. The neck now has two rows of polygons. Next, select the first edge on the top nearest where the Adam's apple would be, and extrude-move to create a new polygon. Move the edge up along the *Z* axis, as shown in Figure 9.3.

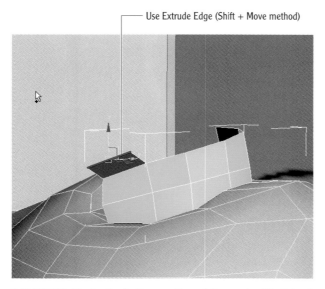

FIGURE 9.3 Begin the creation of the neck with Extrude.

Outlining the Head

In the following steps, you will create an outline of the head by creating one strip of polygons and then forming them to the side image plane. You will extrude 15 times, and move the edges to create the general form of a head. Be sure to keep the outer edge of the head inside the edges of the image plane; that way, you'll have room to fit the head accessories.

1. You should still have the edge selected from the previous exercise. Use extrude-move again, but when you finish one polygon, release the mouse button; then click again and move the edge to create another extruded polygon. You'll do this 14 more times, following the form of the head in the image plane, as shown in Figure 9.4.

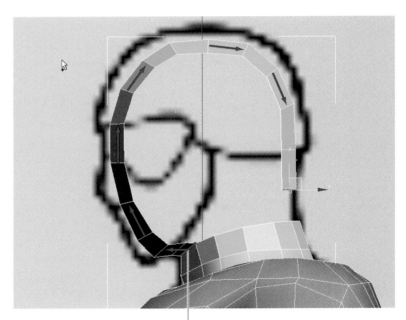

Use the Extrude Edge (Shift + Move method). Do this 15 times, following the form of the head in the image plane.

FIGURE 9.4 Create the head outline using the Shift+Move method, following the image plane.

2. In the Front viewport, select the edge on the top base of the neck about where the ear might be. Using Shift+Move, position a polygon strip as you did in step 1, but this time for the side of the head.

Extrude a total of five segments up from the neck. In Edge mode, use Bridge (on the Graphite Modeling Tools ribbon, choose Edges ➤ Bridge) to fill the gap between the side of the head and the nearest edge on the top of the head, as shown in Figure 9.5.

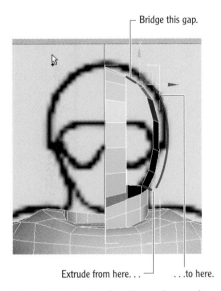

Bridge this gap.

Extrude from here. . .   . . .to here.

FIGURE 9.5 Creating polygons for the side of the head

3. To build the front of the face, start by selecting the two edges just under the chin and use Shift+Move to extrude them out to the right, as shown in Figure 9.6. In Vertex mode, select the Graphite Modeling Tools ribbon and choose Vertices ➤ Target Weld. To use Target Weld, click on one vertex and drag a line to the other to fuse the vertices together. So first click the vertex on the new polygon closest to the neck, and then click on the neck vertex, shown in Figure 9.6. This will fuse the new polygons for the jowls to the neck.

4. Back in Edge mode, select the two rightmost edges of the polygons you just created for the jowls, and then use Shift+Move to extrude those edges up on the Z axis. Match the number of segments with the segments on the outer head strip you already created. The result is shown in Figure 9.7.

5. Select the edges shown on the left side of Figure 9.8. Use Bridge to curve the strip toward the forehead, as shown in Figure 9.8.

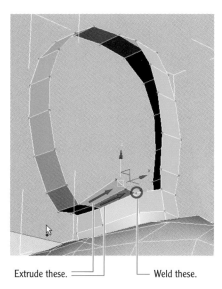

Extrude these.   Weld these.

FIGURE 9.6 Extrude edges to the right and weld the neck vertices.

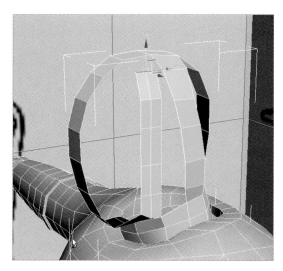

FIGURE 9.7 Extrude a new strip; match the segments.

6. As you did in step 5, in Edge mode use Shift+Move to extrude another row of polygons in toward the front of the face. Then in Vertex mode, use Target Weld on either side of the front face strip, as shown in Figure 9.9.

Select these edges and use Bridge.

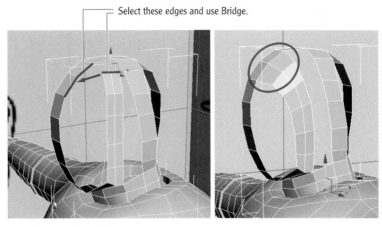

FIGURE 9.8 Use Bridge to close the gap.

Extrude Edge (Shift + Move method)

Target Weld the vertices.

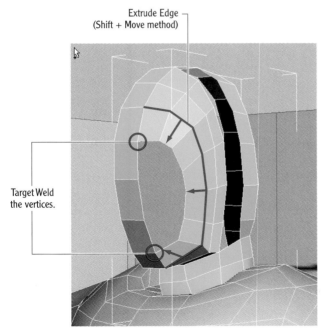

FIGURE 9.9 Use Shift+Move, and then use Target Weld.

7. Looking at the ring of edges from the front of the strip of the head to the side of the head, it's clear you don't have enough horizontal edges. Select the edge closest to where the bridge of the nose would be, and then use Chamfer (from the Graphite Modeling Tools ribbon, choose Edges ➢ Chamfer Settings ➢ Chamfer Settings) with an Edge Chamfer Amount value of 1.346, and then click OK. Try to keep the edges equally spaced, as shown in Figure 9.10.

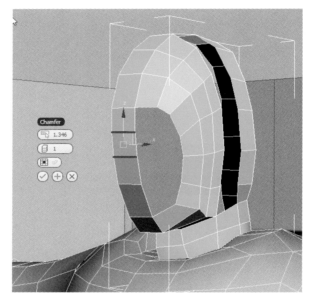

FIGURE 9.10 Chamfer the edge that falls at the bridge of the nose.

8. Select the eight edges on the front of the face and the side of the face, and then use Bridge, as shown in Figure 9.11. Notice that there is nowhere to weld to on the vertical edge on the top of the head. You need to create another edge running down the front of the face and then weld the vertices together to close the head.

9. From the Graphite Modeling Tools ribbon, choose Edit ➢ Cut to access the Cut tool. Then cut from the dead-end edge at the top of the head down to the bottom of the neck, as shown in Figure 9.12. Make sure you start and end the cut directly on the vertices.

10. In Vertex mode, select the two vertices at the top of the cut, and from the Graphite Modeling Tools ribbon, choose Vertices ➢ Weld and modify the Weld Threshold setting until the two vertices are welded together.

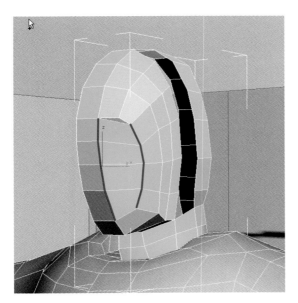

FIGURE 9.11 Select edges and use Bridge.

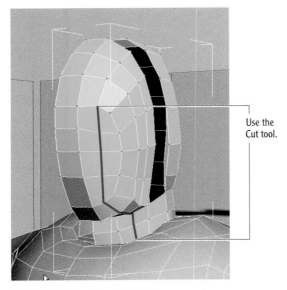

Use the Cut tool.

FIGURE 9.12 Cutting the new edge

Rounding Out the Face

You will now take some time to round out the face a bit. The face doesn't have to be perfectly round, but it will help if the face is close to a round shape. The majority of the head mesh you will create will be covered with the goggles, helmet, and face mask. However, you can use the geometry you create to fit and form those accessories.

1. In Edge mode, select the edges around the ear and use Bridge to close the gap, as shown in Figure 9.13.

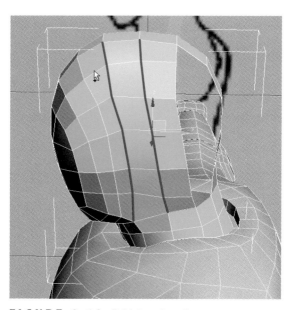

FIGURE 9.13 Bridging the edges

2. Looking at the back of the head, you can see an edge open on the bottom. Use the Cut tool to add another vertical edge, as shown in Figure 9.14.

3. Select the edges on the inside of the gap closest to the back of the head and use Shift+Move to extrude more faces toward the ears, as shown in Figure 9.15. Then switch to Vertex mode and use Target Weld to weld the loose vertices at the top and bottom, also shown in Figure 9.15.

Use the Cut tool to create an edge.   Readjust the spacing here.

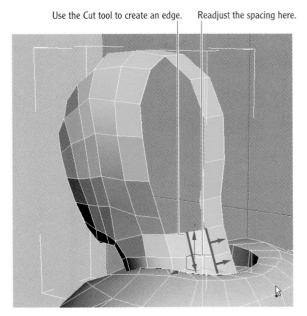

FIGURE 9.14 Create a new edge for the back of the head/neck using the Cut tool.

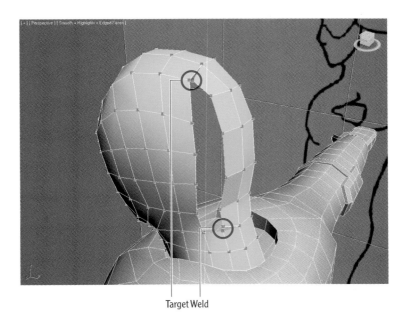

Target Weld

FIGURE 9.15 Extrude edges and use Target Weld on the loose vertices.

Creating the Back of the Head

You have the same problem with the back of the head as you did with the front of the face: There are not enough horizontal edges.

1. Chamfer a horizontal edge near the top of the back of the head, as shown in Figure 9.16. In Figure 9.16, you can visualize how the polygons will bridge over. In this case, after you create the chamfer, you will have five segments that can bridge in the next step.

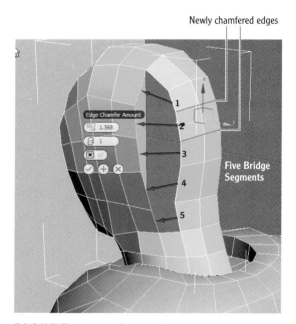

FIGURE 9.16 Chamfer the edges.

2. Bridge the vertical edges of the gap, as Figure 9.17 shows. This time you have the exact amount needed to create a solid head shape.

3. Go into the Right viewport and notice how the edges are closer to the front of the head than the back, as shown in Figure 9.18 (left). Select and move edges or vertices until the vertices are more evenly spaced (Figure 9.18, right).

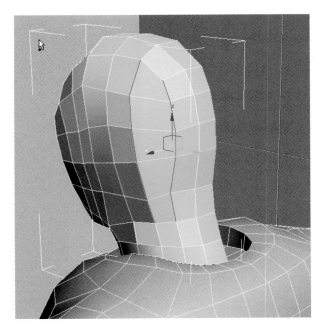

FIGURE 9.17 Bridge the vertical edges to fill the last hole.

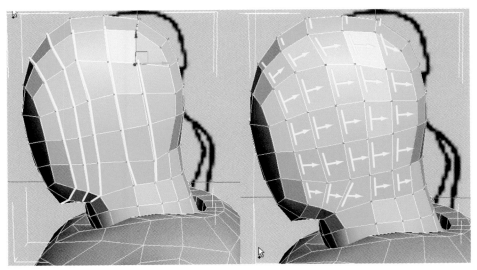

This geometry needs fixing.   Evenly space these.

FIGURE 9.18 Move edges or vertices to evenly space the edges.

Mirroring the Head

Now make any necessary adjustments to your mesh to get it just right. Again, it's not terribly vital that this part be perfect because you will cover it up with accessories in the upcoming steps. Once you're satisfied, continue with these steps:

1. Adjust the head's pivot to the left edge of the geometry and mirror the half over on the X axis as a copy.

2. From the Graphite Modeling Tools ribbon, choose Geometry (All) ➢ Attach, and then select the other side of the head to attach them. Now in Vertex mode, turn off Ignore Backfacing; then select all the vertices in the center vertical seam of the head. From the Graphite Modeling Tools ribbon, select Vertices ➢ Weld Settings ➢ Weld Settings. Use a higher Weld Threshold value to be sure all the vertices are welded when you click OK.

3. Going into the Front viewport, you can see our head is a little wide compared to the image plane. Scale it just a bit to fit on the X axis so you have room to put on the helmet. Our base head is complete; now you can add the details.

Merging In and Attaching the Head's Accessories

The remaining accessories for the soldier are the helmet, goggles, and face mask. To create these you'd repeat the same methods you've already used, so we'll cut a little time and merge in the finished pieces.

The finished models for the helmet, goggles, and face mask have been created separately and can be merged into your final model. The process is the same as the one used in Chapter 5, "Animating a Bouncing Ball," for the Red Rocket project. Keep in mind that if you changed the design of the soldier as you built him in your scene, the accessories for the head may not fit perfectly to your particular model. If this is the case, you may wish to use the scene file provided in the following steps, or create your own accessories to fit your design.

Continue with the previous exercise's scene file, or open the `Soldier_v10.max` scene file in the Soldier project's Scenes folder from the book's web page.

1. Click the Application menu and select Import ➢ Merge; in the Merge File dialog box, choose the file `Soldier_Accessories.max` in the Scenes folder of the Soldier project from the web page. Click Open. In the Merge dialog box, as shown in Figure 9.19, select all the objects

in the list, and click OK. You might see a warning about materials, as shown in Figure 9.20, so just click Use Scene Material. The object will appear in the scene, lined up with the model.

FIGURE 9.19 Merge dialog box

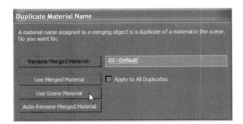

FIGURE 9.20 You might see this warning.

Now you need to attach all the accessories to the main body. This means the entire soldier model is a single mesh and can be used to create the UVW mapping for the model in Chapter 11: "Textures and UV Workflow: The Soldier."

2. Select the body and from the Graphite Modeling Tools ribbon, choose Geometry (All) ➤ Attach (arrow) ➤ Attach From List to open the Attach List dialog box. Using this dialog box makes it easier to attach when you have multiple objects.

3. Because you selected the body when you opened the Attach List dialog box, the window won't show the body as an object that you can select. Select the four objects, but not the image planes, in the list and click Attach.

The soldier is complete—well, at least the model. Now that the head objects are attached to the body, they cannot be selected individually. As a matter of fact, the entire soldier is one object, from the boots to the helmet. You have to select the boots, hands, or any accessories you added to the model by using Element mode from the modifier stack. You will see this approach in action in Chapter 11 as you lay out UVs for the soldier. Figure 9.21 shows the completed model of our special operations soldier with some added accessories, elbow and knee pads, and with the head's accessories.

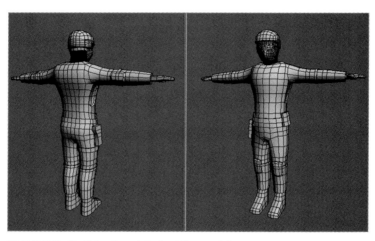

FIGURE 9.21 Completed soldier model

Go grab a beverage; you've earned it!

THE ESSENTIALS AND BEYOND

This chapter explored several tools used in modeling. From a simple box, you formed a torso to match the general shapes shown in the images. The arms and legs were extruded and shaped. Using Mirror required you to model only half of the soldier character at a time. The head modeling came next, and then you merged in already completed accessories from another scene file to add detail to the model's head.

ADDITIONAL EXERCISES

Although we used a fairly low polygon count soldier character in this chapter, this toolset can be utilized for any type of model. Try variations on the same themes, such as:

▶ Design and build another special operations soldier to form a team.

▶ Build different accessories for the soldier, such as a rifle.

CHAPTER 10

Introduction to Materials: Red Rocket

A material defines an object's look—its color, tactile texture, transparency, luminescence, glow, and so on. Mapping is the term used to describe how the materials are wrapped or projected onto the geometry (for example, adding wood grain to a wooden object). After you create your objects, 3ds Max assigns a simple color to them, as you've already seen.

You define a material in 3ds Max by setting values for its parameters or by applying textures or maps. These parameters define the way an object will look when rendered. Much of an object's appearance when rendered also depends on the lighting. In this chapter and in Chapter 14, "Introduction to Lighting: Red Rocket," you will discover that materials and lights work closely together.

Topics in this chapter include the following:

▶ **Materials**

▶ **Compact Material Editor**

▶ **Mapping the rocket**

▶ **Bring on the nose, bring on the funk**

Materials

Materials are useful for making your objects appear more lifelike or for adding detail to a model. If you model a table and want it to look like polished wood, you can define a shiny material in 3ds Max and apply a wooden texture, such as an image file of wood, to the diffuse channel of that material.

The primary force in a material is its color. In 3ds Max, three main parameters control the color of a material: ambient color, diffuse color, and specular color.

Ambient Color   This is the color of a material when it is exposed to ambient light. An object will appear this color in indirect light or in shadow.

Diffuse Color   This is the color of a material when the object is exposed to direct light. Typically, ambient and diffuse colors are not too far apart. By default, they are locked together in the Material Editor.

Specular Color   This is the color of a shiny object's highlight. The color sets the tone of the object and, in some cases, the degree and look of its shine.

For example, in a new scene, open the Material Editor by choosing Rendering ➢ Material Editor ➢ Compact Material Editor. The spheres you see in the Material Editor are sample slots where you can edit materials.

Each tile, or slot, represents one material that may be assigned to one or more objects in the scene. As you click on each slot, the material's parameters are displayed below. You edit the material through the settings you see in the Material Editor.

Select one of the material slots. Let's change the color of the material. In the Blinn Basic Parameters rollout, click the gray color swatch next to the Diffuse parameter. This opens the Color Selector dialog box. Use the sliders on the right to set the red, green, and blue values for the color, or control the color using the Hue, Sat (saturation), and Value levels.

In addition, you can add textures to most of the parameters for a material. Notice the blank square icon next to the diffuse color swatch. Click that icon, and you will get the Material/Map Browser, which is discussed later in this chapter.

Compact Material Editor

The Material Editor is the central place in 3ds Max where you do all of your material creation and editing. You can assign materials to any number of objects as well as have multiple materials assigned to different parts of the same object.

In 3ds Max 2012, there are two interfaces to the Material Editor: the Slate Material Editor (or Slate) and the Compact Material Editor.

The Compact Material Editor is the interface you will be using in this exercise. It is a smaller dialog box than the Slate, and it gives you quick previews of various materials, as shown in Figure 10.1.

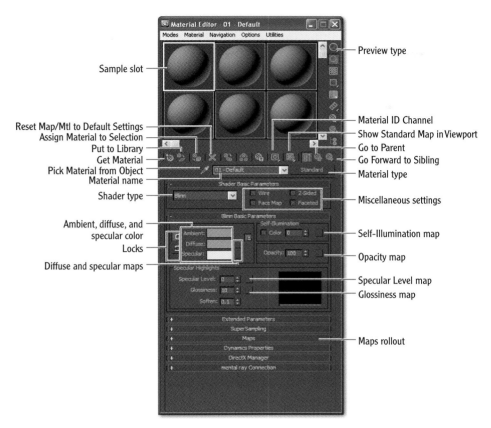

Sample slot

Reset Map/Mtl to Default Settings
Assign Material to Selection
Put to Library
Get Material
Pick Material from Object
Material name

Shader type

Ambient, diffuse, and
specular color
Locks
Diffuse and specular maps

Preview type

Material ID Channel
Show Standard Map in Viewport
Go to Parent
Go Forward to Sibling
Material type

Miscellaneous settings

Self-Illumination map

Opacity map

Specular Level map
Glossiness map

Maps rollout

FIGURE 10.1 The Compact Material Editor

You can access the Compact Material Editor by opening the Slate and then in the Slate's menu bar, selecting Modes ➢ Compact Material Editor. You can switch back to the Slate through the same Modes menu.

Each material is displayed on a sphere in one of the tiles (or slots) in the Material Editor dialog. Right-clicking on any of the materials gives you a few more options, including the ability to change how many sample tiles you can see in the Material Editor.

The Standard material is the default material type and is fine for most uses. However, when you require a more complex material, you can change the material type to one that fits your needs.

Standard

Standard material is the default type for the materials in the Material Editor. With it, you can imitate just about any surface type you can imagine.

Shaders

In 3ds Max, you can control what kind of surface you work with by changing the shader type for a material. In either the Compact Material Editor or the Slate Material Editor, you will find Shader Types as a pull-down menu in a material's Shader Basic Parameters rollout.

The Blinn shader is the default shader in 3ds Max, because it is a general-purpose, flexible shader. The Blinn shader creates a smooth surface with some shininess. If you set the specular color to black, however, this shader loses its shininess and does not display a specular highlight, making it perfect for regular dull surfaces, such as paper. Figure 10.2 shows the Blinn shader controls in the Material Editor.

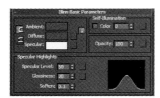

FIGURE 10.2 The Material Editor for the Blinn shader

Because this is the most often used shader, let's look at its Material Editor controls. You can set the color you want by clicking the color swatch, or you can map a texture map to any of these parameters by clicking the Map button and choosing the desired map from the Material/Map Browser.

Mapping the Rocket

Now let's dive into creating material for the rocket we modeled in Chapter 3, "Modeling in 3ds Max: Part I," and Chapter 4, "Modeling in 3ds Max: Part II," to get it ready for lighting and rendering in later chapters.

We will use the Compact Material Editor to create materials and map the Red Rocket model. We will then use the Slate when we map the soldier in Chapter 11, "Textures and UV Workflow: The Soldier."

Study the full-color image of the rocket shown in Chapter 3 in Figure 3.1. That will give you an idea of how the rocket is to be textured. Let's begin with the wheels.

The Wheels

The wheels of the real toy rocket are made of plastic that is fairly smooth, shiny, and reflective. The black tires are different from the wheels: they have a rough, bumpy surface, as shown in Figure 10.3.

The black part of the tire has a slight bumpiness, which changes the shininess, making the surface appear more matte.

Just a simple shiny white plastic

A simple shiny red plastic

FIGURE 10.3 The tire is a rough, black plastic.

The tire is a single object, so we are going to use a texturing technique using Multi/Sub-Object (MSO) materials to apply different materials to polygons of a single 3D object.

Creating a Multi/Sub-Object Material

First you will create the MSO material for the wheel, consisting of three distinct parts: black tire, white hubcap, and red bolt. Start by opening your final rocket model from your work in Chapters 3 and 4, or open the rocket_material_wheel_start.max file from the Scenes folder of the Red Rocket project downloaded from the book's web page at **www.sybex.com/go/3dsmax2012essentials**. This file has the rocket and all its parts showing. When you open this file, select the wheel and press Alt+Q to enter Isolate Selection mode.

1. Open the Compact Material Editor and select a sample sphere. We will start with the red material for the bolt. Name the material **Red Bolt**.

2. In the Blinn Basic Parameters rollout, select the color box next to Diffuse, as shown in Figure 10.4. This controls the base color of an

object. When the Color Selector opens, create a red color with the values of Red: 200, Green: 0, Blue: 0; then click OK.

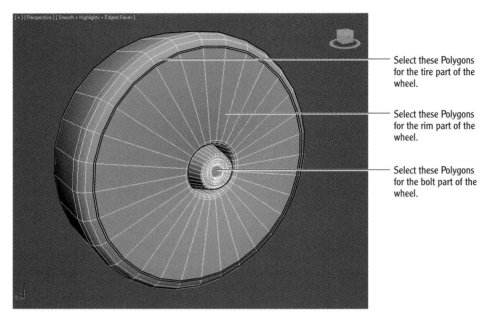

Select these Polygons for the tire part of the wheel.

Select these Polygons for the rim part of the wheel.

Select these Polygons for the bolt part of the wheel.

FIGURE 10.4 Select the color box next to Diffuse.

3. Change the specular highlights to make the surface appear shiny. Set the Specular Level value, which controls the intensity of the highlight, to 90 and set the Glossiness value, which controls the size of the highlight, to 80.

4. Select another sample sphere and name it **Wheel White**. Change the diffuse color to white. Set Specular Level to 90 and Glossiness to 80, as with the red material.

5. Select a third sample sphere in the Material Editor and name it **Wheel Black**. Change the diffuse color to black. Because the highlights on the tire will be different, set Specular Level to 50 and Glossiness to 20.

Selecting Polygons

With an MSO material, you select the polygons on the objects you want to assign a particular type of material, as opposed to selecting the entire object.

1. Press F4 so you can see the edges on the shaded model and then press F2 so you can see just edges around the poly when you select them.

2. Select the wheel object and go to the Polygon Modeling tab of the Graphite Modeling Tools ribbon. If this ribbon doesn't show up, click the Modify tab. Select Polygon to enter Polygon Selection mode (you can also press 4 for Polygon mode).

3. Click the Select Object tool () in the Main toolbar. Then select the polygons that make up the tire portion of the wheel, as shown in Figure 10.5.

FIGURE 10.5
The wheel is composed
of three distinct sections.

> Pressing the Ctrl key lets you add polygons to your selection, and pressing the Alt key lets you remove polygons from your selection.

4. Go to the Material Editor, select the Black Wheel material, and drag it to the selected polygons to assign it to those polygons. You should see the Wheel change black.

5. Select the polygons for the white hubcap as shown in Figure 10.5; then return the Material Editor, grab the Wheel White material, and drag it to the selected polygons, assigning the material to the hubcap portion of the wheel.

6. Select the polygons for the bolt portion of the wheel (Figure 10.5). Drag the Red Bolt material from the Material Editor to the selected polygons.

> Use the Select Object tool and not the Select And Move tool. You do not want to accidentally move any of the polygons while you are trying to select them.

Your wheel now has three distinct materials applied to its appropriate parts. Save your work! You have created an MSO material, even though it may not appear that way.

Loading the MSO Material into the Material Editor

The three materials you see in the Material Editor are now just instances of the main or *parent material* called the Multi Sub-Object material. In the following steps, you will load this material into the Material Editor so you can see it:

1. Exit Polygon mode by clicking the polygon icon in the Graphite Modeling Tools ribbon. Open the Compact Material Editor, and select a sample sphere that isn't being used.

2. Next to the material title is an eyedropper icon (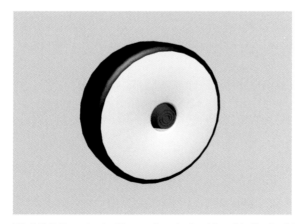). Click the eyedropper, and then click the wheel. The MSO material should be loaded into the Compact Material Editor.

3. In the Compact Material Editor parameters for the wheel's MSO material, change the name of the MSO material to **Wheel**.

Fine-tuning the Materials

Continue with your own scene file. Select the Perspective viewport and press F9 for a Render Last of the wheel (F9 is the shortcut key for a Render Last). Keep in mind that the rest of the rocket is hidden and accessible through the Layer Manager.

The rendered result as shown in Figure 10.6 looks a bit flat. Specular highlights help make a 3D object look real, but highlights don't show up on flat surfaces.

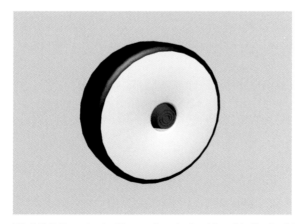

FIGURE 10.6 The rendered wheel is a bit flat looking.

For example, in Figure 10.7 you can see three cylinder objects of varying flatness. The cylinder with the most rounded sides shows the highlight the most.

Usually shiny objects are also reflective, so if you add reflections to the flat hubcap surface, the render would look more convincing.

To assign a reflection map to the wheel, follow these steps.

1. In the Compact Material Editor, select the Red Bolt material. Go to the Maps rollout; click None (to the right of Reflection) as shown in Figure 10.8. Choose Bitmap from the Material/Map Browser; it should be at the top. Navigate to the SceneAssets\Images folder in the Red Rocket project, and select the rocket Rocket Refmap Blur.jpg image file. If you don't see this map, make sure the Files Of Type field is set to JPG.

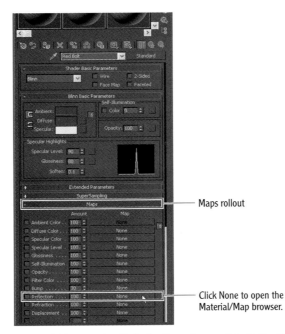

FIGURE 10.7 Flat objects do not show off their specular highlights particularly well.

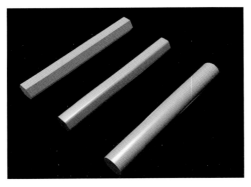

Maps rollout

Click None to open the Material/Map browser.

FIGURE 10.8 Click the None bar next to Reflection in the Maps rollout to access the Material/Map browser.

2. Render a frame of the wheel bolt. Now the wheel's bolt will look like a perfect mirror, because the Reflection amount is being used at 100 percent.

3. In the Material Editor tools, navigate up a level by clicking the Go To Parent icon below the Sample Slots ( ) in the Maps rollout and change Reflection Amount to 30, as shown in Figure 10.9.

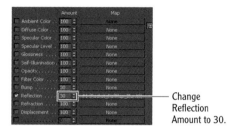

Change Reflection Amount to 30.

FIGURE 10.9 **Change Reflection Amount to 30.**

Figure 10.10 shows the wheel rendered with the mapped reflection. You should notice a subtle difference between Figure 10.10 and Figure 10.7, which shows the wheel with no reflections. You can adjust the Reflection Amount setting to taste.

FIGURE 10.10 **The wheel rendered with mapped reflections**

The mapped reflection helps give the wheel more substance, as it makes the material more convincing when rendered.

Applying a Bump Map

Bump mapping adds a level of detail to an object fairly easily by creating bumps and grooves in the surface and giving the object a tactile element, which this object needs (refer back to Figure 10.3). Bump mapping uses the intensity values (aka the brightness values) of an image or procedural map to simulate bumpiness on the surface of the model, without changing the actual topology of the model itself. To add a bump map to the tire, follow these steps:

1. In the Compact Material Editor, you should have the Wheel Black material selected and the Maps rollout open from the previous series of steps.

2. Click the None button next to the Bump map. In the Material/Map Browser, choose Noise.

3. When you place the noise map in the Bump map slot, you are automatically taken to the parameters for the noise map in the Compact Material Editor. Change the Size value to 0.02. Click the Go To Parent icon to move up a level to the main Material parameters.

4. Go to the Maps rollout and increase Bump Amount from 30 (the default) to 60.

5. Render; you should now see a texture on the tire that resembles the real bumpiness of the tire in Figure 10.4.

Noise is a map of color patterns that is generated procedurally in three dimensions so you don't have to fuss with mapping coordinates.

Now you'll need to apply the MSO material you created to the other three wheels. The easy way is to make three clones of the finished wheel, place them where the other three wheels are located, and delete the original wheels.

Mapping the Fins: Introduction to Mapping Coordinates

An image map is two-dimensional; it has length and width but no depth. Geometry in 3ds Max, however, extends in all three axes. Mapping coordinates define how and where image maps are projected onto an object's surfaces and whether the maps are repeated across those surfaces.

Mapping coordinates can be applied to objects in several ways. The Generate Mapping Coords option is on by default. When primitive objects are created and the Generate Mapping Coords option is checked at the bottom of the Parameters rollout, the appropriate mapping coordinates are created automatically.

The Base Material

The top vertical fin on the rocket's tail is white plastic that is just a bit shiny and has a decal, as you can see in Figure 10.11. At this point, you easily can create the material itself:

FIGURE 10.11 The top vertical fin of the rocket

1. Open the rocket_material_fin_start.max file from the Scenes folder of the Red Rocket project, or continue with rocket_material_ wheel_final.max or the file you have created. When you open this file, select the fin and enter Isolate Selection mode.

2. Open the Compact Material Editor and select an available sample sphere. In the Blinn Basic parameters, click the color swatch next to Diffuse, and make it white.

3. Name the material **Fin_Decal**. Unlike the side fins, the top fin has a decal on its side, so it will have its own material. Apply the material to the fin object by dragging and dropping the sample sphere from the Material Editor to the fin.

4. Back in the Material Editor, in the Specular Highlights group of the Basic Blinn parameters, set Specular Level to 80 and Glossiness to 60.

5. You need to add reflections for the fin. Go to the Maps rollout in the Material Editor, click None next to the Reflection map, and select Bitmap from the Material/Map Browser. Navigate to the SceneAssets\Images folder in the Red Rocket project and select Rocket Refmap Blur.jpg to assign it as the reflection map.

6. The Compact Material Editor will display the Bitmap Parameters rollout. Go up a level by clicking the Go To Parent icon. Go to the Maps rollout and turn the Reflection Amount value down to 35.

Adding the Decal

The decal is an image that you need to add to the material. The image is a 2D image and won't be as easy to apply as the 3D noise map you used earlier for the bump map of the tire. The decal will become a part of the diffuse color; you will replace the color you created for Diffuse with the image itself.

1. In the Compact Material Editor, select the Fin_Decal sample sphere. Make sure you are at the top level of the material and can see the Maps rollout.

2. Click None next to the Diffuse color map. Choose Bitmap from the Material/Map Browser, navigate to the SceneAssets\Images folder in the Red Rocket project, and choose RedRocketDecal.tif.

3. In the Material Editor toolbar, click the Show Standard Map In Viewport icon (▦). This allows the decal to be displayed in the viewport.

4. Drag the Fin_Decal Sample Slot onto the fin. Now you can see the mapped decal on the fin.

Using a UVW Mapping Modifier

We are going to use a modifier to replace those coordinates on the geometry. The *UVW Mapping modifier* makes the decal act more like a real decal that we can control by moving a modifier gizmo around to place the coordinates as we please.

The UVW Mapping modifier is commonly used to apply and control mapping coordinates. You select the type of mapping projection, regardless of the shape of the object, and then set the amount of tiling in the modifier's parameters. The mapping coordinates applied through the UVW Mapping modifier override any other mapping coordinates applied to an object, and the Tiling values set for the modifier are multiplied by the Tiling value set in the assigned material.

To use the UVW Mapping modifier to properly map the decal to the fin, follow these steps:

1. Select the fin and go to the Modify panel. From the Modifier List drop-down, choose UVW Map.

2. In the modifier stack, you can see the UVW Map modifier stacked on top of the editable poly. You will also see an orange gizmo around the fin geometry.

3. Go to the UVW Mapping modifier parameters, and in the Alignment section, click the Bitmap Fit button, as shown in Figure 10.12.

FIGURE 10.12 The Alignment section for the UVW Mapping modifier parameters

4. This will take you to the Select Image dialog box. Navigate to the SceneAssets\Images folder in the Red Rocket project and select the file RedRocketDecal.tif. This will change the size of the UVW Mapping gizmo to the size and aspect of the image rather than the geometry.

Now let's adjust the UVW Mapping gizmo:

1. In the modifier stack, click the plus sign in the black box next to the UVW Mapping modifier and select Gizmo.

2. Now look at the top fin in the viewport, and you should see the plane-shaped Modifier gizmo. You will now be able to transform the gizmo to where you need the decal on the fin.

3. Switch to the Rotate tool, and rotate 75 degrees on the *X* axis.

4. Switch to the Scale tool (press R), and scale down the gizmo to 40 percent. Then switch to the Move tool (W) and center the decal on the fin. In the viewport, the decal looks like a bright white rectangle, whereas the rest of the top fin is gray. That is okay.

While the decal on this side of the fin looks fine, if you look on the other side of the fin, the decal is flipped. The type of UVW Mapping modifier projection you are using (planar mapping) is useful only when one side of an object needs to be mapped. In this case you need the decal to show up correctly on the other side of the fin. What do you do now?

1. Go to the UVW Mapping modifier parameters, and select Box Under Mapping.

2. This works, but now you have the decal in places you don't want, as shown in Figure 10.13. This is because Box mapping projects the image from six sides, using a planar map for each side, but uses the sided-surface normal (a vector that defines which way a face or vertex is pointing) to decide the mapping direction. So, you are going to trick the modifier and remove the depth.

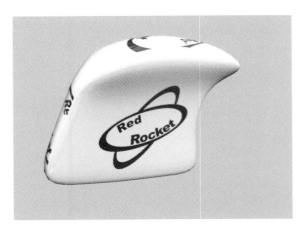

FIGURE 10.13 The decal shows in places you don't want.

3. In the parameters for the UVW Mapping modifier, change the Height parameter to 0.01. Don't go to 0; the modifier won't work correctly.

4. The copies of the decals you don't want on the fin should disappear. On the sides where you don't want the decal, you have scaled the Box Projection gizmo down to almost nothing; the projections for those

sides are actually still there but now they are very small and not noticeable on the fin. This isn't the most sophisticated way to fix the issue, but it works for our needs. In CG, whatever works is the best course of action. See Figure 10.14 for final results.

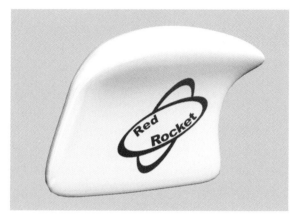

FIGURE 10.14 Fin with final materials

Mapping the Body

The rocket body is made up of three material areas:

The Main Body   Red with a white decal

The Control Panel   A gray metallic material

The Nose   A white plastic with teardrop embossed features

The easiest way to texture is to use the Multi/Sub-Object material technique you used on the wheel. The body has a logo on it, so it will have the same issue as the fin: the logo image will appear on the opposite side of the object when you use planar mapping. Another way of dealing with the logo-flipping issue is to apply the material to each side separately. You would apply the same material to specific selected polygons on each side of the object, but 3ds Max lets you apply two maps and two UVW Mapping modifiers instead of one. This gives you independent control over each side of the rocket body.

1. Open the file `rocket_material_body_start.max`. Select the rocket and enter Isolate Selection mode.

2. Select the rocket and select the modeling ribbon. Go to Polygon mode and select the polygons on one half of the rocket. This is accomplished most easily in the Top viewport.

The seat and control panel polygons are also selected now. You want to deselect them for now. To do this, go to the modeling ribbon, and under Polygon Modeling select Ignore Backfacing; see Figure 10.15.

FIGURE 10.15
Selecting Ignore Backfacing

This allows you to select only the polygons facing you. Hold down Alt while you select what you want to subtract from any selection. This process can be a bit tedious, but it must be done. Once finished, your selection should resemble Figure 10.16. In the figure the rocket color has been changed to gray to better show the selection.

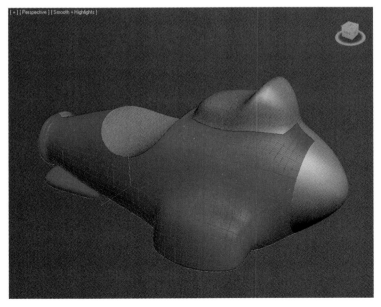

FIGURE 10.16 Select one half of the rocket's body, without the seat or control panel polygons.

Creating the Material

You'll begin by creating a material for the red body.

1. Open the Compact Material Editor, select a sample sphere, and click on the color swatch next to Diffuse. Change the color to red (with values of R: 200, G: 0, B: 0). Name the material **Rocket Body Right**.

2. Drag and drop the new material onto the selected polygons of the rocket to assign the material to that half of the rocket.

3. Go to the Maps rollout and click on None next to Diffuse color. Choose Bitmap from the Material/Map Browser and navigate to the SceneAssets\Images folder in the Red Rocket project. Select the file RocketBodyRight.tif. On the toolbar, click the Show Standard Map In Viewport icon. Don't worry if the map doesn't look correct.

4. Click the Go To Parent icon in the Material Editor toolbar and navigate to the top level of the material. In the Specular Highlights section of the Material Editor, change Specular Level to 90 and Glossiness to 80.

5. Go to the Maps rollout and click None next to Reflection, and from the Material/Map Browser choose Bitmap. Navigate to the SceneAssets\Images folder in the Red Rocket project and select the file Rocket Refmap blur.jpg for the reflection. Go back to the Maps rollout and change the Amount value next to Reflections to 20.
   The decal will probably be tilting, so you see part of it toward the front and the seat of the rocket.

6. Go back to the Material Editor, and in the Coordinates rollout of the RocketBodyRight.tif map, uncheck the Tile UV boxes to turn off tiling. Don't worry if the map doesn't look quite right yet. The map on the rocket may appear in a strange layout, such as shown previously, or may even be a strange color (in some rare cases).

The model still needs mapping coordinates. You will get to them soon.

Flipping the Decal

In the following steps, you will create a copy of the one side's material and flip it for the other side.

1. Go back to the modeling ribbon, and select the polygons on the opposite side of the rocket. Remember to deselect the seat and control panel polygons.

2. In the Compact Material Editor, drag and drop the Rocket Body Right material sample sphere onto an available sample sphere to make a copy of the material. Rename the material **Rocket Body Left**.

3. Go to the Maps rollout for this new material and click the button next to Diffuse color to take you to the bitmap parameters. Click the bar with the image path and, in the file selection window, select RocketBodyLeft.tif for a flipped version of the previous color map.

4. In the Coordinates rollout, change the Map Channel parameter to 2, as shown in Figure 10.17. This lets you have many different sets of coordinates on the same object simultaneously. Don't worry that the Red Rocket graphic disappears; it will return when you add the UVW Mapping modifier for the left of the rocket.

FIGURE 10.17 Change to Map Channel 2 in the Coordinates rollout of the bitmap.

5. Drag and drop the flipped material onto the selected polygons of the rocket (representing the other side of the rocket).

    You are now adding the mapping coordinates. You have two materials for each side of the rocket. The right side of the rocket has Map Channel 1 (which is the default) and the left side has Map Channel 2. You are going to start by adding and editing the mapping for the right side with Map Channel 1.

6. Go into the Modify panel and click the Editable Poly entry to leave the sub-object selection level. Then, from the Modifier List, choose the UVW Map modifier. We are going to keep it on the default mapping setting, which is Planar. In the Alignment parameters of the modifier, change to the X axis, as shown in Figure 10.18.

7. Click the Bitmap Fit button, navigate to the SceneAssets\Images folder in the Red Rocket project, and select the file RocketBodyRight .tif. This will change the Modifier gizmo to make it the same size as the bitmap image, keeping the image's scale proportional.

FIGURE 10.18
Change to the *X* axis in
the Alignment parameters
of the UVW Map modifier.

8. In the Modify panel, go to the modifier stack and click on the black box with the plus sign next to the UVW Mapping modifier. Click Gizmo to allow you to transform the image (via the gizmo) without affecting the object.

9. Move the Modifier gizmo so the white stripe in the decal is lined up approximately with the front of the rocket.

10. Exit the UVW Mapping modifier gizmo subobject mode by clicking the modifier in the stack.

11. Add a second UVW Mapping modifier onto the rocket, and change the Map Channel to 2, as shown in Figure 10.19.

FIGURE 10.19
Select Map Channel 2
in the UVW Mapping
modifier.

12. In the Alignment parameters of the second UVW Mapping modifier, change to the *X* axis. Click the Bitmap Fit button, navigate to where the RocketBodyLeft.tif bitmap is located, and click Open.

13. Go to the modifier stack, click the Gizmo subobject, and move the bitmap gizmo to line up the image with the map on the opposite side of the rocket.

If you render, you should now see the stripe decals on the side of the rocket, as shown in Figure 10.20.

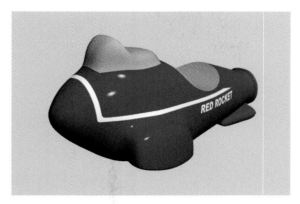

FIGURE 10.20 A render of the rocket shows how the decal is mapped on the body.

The Control Panel

In this section, you will texture the control panel:

1. As you have done before, create a new material in an available sample sphere in the Material Editor and set its color to gray. If you prefer, you can just use the default gray (R150, G150, B150).

2. Set the Specular Level value to 50 and Glossiness to 20.

3. Name this new material **Control Panel**.
   For the control panel, you should add just a bit of bumpiness to the surface to give the panel a better feel.

4. Select the Control Panel material in the Material Editor. In the Maps rollout, change the Bump Amount value to 20 and click None to create a map.

5. Select Noise from the Material/Map Browser to add a noise texture to the bump map.

6. In the Noise Parameters rollout for the noise map, change Size to 0.02.
   Finally, you'll add a reflection map to the control panel, as you did with the body of the rocket.

7. In the Material Editor, click Go To Parent; then select the Maps rollout, set Reflection Amount to 10, and click None next to Reflection to add a map.

8. Select Bitmap from the Material/Map Browser and navigate to the Red Rocket project's `SceneAssets\Images` folder to select `Rocket Refmap blur.tif`.

9. In a viewport, select the rocket, enter Polygon mode, and select the polygons that make up the control panel. Drag the Control Panel material onto the selected polygons to assign the material.

10. Click on the Editable Poly level when you are finished. If you don't, the two UVW Mapping modifiers will be applied only to the control panel polygons.

Because the buttons of the control panel are separate objects, you can easily create colorful materials for them. Simply assign each button its own material for its own distinctive color. If you are using `rocket_material_body_start.max`, the finished control panel buttons are hidden in their own layer. Open the Manage Layer dialog box and unhide the layer.

Bring on the Nose, Bring on the Funk

The material for the nose is pretty similar to the material you just created for the control panel, except that the diffuse color should be white.

1. Copy the Control Panel material by dragging it onto an empty sample sphere in the Compact Material Editor and changing its diffuse color to white. Feel free to adjust the Specular settings as you see fit. (A Specular level of 90 and a Glossiness value of 80 work very well.) Name the new material **Nose**.

   The control panel had a slight bump map on the material. Let's remove that from the Nose material.

2. Select the Nose material in the Compact Material Editor. Right-click on the map bar next to the Bump parameter, and select Clear from the context menu.

   The Nose material now has no bump map, but it retains the reflection map from the control panel's material, saving you a little bit of work.

3. Select the polygons of the nose, and drag the material from the Material Editor to the selected polygons to assign the material. When you're finished, click Editable Poly to return to object mode.

4. Save your work, and be sure to save a new version the file as not to overwrite your previous scene file. The rocket's side decals will look wrong until you click the top UVW Mapping modifier.

You don't have to worry about mapping the polygons of the seat for the rocket because you have a model of a seat to add.

Go to the Application menu and choose Import ➢ Merge, navigate to the Scenes folder in the Red Rocket project, select the file SEAT.max, and click Open to merge in the seat geometry. In the Merge dialog box, select the SEAT object and click OK. The extra geometry adds detail to the model by giving it a nicer seat. If you had to, you could forgo the seat geometry, instead selecting the seat polygons and assigning a glossy black material to them.

Now exit Isolation mode and render a frame of the fully textured rocket, as shown in Figure 10.21 and Figure 10.22.

FIGURE 10.21 The rocket!

FIGURE 10.22 The rocket from behind

Save your work, pat yourself on the back, and have a nice smoothie to celebrate.

THE ESSENTIALS AND BEYOND

Creating materials can give you a sense of accomplishment because it is essentially the last step in making the object look as you envisioned—aside from lighting and rendering

Finding the right combination of maps, shader types, and material types can make a world of difference in the look of your scenes. In this chapter, you learned the basics of materials, you mapped the entire rocket you modeled in Chapter 5, "Animating a Bouncing Ball," and you readied it for its next step: lighting in Chapter 11.

ADDITIONAL EXERCISES

▶ Go back and adjust all the materials on the rocket with different types of materials, colors, and settings to see how they affect the render of the rocket.

▶ The thruster was not done in the exercise. Unhide it and create a material based on the images.

▶ The buttons on the control panel were also left out of the exercise for the same reason. Create materials for them.

CHAPTER 11

Textures and UV Workflow: The Soldier

Materials in 3ds Max simulate the natural physics of how we see things by regulating how objects reflect and or transmit light. You define a material in 3ds Max by setting values for its parameters or by applying textures or maps. These parameters define the way an object will look when rendered. In this chapter and in Chapter 14, "Introduction to Lighting: Red Rocket," you will discover that materials and lights work closely together.

Topics in this chapter include:

▶ **Mapping the soldier**

▶ **UV unwrapping**

▶ **Seaming the rest of the body**

▶ **Applying the color map**

▶ **Applying the bump map**

▶ **Applying the specular map**

Mapping the Soldier

In this chapter, you will apply materials and maps to the soldier model from Chapters 7–9. You will first set up the model to accept textures properly through a process called UV-unwrap. This allows you to lay out the colors and patterns for the soldier's uniform and general look. This process essentially creates a flat map that can be used to paint the textures in a program such as Photoshop.

We have already used Adobe Photoshop to create the textures (i.e., the maps) you'll use for the soldier.

We will then show you how to prepare the model for proper UVs and how to apply the maps you have already painted. We will not demonstrate the actual painting process in Photoshop, because that discussion goes beyond the purposes of this book.

UV Unwrapping

Set your project to the Soldier project downloaded from the companion web page at **www.sybex.com/go/Essential3dsmax2012**. Open the scene file SoldierTexture_ v01.max from the Scenes folder of the project, or use your own final model scene file from Chapter 9, "Character Poly Modeling: Part III." Keep in mind that any design changes you made to your own soldier model may cause discrepancies in the UV unwrapping and mapping steps in the following sections.

You will begin by creating seams to define the shapes of the arms, so you know where in Photoshop to paint the sleeves of the uniform. In this file the image planes are hidden; if you want them back, right-click in the viewport and choose Unhide All from the context menu.

Begin defining UVs with the following steps:

1. Turn on Smooth + Highlights + Edged Faces view (F4) for your viewports. Remember, if you are running 3ds Max through the Nitrous driver, turn on Realistic in your viewport.

2. With your model selected, choose Unwrap UVW from the modifier list.

3. Expand the Unwrap UVW modifier in the modifier stack by clicking on the plus sign in the black box next to the Unwrap UWV title. Enter Face mode.

4. In the Configure rollout, uncheck Map Seams, as shown in Figure 11.1. Doing so turns off the green highlight on the edges, which is generated by default and is not useful in its current state.

FIGURE 11.1
Uncheck Map Seam in
the Configure rollout.

5. Click the Point To Point Seam button toward the bottom of the Command panel under the Map Parameters rollout, as shown in Figure 11.2. This tool lets you reroute the seams to where you want them.

FIGURE 11.2
Click the Point To Point
Seam button.

6. With Point To Point Seam enabled, click on the center of a pair of intersecting edges about where you want to define the left shoulder, as shown in Figure 11.3 (left image). A dashed-line "rubber band" appears next to your cursor, letting you know that the tool is waiting for the next point to be selected.

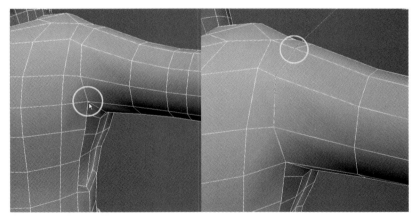

FIGURE 11.3 Pick this edge intersection to begin defining the seam (left). Choose the next point at the upper shoulder (right).

While Point To Point Seam is active, you can navigate using all the viewport navigation tools to look around the model. 3ds Max remembers the last intersection you clicked and draws an accurate seam at the next click.

7. Select the next intersecting edges in the loop around the shoulder. This creates a blue highlight across the edges, as shown in Figure 11.3 (right image).

8. Continue around the shoulder until you have a complete loop, ending with the intersection you started with in step 6. Also, you can right-click and then start or continue the picks without overlapping them.

9. Select the bottommost edge intersection on the underarm and continue selecting edge intersections all the way to the middle point of the wrist, as shown in Figure 11.4. You will have to switch to Wireframe view (press F3) to pick the last point, as shown in Figure 11.5, at the end of the forearm.

10. Right-click to deactivate the Point To Point Seam tool's rubber banding but still keep the button active; then continue cutting a new set of UVs for the right arm, just as you did for the left arm.

11. Right-click and box out areas under the arms on both sides, as shown in Figure 11.6. In Figure 11.6, you can see the seams block out the area under the arm and continue down to the belt line and across the top of the belt line around the waist. If you pick a point by mistake, you can use the Undo button.

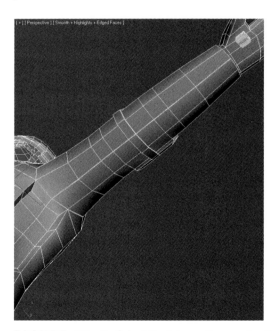

FIGURE 11.4 Select the intersections under the arm.

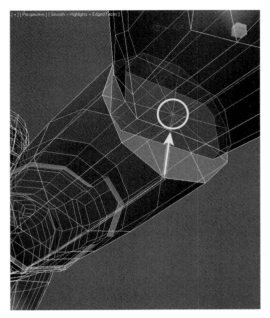

FIGURE 11.5 Switch to Wireframe view to pick the last intersection for the forearm/wrist.

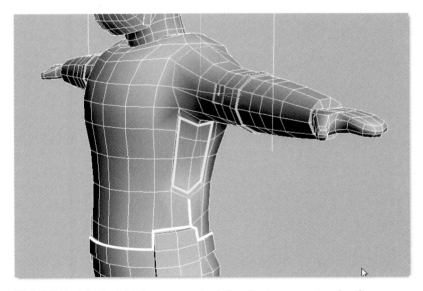

FIGURE 11.6 Add these seams to define the torso areas under the arm.

12. Using the Point To Point Seam tool, cut seams for the two gloves lengthwise down the middle from wrist to wrist. You can see this progression for the left-hand glove start in Figure 11.7. Begin at the wrist on the side of the thumb and work your way around to the opposite side of the wrist. Remember, you may need to enter Wireframe view (press F3) to select the proper edge intersection points. Figure 11.8 shows the seam working around the hand.

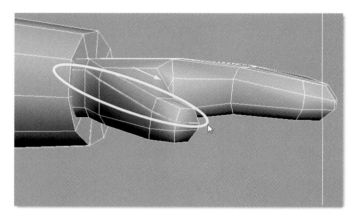

FIGURE 11.7 Cut a new seam along the glove, starting as shown.

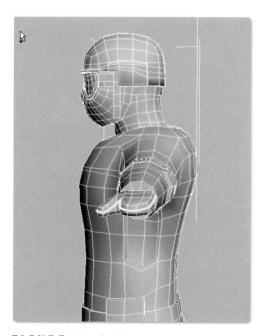

FIGURE 11.8 Work your way around the glove.

13. Open the Slate Material Editor. If the Compact Material opens, choose Modes ➤ Slate. In the Material/Map Browser, choose the Materials rollout. On the Standard rollout, double-click on Standard. Doing so loads a Standard Material node into the Active View panel in the center of the Slate interface. The dots running along the left side of the Material node are called Input Sockets and are used to connect other nodes such as textures into the material's parameter. The dot on the right side of the node is the output socket, used to connect this node to the input of another.

14. Double-click on the Diffuse Color input socket of the material, as shown in Figure 11.9; the Material/Map Browser opens again. Under Maps, select the Standard rollout, click Checker, and then click OK.

FIGURE 11.9 Double-click the Diffuse Color input socket.

SLATE MATERIAL EDITOR

The Slate Material Editor, also called the Slate for short, is a dialog box in which materials and maps appear as graphical nodes that you can connect, or "wire," together to create material trees using input and output sockets. If you are designing new materials, the Slate is especially powerful since it

(Continues)

SLATE MATERIAL EDITOR   *(Continued)*

gives you a graphical view into how your maps and materials are connected to each other. The Slate also includes search tools to help you manage scenes that have a large number of materials. The Slate is made up of elements, including the Material/Map Browser, which allow you to browse for materials and maps; the currently active view, where you do the work of connecting materials and maps; and the Parameter Editor, where you can alter the values for material and map parameters.

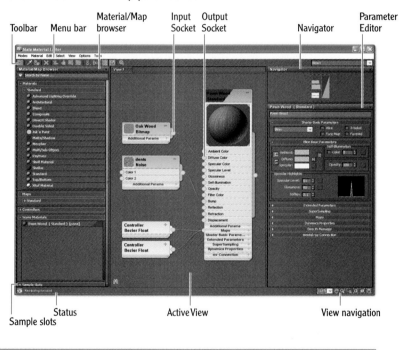

15. In the Slate, double-click the Checker Map title bar to open its parameters on the right of the Slate interface in the Parameter Editor. Change the U and V Tiling parameters for the Checker map from 1 to 5, as shown in Figure 11.10.

FIGURE 11.10 Set the U and V Tiling to 5.

16. Click and drag from the Material output slot onto the Soldier model to assign the material and see the texture on the model to give you better visual feedback as to how your UVs are coming along as you fix them.

17. At the top of the Slate, click Show Standard Map In Viewport (image) if you cannot see the map on your model in the viewports.

Pelting the Left Arm UVs

Save your work now before continuing with the next set of steps to unfold the UVs for the arms into usable patterns to paint the textures. You can pick up with the scene file SoldierTexture_v02.max from the Scenes folder of the Soldier project from the book's web page to check your work so far or to skip to this point. In this file the image planes are hidden; if you want them back, right-click in the viewport and choose Unhide All from the context menu.

1. With Face mode selected in your Unwrap UVW modifier and Point To Point Seam toggled off, click on a polygon on the left forearm of your model. Then in the Peel rollout, click the Expand Face Selection To Seams icon (image). If the seams were created correctly in the previous set of steps, a selection of faces on the arm will turn red in your viewport, as shown in Figure 11.11.

FIGURE 11.11 The arm's faces are selected.

2. You need to unfold the UVs to create the pattern to paint on in Photoshop (or another image editor). To unfold the UVs into a usable pattern, click the Pelt Map icon ( ) in the Peel rollout.

3. When you click Pelt Map, an Edit UVWs dialog box as well as the Pelt Map dialog box will open. In the Edit UVWs dialog box, click the View menu and toggle off Show Grid and Show Map to simplify the UV view, as shown in Figure 11.12.

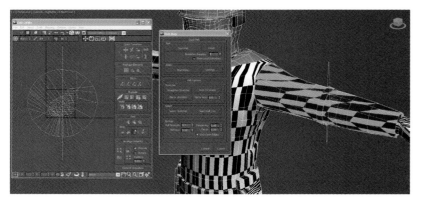

FIGURE 11.12 The Edit UVWs and Pelt Map dialog boxes showing the arm UVs.

4. To unfold the map, click the Start Pelt button in the Pelt Map dialog box. Doing so moves the UVs in the Edit UVWs dialog box in real time. This procedure keeps unfolding the UVs until you stop it, so wait a couple of seconds for the UVs to stop moving, and then click Stop Pelt.

5. You're almost done with the arm, but if you check the checkerboard texture in your viewport you can see that some of the checks are bigger than others. To fix this, click the Settings box next to the Relax button in the Pelt Map dialog box, and change the drop-down option to Relax By Face Angles, as shown in Figure 11.13.

FIGURE 11.13 Set the drop-down menu to Relax By Face Angles.

6. Now, click Start Relax. Wait until the UVs stop moving and then click Stop Relax; then click Apply. Close the Relax Tool dialog box. Checking your texture in the viewport now shows the checkerboard how you want it.

7. Click the Commit button at the bottom of the Pelt Map dialog box, or your changes won't take effect. Also, you want to close the Edit UVWs dialog box.

Pelting the Right Arm UVs

Repeat Steps 1–7 for the right arm. You can see in Figure 11.14 that both arms are now laid out—pelted and relaxed.

FIGURE 11.14 Both arms are pelted and relaxed.

Unwrapping and Using Pelt for the Head

Save your work now before continuing with the next set of steps to unfold the UVs for the head. You can pick up with the scene file `SoldierTexture_v03.max` from the `Scenes` folder of the Soldier project downloaded from the book's web page to check your work so far or to skip to this point.

For this section, since it is a bit hard to see where to seam, you went into the Material Editor to the Standard Checker material. In the Maps rollout, you unchecked Diffuse Color to turn off the checker pattern.

The head poses a problem: Each part (helmet, goggles, mask) is a separate object modeled in Chapter 9 that was attached into one editable polygon. That means when you look closely at the geometry, there is some object penetration, making it difficult to clearly see some of the areas you need to seam. You will use a subobject visibility technique to control what you are viewing in the following steps:

1. Select the Soldier, and in the Modify panel's modifier stack, choose Editable Poly and select Element. Element mode allows you to select separate objects that are attached together into a single object.

   When you do this, you will get the warning shown in Figure 11.15. Select Yes. Every time you move between the Unwrap UVW modifier and the Editable Poly modifier, you will see this warning; if that gets annoying, check the Do Not Show This Message Again option. The warning tells you that any changes you make to that level of the model will ripple throughout the rest of the stack and may mess up other parts of your work. Since you are simply using Element mode to hide parts of the head of the model to make seaming easier to see, you need not worry that anything will change.

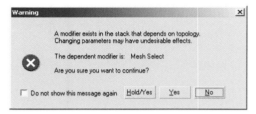

FIGURE 11.15 Topology dependency warning

2. Select the helmet, and then in the modeling ribbon go to the Visibility tab and click Hide Unselected. Doing so hides all unselected elements in the model, leaving the helmet as the only visible object.

3. Exit Element mode by clicking Editable Poly in the modifier stack. Now go back up to the Unwrap UVW modifier and click Face. Move down to the Peel rollout and click the Point To Point Seam button. Following the line in Figure 11.16, create a new seam on the helmet.

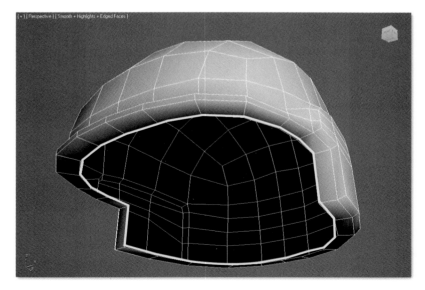

FIGURE 11.16 Create a new seam on the helmet.

4. When the seam has been created, click Editable Poly and select
   Element mode in the modifier stack, and in the Visibility tab click
   the Unhide All button. Then select the goggles, click the Visibility
   tab, and click the Hide Unselected button. Repeat step 3 on the goggles using Figure 11.17 as your guide for the seams.

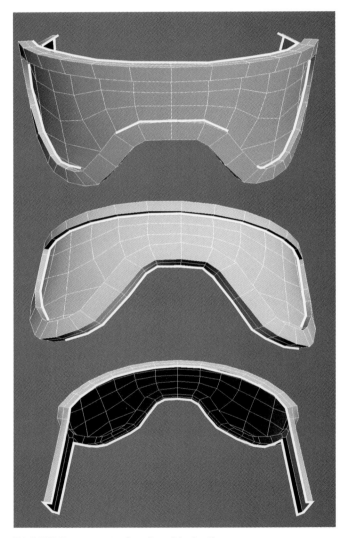

FIGURE 11.17 Goggle guide for the seams

5. Repeat the process individually for the mask, the head, and the helmet straps, using Hide Unselected to isolate each of the three elements as you work on them. Then follow the same process as before to create the seams shown in Figure 11.18 for the face mask, Figure 11.19 for the head, and Figure 11.20 for the helmet strap.

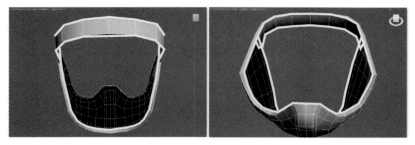

FIGURE 11.18 Seams for soldier face mask

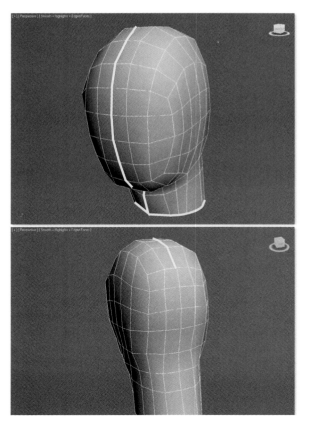

FIGURE 11.19 Seams for the soldier head

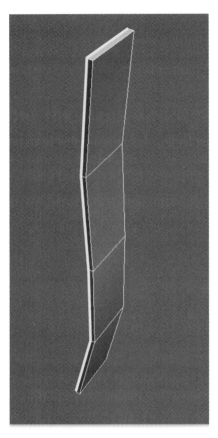

FIGURE 11.20 Seams for the soldier helmet strap

6. Open the Material Editor, and in the soldier's checker material go to the Maps rollout and check the box next to Diffuse Color to turn on the checkers again. You will need the checkers when you pelt the model.

Seaming the Rest of the Body

Use the Point To Point Seam tool to block out the rest of the model's parts and then use the Pelt Map steps above as you did for the arms. Refer to Figure 11.21 and Figure 11.22 for the placement of seams on the model's body.

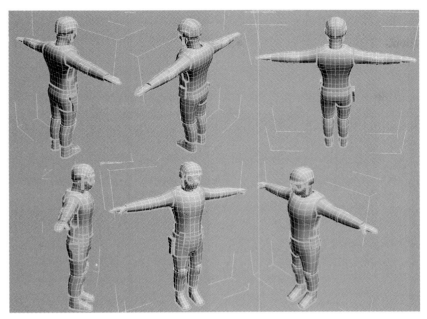

FIGURE 11.21 Follow these outlines to create the rest of the model's seams.

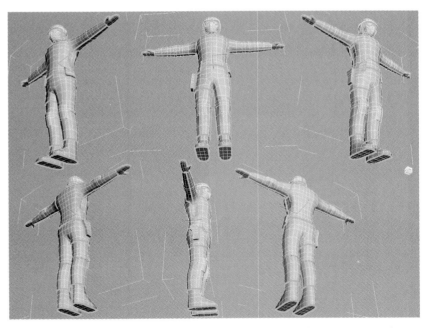

FIGURE 11.22 Follow these outlines taken from a different vantage point to create the rest of the model's seams.

Unfolding the Rest of the Body

Save your work. You can pick up with the scene file SoldierTexture_v04.max from the Scenes folder of the Soldier project downloaded from the book's web page to check your work so far or to skip to this point.

1. In the Modify panel, click the Face button. Then click a single polygon on the helmet. Then in the Peel rollout, click the Expand Face Selection To Seams icon (🖾). Doing so selects all the polygons associated with the seams you created for the helmet.

2. Click the Pelt Map icon (🖾) to open the Edit UVWs dialog box and the Pelt Map dialog box. First click Start Pelt. You will see the UVs moving around; when they stop moving, click the Stop Pelt button.

3. Now click the Settings button next to the Start Relax button. Make sure the drop-down menu is set to Relax By Face Angles, click Apply, and then close the Relax Tool dialog box.

4. Click the Start Relax button again, and when the UVs stop moving, click Stop Relax. For the remaining objects you don't have to go into the Settings box—just click Start Relax.

5. Click the Commit button. The checkers pattern on the helmet should look organized and even.

Now that you are finished with the helmet, make your way down the body using Pelt and Relax to lay out the UVs on the remaining parts of the body, checking each one off as you go.

Save your work. You can pick up with the scene file SoldierTexture_v05.max from the Scenes folder of the Soldier project to check your work so far or to skip to this point.

As you can see in Figure 11.23, when the UVs are finished, the checker pattern for each separate part of the soldier is a different size. In the following steps we will set all the sizes to be the same showing that the UVs are now uniform.

1. In the Modify panel, click the Face button if it isn't already selected. Then click away from the Soldier model and drag a selection box around the whole model to select all the polygons, as shown in Figure 11.23.

2. In the Unwrap UVW modifier, go to the Edit UVs rollout and click the open UV Editor button. What you will see is a mess; these are all the unwrapped UVs piled on top of each other.

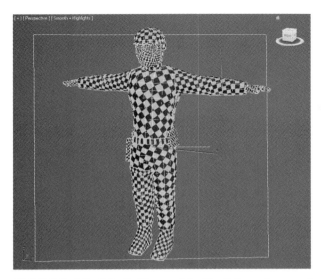

FIGURE 11.23 Soldier model with all the polygons selected

3. In the Edit UVWs menu, choose Tools ➤ Relax. Click Start Relax. Be patient and wait for the movement to slow down or stop before clicking Stop Relax. Then close the Relax Tool dialog box. This will relax all of your UVs together uniformly, ensuring that they all have the same UV real estate. This is important so that all the elements carry the same relative texture space, as shown in Figure 11.24.

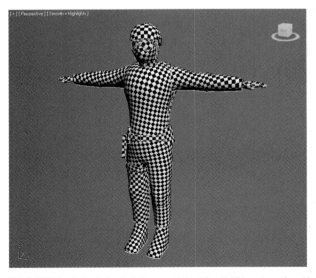

FIGURE 11.24 Soldier model with all UVs relaxed uniformly

4. Keep the Edit UVWs dialog box open. Deselect the UVs by clicking away from the model. Figure 11.25 shows what you should see now.

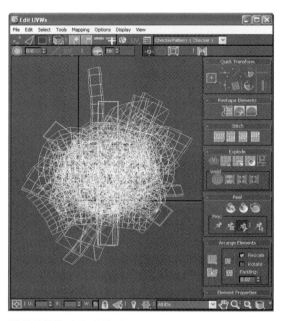

FIGURE 11.25 The Edit UVWs dialog box with the soldier UVs in a pile

Because you are still in Face mode in the Unwrap UVW modifier, if you click anywhere on the pile of UVs you will select a face. What you want to do now is select an individual element's full set of UVs so that you can lay them out separately, giving them some space on the flat blank canvas that can be used later for painting the textures for those parts of the body. The easiest way is to select a face, then go to the toolbar at the top of the Edit UVWs dialog box and click Select By Element, as shown in Figure 11.26.

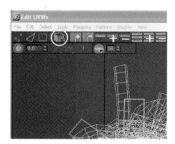

FIGURE 11.26 Clicking Select By Element

At this point, you can select all the UVs associated with an element (such as the helmet only). When you select something in the Edit UVWs dialog box, it shows up selected on the model in the viewports, as shown in Figure 11.27. This will help you know what parts you are moving around in the Edit UVWs dialog box. Also in the Edit UVWs dialog box, you can use all the navigation tools you use in the viewports to pan and zoom. In the following steps, you will start placing the UVs for each element within the thick blue bordered box in the Edit UVWs dialog box to lay out the entire soldier's UVs for textures.

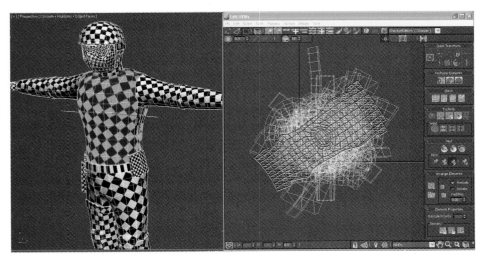

FIGURE 11.27 Select an element in the Edit UVWs dialog box, and it will show as selected on the model.

1. In the Edit UVWs dialog box, drag a selection box around all the UVs. From the Arrange Elements rollout on the right side of the Edit UVWs dialog box, change the Padding type-in to 0.0 and then click the Pack Normalize button, as shown in Figure 11.28. Now you should be able to see the blue border box in the Edit UVWs dialog box with the UVs laid out correctly, as shown in Figure 11.29.

Pack
Normalize
button

Padding
field

FIGURE 11.28 The Arrange Elements rollout

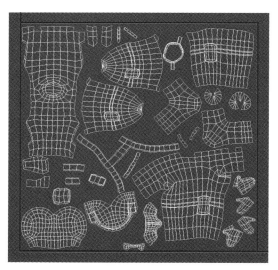

FIGURE 11.29 UVs correctly placed within the
UV space

The goal is to fit the UVs into this box without going outside of it
and without overlapping any of the UVs. Anything outside this box
ends up tiling (or having no texture at all), and any overlapping UVs
share parts of the texture from another element. Either way, that's
not good. Once you have the layout, you can select and move UVs
around.

2. In the Edit UVWs dialog box, select Tools ➤ Render UV Template to
open the Render UVs dialog box. In that dialog box, click the Render
UV Template button to create an image of your UVs, as shown in the
Render Map dialog box in Figure 11.30.

3. Save the UV layout image by clicking the Save Image icon in the
Render Map dialog box, as shown in Figure 11.31. Once saved, this
image can be opened in your favorite image editor and you can use
the pieces as guides to paint the soldier's textures.

With the UV layout image saved, you can go into Photoshop (or the image-
editing software of your choice) and create a texture to place on your model.
We took the UV image into Photoshop and with a combination of painting and

cutting and pasting of photos, we created the final map for the soldier, as shown in Figure 11.32.

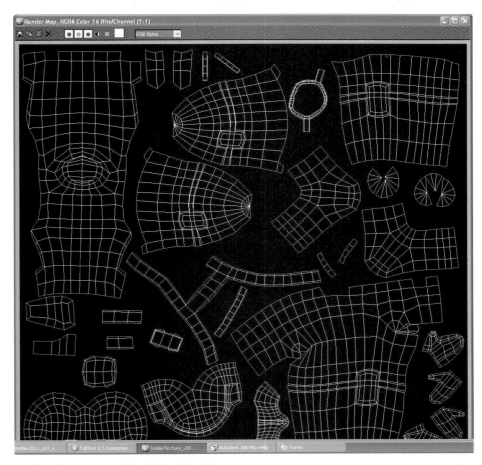

FIGURE 11.30 The UV rendered image

FIGURE 11.31
Save the UV image.

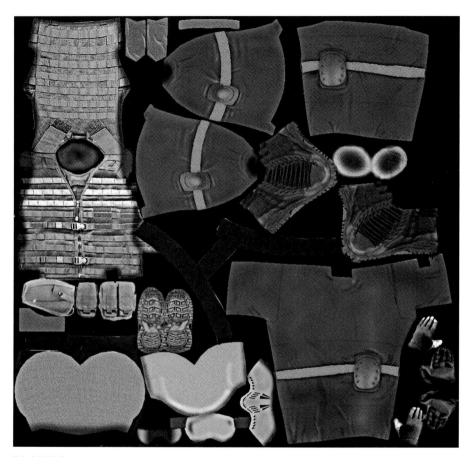

FIGURE 11.32 The final map for the soldier

The texture map, as you can see, places painted parts of the soldier's body according to the UV layout you just created. For example, you can clearly see the soldier's vest painted in the upper-left corner of the texture image file.

The more you unwrap UVs for models, the easier it becomes to anticipate how to paint the textures.

Applying the Color Map

Save your work before continuing with the next set of steps. You can pick up with the scene file SoldierTexture_v06.max from the Scenes folder of the Soldier project to check your work so far or to skip to this point.

Now it is time to use the map you put so much effort into:

1. Open the Slate. You should see the checker material you created for the soldier to help with the UVs. In the Material/Map Browser, choose the Materials rollout. On the Standard rollout, drag and drop a Standard material to the Active View area.

2. Double-click on the Diffuse Color input socket of the material to open the Material/Map Browser. In the Maps rollout, select the Standard rollout and click Bitmap. When the Select Bitmap Image File dialog box appears, navigate to the \SceneAssets\images folder for the Soldier project and select the Soldier_Color_V04.tif file.

3. Apply the material to the soldier and click Show Standard Map In Viewport; the result is shown in Figure 11.33. Bam! Now wasn't all that hard UV work worth it?

FIGURE 11.33 The soldier with the material applied

Applying the Bump Map

Bump mapping makes an object appear to have a bumpy or irregular surface by simulating surface definition. When you render an object with a bump-mapped material, lighter (whiter) areas of the map appear to be raised on the object's surface, and darker (blacker) areas appear to be lower on the object's surface, as shown in Figure 11.34.

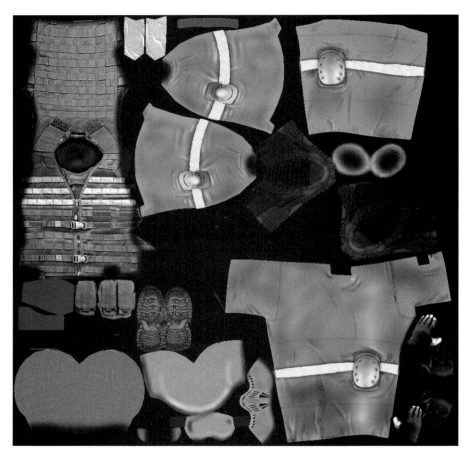

FIGURE 11.34 Bump map created in Photoshop by desaturating the original color map to create light and dark areas that conform to the original color texture

Normal mapping is a technique used for faking the lighting of bumps and dents. A normal map is usually used to fake high-resolution geometry detail while it's actually mapped onto a low-resolution mesh for efficiency. This vector is called a *normal* (or simply, a direction) that describes a high-resolution surface's slope at that very point on the surface. The RGB channels of a normal map control the direction of each pixel's normal, enabling you to fake a high degree of surface resolution when applied to a low-polygon mesh. A normal map for the soldier is shown in Figure 11.35.

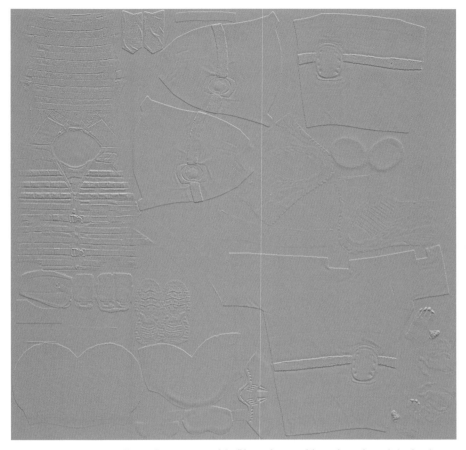

FIGURE 11.35 Normal map created in Photoshop and based on the original color map

You can use one or both of these mapping techniques to create additional surface detail. Bump maps are simpler to create, since you can usually take the color map and just desaturate it to make a grayscale image file. We have both a normal map and bump map for you to use. You will continue with the Soldier material you created in the previous exercise as you add these new maps in the following steps:

1. Double-click on the Bump input socket of the material to open the Material/Map Browser. Under the Maps rollout, select the Standard rollout and choose Normal Bump.

2. Click on the title bar of the Normal Bump node to bring up the Parameters rollout shown in Figure 11.36. Click the None button next to Normal. Doing so once again brings up the Material/Map

Browser. Under the Maps rollout, select the Standard rollout and choose Bitmap. When the Select Bitmap Image File dialog box appears, navigate to the /SceneAssets/images folder of the Soldier project and select the Soldier_Normal_V01.tif file.

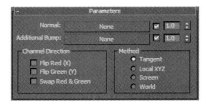

FIGURE 11.36 The Normal Bump node's Parameters rollout

3. Back in the Normal Map parameters, click None next to Additional Bump to open the Material/Map Browser. Under the Maps rollout, select the Standard rollout and choose Bitmap. When the Select Bitmap Image File dialog box appears, navigate to the /SceneAssets/images folder of the Soldier project and select the Soldier_BS_V01.tif file.

4. Double-click on the Materials title bar to show the main material parameters. In the Maps rollout, set the Bump Amount to 100.

The normal map is applied and finished. See Figure 11.37 for images that compare the soldier rendered with and without the normal map. You may notice that the normal and bump maps have created a lot more detail in the soldier's body, particularly in his vest. You will notice the difference even better in your own renders.

FIGURE 11.37 The left image is a render of the soldier without the normal and bump maps. The right image is rendered with the normal and bump maps.

Applying the Specular Map

Highlights in objects are a reflection of a light source. Specular maps are maps you use to define a surface's shininess and highlight color, without the complex calculations of reflections in the render. The higher a pixel's value (from black to white, or 0 to 1, respectively), the shinier the surface will appear at that location.

You will be adding a specular map to the soldier to further the amount of detail you can get from the render. You are going to reuse the image that you used for the bump map to give the soldier a bit of bling on his vest and buckles.

In the Slate, drag from the output socket of the Additional Bump bitmap to the Specular Level input socket of the Soldier material already in your scene, as shown in Figure 11.38.

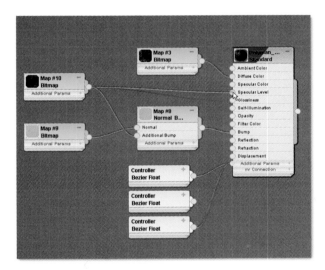

FIGURE 11.38 Dragging from the bump map to the Specular Level slot

The final render of the soldier is shown in Figure 11.39. You can see the improvement to the look of the soldier's vest with the added specular color map.

You will use the soldier for rigging and animation with Character Studio in Chapter 12, "Character Studio: Rigging."

FIGURE 11.39 Final render of the soldier

THE ESSENTIALS AND BEYOND

In this chapter you set up the soldier's UV layout using UV unwrapping and the Pelt toolset. Then you assigned materials and maps created specifically for the soldier, all the while getting to know the Slate Material Editor.

ADDITIONAL EXERCISES

▶ Create a new uniform color scheme for the soldier to make him/her more suitable for jungle camouflage and map it.

CHAPTER 12

Character Studio: Rigging

At one time or another, almost everyone in the 3D community wants to animate a character. This chapter examines the 3ds Max 2012 toolsets used in the process of setting up for character animation using Character Studio, a full-featured package incorporated into 3ds Max that is mostly for animating bipedal characters, including humans, aliens, robots, and anything else that walks on two feet—though you can have characters with more than two feet in certain situations.

Topics in this chapter include the following:

▶ **Character Studio workflow**

▶ **Associating a biped with the soldier model**

Character Studio Workflow

Character Studio is a system built into 3ds Max to help automate the creation and animation of a character, who may or may not be exactly a *biped* (two-footed creature). Character Studio consists of three basic components: the Biped system, the Physique and Skin modifiers, and the Crowd system. Biped and Physique are used to pose and animate a single character, and the Crowd system is used to assign similar movements and behaviors to multiple objects in your 3ds Max scene. This chapter covers the Biped and Physique features; the Crowd system is beyond the scope of this book.

The first step in the Character Studio workflow is to build or acquire a suitable character model. The second step is to *skin* (bind) the character model to the skeleton so the animation drives the model properly.

Models should typically be in the reference position known as the "da Vinci pose," where the feet are shoulder width apart and the arms are extended to the sides with the palms down, as shown in Figure 12.1. This allows the animator to observe all of the model's features, unobstructed by the model itself, in at least two viewports.

FIGURE 12.1 A bipedal character in the
reference position

In 3ds Max, a *biped* is a predefined, initially humanoid, structure. It is important to understand that you animate the biped that is associated with your model, and not the model itself. Once the model is bound to the skeleton, the biped structure *drives* the model. You use the Physique modifier in Character Studio to create that relationship between the skeleton and the model.

You will work with attaching a model to a biped using Physique later in this chapter. You can also use another 3ds Max methodology, the Skin modifier, to attach the model to the biped skeleton; however, only Physique is covered here.

General Workflow

The default biped, shown in Figure 12.2, consists of legs, feet, toes, arms, hands, fingers, pelvis, spine, neck, and head. After your model is ready, you will create a biped and, using its parameters and the Scale transform, fit the biped closely to the model. The better the biped to model relationship, the easier the animation will be.

Once the biped is fit snugly to the model, you select all the components of the model, not the biped skeleton, and apply the Physique or Skin modifier in a process often referred to as *skinning*. It may take a while to properly test and refine the relationship between the model and the biped to get it to an acceptable level.

FIGURE 12.2
The default biped

BONES AND SKIN

The Bones system and Skin modifier have capabilities similar to those found in Character Studio. Bones is a series of linked, hierarchical components that are used, in conjunction with the Skin modifier, to control the displacement of a model similar to the Biped and Physique method. The Bones system requires a more tedious setup process to create a skeleton than Biped and is not covered.

The final step is animating your character. You can accomplish this by adding to the biped any combination of default walk, run, and jump cycles included with Character Studio, then applying any freeform animation to the character, and finally refining the animation keyframes in the Dope Sheet. Don't expect the default walk, run, and jump cycles to create realistic motion, though. They are just a starting point and must be tweaked to achieve acceptable movements.

The best way to start is to jump in and examine the tools available. In the next section, you will work with a biped and adjust the parameters and components to modify it.

Associating a Biped with the Soldier Model

The purpose of a biped is to be the portal through which you add animation to your model, rather than animating the model itself using direct vertex manipulation or deforming modifiers. Any motion assigned to a biped is passed through it to the nearest vertices of the associated model, essentially driving the surfaces of the model. For this reason, it is important that the biped fit as closely as possible to the model.

Creating and Modifying the Biped

In the following steps, you'll create and adjust a biped to fit to a character model. Set your project to the Soldier project available for download from this book's web page at **www.sybex.com/go/3dsmax2012essentials**. You can then open the CSSoldier.max file from the Scenes folder of the Soldier project. It contains a completed soldier model in the reference position. Be sure to set the project folder to the root folder for the CSSoldier project.

With the soldier model file open, select the character, right-click in a viewport, and choose Freeze Selection. This will prevent you from inadvertently selecting the soldier instead of the biped.

VIEWING FROZEN OBJECTS

If your background color is similar to the default shade of gray that 3ds Max uses to depict frozen objects, the model may seem to disappear against the background. There are several solutions to this situation:

- ▶ You can go to Object Properties, turn off Show Frozen As Gray, turn on See-through, and set all viewports to Smooth + Highlights mode. If you are using the Nitrous display driver, you will need to select the Realistic mode.

- ▶ You can change the shaded color in the Customize User Interface dialog box (Customize ➤ Customize User Interface ➤ Colors).

- ▶ You can change the viewport background color in the Customize User Interface dialog box (Customize ➤ Customize User Interface ➤ Colors).

Follow these steps to create and adjust a biped:

1. From the Command panel, select Create ≻ Systems ≻ Biped.

2. The first click sets the insertion point. Dragging defines the height of the biped system and defines all of the components. All of the biped's components are sized relative to the biped's Height parameter.

3. Create a biped with a height about the same as the soldier's. This will size most of the biped's parts similar to those of the soldier, as shown in Figure 12.3.

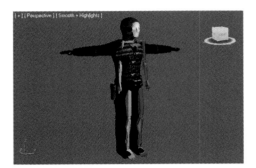

FIGURE 12.3 Create a biped about the same height as the soldier model.

Click any part of your biped to select it. Bipeds react differently than other objects. Selecting any single component of the biped opens the entire Biped object for editing.

4. With the biped still selected, click the Motion tab (⊙) of the Command panel and enter Figure mode, as shown in Figure 12.4. Changes to the biped's features or pose must be made in Figure mode to be retained by the system.

FIGURE 12.4
Enter Figure Mode
in the Biped rollout.

5. Use the Body Vertical and Body Horizontal buttons in the Track Selection rollout, as shown in Figure 12.5, and the Move Transform

gizmo to position the biped's pelvis in the same location as the model's pelvis, as shown in Figure 12.6. With the pelvis located properly, scaling the legs or spine to match the model's proportions will be much easier. Check to make sure the location is correct in all of the viewports.

FIGURE 12.5
Track Selection rollout

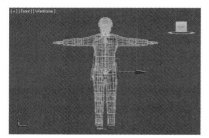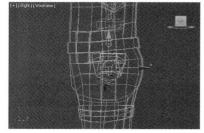

FIGURE 12.6 Match the positions of the biped pelvis and the model pelvis.

Now you will modify one side of the biped to fit the model and then paste that posture to the other side.

6. Make sure the coordinate system for the Scale transform is set to Local in the main toolbar, as shown in Figure 12.7. In the Front viewport, select the pelvis and scale its width so that the biped's legs fit inside the soldier's legs. Scale the pelvis in the Right viewport so that it roughly encompasses the soldier's lower region. See Figure 12.8.

FIGURE 12.7
Set the coordinate system to Local.

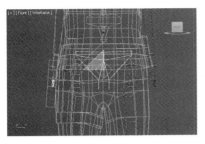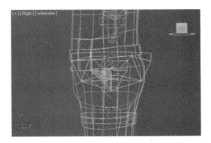

FIGURE 12.8 Scale the pelvis to fit.

7. Select the biped's left upper leg, and then scale it along the X axis until the knee aligns with the soldier's knee. Scale it on the Y and Z axes until it is similar in size to the soldier's thigh.

8. Select the biped's left calf. In the Right viewport, rotate the calf to match the model and then scale it on the X axis until the biped's ankle matches the soldier's ankle. You may need to select the left foot and use the Move transform, in the Front viewport, to orient the calf to the model. Scale the calf to match the proportions of the soldier's calf.

9. Continue working down the leg by scaling the biped's foot to match the soldier's. Be sure to check the orientation of the foot in the Top viewport. In the Structure rollout, use the Ankle Attach parameter to move the biped's ankle slightly backward, as shown in Figure 12.9.

> Moving the foot as described in the previous step may require that the upper leg's proportions be readdressed. Don't expect to perform this task quickly without making any revisions to components on which you have previously worked.

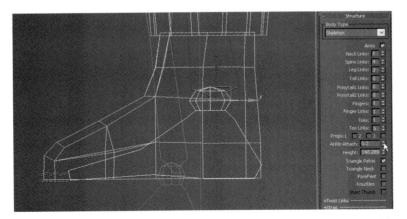

FIGURE 12.9 Increasing the Ankle Attach parameter to move the ankle

10. In the Structure rollout, change the number of toes to 1 and toe links to 2. Because the soldier is wearing boots, a single, wide toe will suffice.

11. Scale and move the biped's toe to match the model's boot. Be sure to scale the toe links on the *Z* axis, as shown in Figure 12.10.

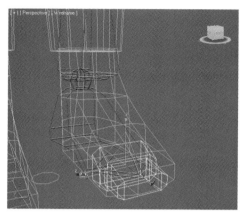

FIGURE 12.10 Match the model's boot and the biped's toe.

12. Double-click the left upper leg to select it and all of the objects below it in the hierarchy.

13. Open the Copy/Paste rollout.

14. Postures must be saved as collections prior to being pasted. Click the Create Collection button, as shown in Figure 12.11, and then rename the collection from the default Col01 to **Left Leg**.

FIGURE 12.11
Create the collection.

15. Click the Copy Posture button just below the Posture button to copy the selected posture to the clipboard. A preview of the copied posture will appear in the Copied Postures area of the Command panel, as shown in Figure 12.12.

FIGURE 12.12
Copy the posture.

16. Click the Paste Posture Opposite button (![icon]). The size, scale, and orientation of the selected objects will be applied to the reciprocal objects on the opposite side of the biped.

Adjusting the Torso and Arms

Similar to the method used to adjust the legs, you will use the Scale and Rotate transforms to fit the biped to the model. The locations of the arms rely on the scale of the spine links. You can continue with your file from the previous exercise or open CSSoldier2.max from the Scenes folder of the Soldier project available on the book's web page. Just make sure your project is set to the Soldier project.

1. In your scene (or the one from the web page), select the biped, and then access Figure mode, if you need to.

2. Ctrl+click to select each of the spine links in turn, and then rotate and scale them to fit the soldier's torso. Only the lowest spine link can be moved, and this will move all of the links above it as well. Each spine link should be scaled down slightly on the X axis to lower the biped's clavicles to match the model's, as shown in Figure 12.13.

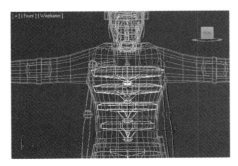

FIGURE 12.13 Match the biped's clavicles to the model.

3. Move, rotate, and scale the left clavicle as required, placing the biped's shoulder socket in the proper location.

4. Scale and rotate the left upper arm and left forearm using the same techniques you used to adjust the biped's legs.

5. Scale and rotate the left hand as required to fit the model.

6. The hands need only two fingers (the second finger is actually the thumb) and two links each. Adjust the biped's fingers to match the model's fingers, as shown in Figure 12.14. This can be one of the most tedious tasks in character animation, depending on the complexity and orientation of the model's fingers. Take your time and get it right. (Would you rather do it right or do it over?)

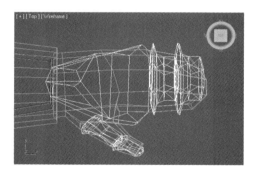

FIGURE 12.14 Match the biped's fingers to the model's.

7. When you are done, paste the posture to the right side of the biped and make any required changes.

Adjusting the Neck and Head

The neck and head will seem easy to adjust when compared to the hands. You need to make sure the neck links fill the soldier's neck area, and scale the head to fit. Follow along here:

1. In the Structure rollout, increase the number of neck links to 2.

2. Move, scale, and rotate the neck links to match the proportions of the model's neck.

> Once the fingers have been adjusted, you cannot go back and change the number of fingers or finger links. If you do, all modifications to the fingers will be lost.

3. Move and scale the head to the approximate size of the soldier's head, as shown in Figure 12.15.

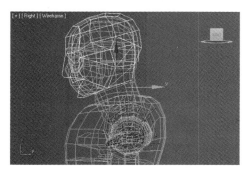

FIGURE 12.15 Matching the head

That's it. The biped has been created and adjusted to fit the 3D model, and half the battle is over. Next you will tie the biped to the model and make adjustments to the skinning process. Now would be a good time to save your work and take a break.

Applying the Physique Modifier

The Physique modifier is the tool used to skin the 3D model to the biped so that all of the biped's animation is passed through to the model. It's important to remember that the modifier is applied to the model and not to the biped. Continue with the previous exercise or open CSSoldier3.max from the Scenes folder of the Soldier project on the book's web page to follow these steps:

1. Right-click in any viewport and select Unfreeze All from the quad menu to unfreeze the soldier model.

2. Select all of the biped's components by double-clicking the Bip001 object.

3. Select the Soldier model and click the Modify tab of the Command panel.

4. Expand the modifier list and select the Physique modifier.

If you have trouble double-clicking the Bip001 in a dense model, try selecting Bip001 using the Select From Scene () dialog box and then pressing Ctrl+Page Down to select everything below it in the hierarchy.

5. In the Physique rollout, click the Attach To Node button (⬛). The button will turn dark and wait for you to identify the root object in the hierarchy that controls the mesh.

6. Press the H key to open the Pick Object dialog box. This method will be easier than trying to click on the object directly in a cluttered scene. Select the Bip001 Pelvis object and click the Pick button.

7. In the Physique Initialization dialog box, accept the defaults and click the Initialize button. The cursor will briefly turn into a coffee cup to indicate that the initialization is in progress. It will return to normal when the process is complete.

Testing the Model

The most time-consuming part of the process is complete. You have created a biped, adjusted all of its component parts to fit your model, and applied the Physique modifier to link the model to the biped. The next step is to test the model by adding animation.

1. Select any element of the biped and click the Motion tab of the Command panel.

2. Enter Footstep mode (⬛).
   The rollouts change to display the tools for adding and controlling a biped's motion. The Footstep mode and Figure mode are exclusive; you cannot be in both modes at the same time.

3. In the Footstep Creation rollout, make sure that the walk gait is selected and then click the Create Multiple Footsteps button, as shown in Figure 12.16, to open the Create Multiple Footsteps dialog box.

FIGURE 12.16 Create footsteps with a walk gait.

4. In the dialog box that appears, you will assign Footstep properties for the number of steps you want, the width and length of each step, and which foot to step with first. Set the number of footsteps to 8, leave the other parameters at their default values, and click the OK button.

5. Zoom out in the Perspective viewport to see the footsteps you just created, as shown in Figure 12.17. Look at the time slider, and note that the scene now ends at frame 123; that's 23 more frames than the 100 frames the scene had at the beginning of this chapter. 3ds Max recognized that it would take the biped 123 frames, or just over 4 seconds, to move through the eight steps that it was given.

FIGURE 12.17 Zoom out and review the footsteps.

6. Click the Play Animation button in the Playback Controls area. What happens? Nothing. The biped must be told explicitly to create animation keys for the steps that you have just added to the scene. Drag the time slider back to frame 0.

7. In the Footstep Operations rollout in the Command panel, click the Create Keys For Inactive Footsteps button shown in Figure 12.18. The biped will drop its arms and prepare to walk through the footsteps that are now associated with it.

FIGURE 12.18
The Create Keys For
Inactive Footsteps button

8. Click the Play Animation button again. This time the biped walks through the footsteps with its arms swinging and its hips swaying back and forth.

Controlling the View

Now the problem is that if you zoom in on the biped and play the animation, it walks off the screen so you cannot see the end of the walk cycle. What good is that? Motion cycles can be very linear and difficult to track, so Character Studio contains the In Place mode to follow a biped's animation. In the In Place mode, the biped will appear to stay in place while the scene moves around it in relation. The In Place mode cannot be used in a Camera viewport, however.

1. Go to frame 0 then zoom in on the biped in the Perspective viewport.

2. At the bottom of the Biped rollout, click the Modes and Display text with the plus sign to the left of it. This is a small rollout located inside of another rollout that expands to show additional display-related tools.

3. In the Modes And Display rollout, click the In Place Mode button, as shown in Figure 12.19.

FIGURE 12.19
Click the In Place Mode
button.

4. Click the Play Animation button again. This time the biped will appear to be walking in place while the footsteps move underneath it. Stop the animation playback when you're ready.

   Using the In Place mode helps you work out the way a character moves without having to navigate throughout 3D space with your viewport, so you won't need to hunt down your biped. The In Place mode is great for tweaking your animation cycle because the viewport moves with the character in 3D space and you can concentrate on how its body is moving.

5. Exit Footstep mode, then select the entire SoldierBiped by double-clicking on the Bip001.

6. Right-click in any viewport and choose Hide Selection from the quad menu to hide the biped and obtain an unobstructed view of the model.

7. Click the Play Animation button. Your soldier will walk through the scene. It should be similar to the rendered soldier shown in Figure 12.20.

FIGURE 12.20
The rendered soldier
during a walk cycle

As you can see, you still need to do a little work to successfully rig this character. Certain parts of the model seem to drag other nearby parts of the model along with them. This issue is particularly visible in the feet and arms. You'll fix it in the next section.

Tweaking Physique

Each element in the biped has an area of influence, called an *envelope,* that determines which parts of the model it affects. The biped's left foot, for instance, should control the movement of only the model's left foot and the lower part of the ankle. In our case, the envelopes extend to affect some of the vertices on the opposite side. To fix the envelopes, follow this procedure:

1. Right-click in the viewport and choose Unhide By Name from the quad menu. In the Unhide Objects dialog box, click Display ➤ Expand All. Select all of the Biped objects, and then click the Unhide button to unhide the biped.

2. Scrub the time slider until the left foot rests on the ground after its first step. In the Right viewport, zoom into the feet and legs, and then render the viewport. Figure 12.21 shows the condition where the left foot drags along some of the vertices from the right foot.

FIGURE 12.21 There is a problem with the feet.

3. Select the mesh, and then in the Modify panel click the Hide Attached Nodes option at the bottom of the Physique Level Of Detail

rollout. Doing so turns off the geometry of the biped temporarily and displays the links as thin orange lines.

4. In the modifier stack, expand the Physique modifier and select the Envelope subobject, as shown in Figure 12.22.

FIGURE 12.22
Select the Envelope subobject level.

5. Select the orange links for the left foot and toes. The inner and outer envelopes appear as shown in Figure 12.23. Also, notice that the model's vertices that are affected by the links are displayed in the viewport as small crosses.

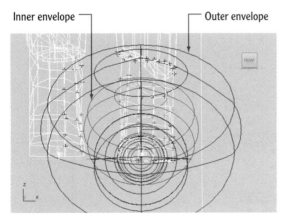

Inner envelope   Outer envelope

FIGURE 12.23 Inner and outer envelopes for the left foot and toes

6. In the Envelope Parameters section of the Blending Envelopes rollout, click the Inner button, then reduce the Radial Scale value as shown in Figure 12.24 until the envelope just encompasses the boot

in the Front viewport. Clicking the Inner button causes changes to affect only the inner bound of the envelope.

FIGURE 12.24
Reduce the radial scale.

7. Repeat the procedure with the Outer button selected and watch the vertices from the opposite foot become unselected as the envelope shrinks.

8. Switch to the Right viewport and use the Strength parameter and the Scale transform, alternately with the Inner and Outer buttons selected, to adjust the size and shape of the envelopes. The goal is to have the foot links affect only the boot and ankle.

9. Repeat this procedure with the remaining links in the model. You can use the Parent Overlap and Child Overlap options to determine how much one link affects the vertices controlled by the links before or after it in the hierarchy. You may also want to add some freeform animation to make the character livelier.

The completed Character Studio Soldier exercise can be found in the `CSSoldierComplete.max` file in the `Scenes` folder of the Soldier project on the book's web page.

Character Studio is a complete character animation package, and we've barely scratched the surface here. There are tools for saving biped configurations and sequences of animation. You can mix animation sequences from different files to create an entirely new motion. When the model does not skin as well as you need, you can use envelopes to refine the skinning process further, define vertices to be excluded from a specific Biped object's influence, or include bulge conditions to define the model's behavior depending on the angle between subsequent biped elements.

The list goes on, but the good news is that the Character Studio tutorials and help system that ship with 3ds Max are very thorough, and you should find the information there to expand your skills once you have a solid footing with the basics. It's important to realize that animation requires nuance, and the best animation with the simplest rig and setup will beat a mediocre animation created with a more wonderful, complicated, and ingenious setup.

THE ESSENTIALS AND BEYOND

This chapter introduced you to the basics of Character Studio and Biped setup for the soldier character. We used Physique to apply the Biped setup to the geometry of the soldier, and adjusted the envelopes for the best results in animation.

ADDITIONAL EXERCISES

▶ Try adjusting the proportions of the soldier model to create a new character design, and adjust the Biped accordingly.

▶ Try adding a tail to the Biped for an interesting creature.

CHAPTER 13

Character Studio: Animating

Character animation is a broad and complex field. This chapter introduces you to the basics of using Character Studio and bones for animation. Further investigation into these tools is a must if you want your animation to be full of life and character.

Topics in this chapter include the following:

▶ **Character animation**

▶ **Animating the soldier**

Character Animation

The character animation CG specialty is one of the toughest specialties to master. To use one word, good character animation comes down to *nuance*.

When you animate a character, you have to have a keen eye for detail and an understanding of how proportions move on a person's body. Setting up a CG character to walk *exactly* like a human being is amazingly complicated.

Character systems such as Character Studio make it a breeze to outfit characters with biped setups and have them moving in a walk cycle very quickly.

Animating the Soldier

Bipeds can be animated in several ways, including footstep-driven animation and freeform animation. With *footstep-driven animation* you add visible Footstep objects to your scene and direct the biped to step onto those footsteps at particular points in time. Footsteps can be added individually or as a set of walk, run, or jump steps; they can be moved or rotated to achieve the desired result and direction. When you use footstep-driven animation, the legs and feet of the biped are not the only things animated; the hips, arms, tails, and all other components are animated as well. However, this approach is rarely the complete solution to your animation needs.

Freeform animation is when you animate the components of the biped manually, as you would animate any other object, such as a bouncing ball.

Animation keys that are added to the selected Biped objects appear in the track bar, just like other objects, where they can be moved, modified, or deleted to adjust the animation.

Adding a Run-and-Jump Sequence

At the end of the previous chapter we completed rigging the soldier model and added footsteps to check the model. New footsteps can be appended to any existing footsteps. In the next exercise, you will add footsteps to the existing animation cycle.

Continue with the previous soldier model or open the CSSoldierComplete00.max file in the Scenes folder of the Soldier project on the book's web page at **www.sybex .com/go/3dsmax2012essentials**. Then select the Bip001 object. If you have trouble, you can either press H or open the Select By Name dialog icon ( ) found on the Main toolbar. Once you've selected the Bip001 object, click Select. Then on the Motion panel choose Footstep mode ( ).

1. Click the Run icon ( ) in the Footstep Creation rollout. This will apply a run gait to any footsteps you add to your current footsteps in the Create Multiple Footsteps dialog box.

2. Click the Create Multiple Footsteps icon ( ) to open the Create Multiple Footsteps dialog box.

3. Change the number of footsteps to 10 and click OK.

4. In the Footstep Operations rollout, click the Create Keys For Inactive Footsteps icon ( ) to associate the new footsteps with the biped.

5. Click the Play Animation button. The biped walks through the first 8 steps and then runs through the next 10. As you can see, the run sequence meets the definition of a run, but it is far from realistic. In the next exercise, you'll learn how to add to or modify a biped's motion with freeform animation to make a better cycle. For now, click the Play Animation button again to turn play off.

6. Click the Jump button in the Footstep Creation rollout, and then click the Create Multiple Footsteps button.

7. In the Create Multiple Footsteps dialog box, set the number of footsteps to 4 and click OK. Because a jump is defined as a sequence with either two feet or zero feet on the ground at a time, four jump steps will equal two actual jumps.

8. Click the Create Keys For Inactive Footsteps icon to associate the new jump footsteps with the biped.

9. Click the Play Animation button. The biped will walk, run, and then end the sequence with two jumps, as shown in Figure 13.1.

The Actual Stride Height parameter in the Create Multiple Footsteps dialog box determines the height difference from one footstep to the next.

FIGURE 13.1 Soldier model with the jump biped applied

Adding Freeform Animation

When you set your keys initially, you will need to edit them to suit good timing and form. When one part of the body is in one movement, another part of the body is in an accompanying or supportive or even opposite form of movement. When you are walking and your right leg swings forward in a step, your right arm swings back and your left arm swings out to compensate.

You can easily add or modify the biped's existing animation keys with free-form animation using the Auto Key button and the Dope Sheet. The following exercises contain examples of freeform animation.

Moving the Head

The following steps will guide you through the process of creating head movement for your biped. Continue with the current project scene or open the CSSoldierComplete01.max file from the Biped Scene Files folder on the book's web page. Because we will be working with the Biped a lot in this exercise, the Biped components have been unhidden and the soldier model hidden.

1. Select the Bip001 object and, if necessary, exit the Footstep mode by clicking the Footstep Mode icon.

2. Drag the time slider to frame 50, approximately the point when the biped lifts its left foot off footstep number 2.

3. Select the biped's head and note the animation keys that appear in the track bar, as shown in Figure 13.2.

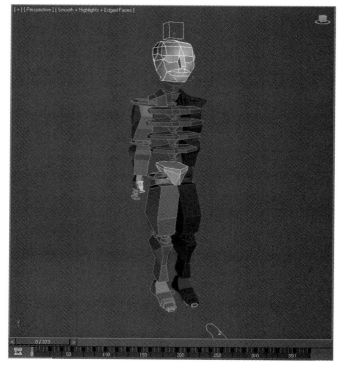

FIGURE 13.2 Selecting the head of the biped reveals all of that object's animation keys in the track bar.

> **Footsteps are numbered, starting with the number 0 and initially alternating from the left to the right side. They are also color-coded, with blue footsteps on the left and green footsteps on the right.**

4. In the track bar, select the two keys on either side of the current frame, right-click either one, and then delete them as shown in Figure 13.3.

FIGURE 13.3
Delete the keys on either side of frame 50.

5. Click the Auto Key button or press N to turn it on.

6. Click the Rotate Transform button and rotate the head, as shown in Figure 13.4, to the left and up, as if the character sees somebody in a second floor window off-screen. A new key will be created at frame 50, recording the time and value of the head's rotation.

FIGURE 13.4 Rotate the head to the left and up.

7. Scrub the time slider back and forth. Watch the head rotate from a neutral position to the orientation that you created and then rotate back to the neutral position.

8. Select all the keys between frame 50 and frame 100 (but not keys at frames 50 and 100). Delete them. Doing so will make room for the new key that you are about to create. If animation keys are too close together, the animation could appear jerky.

9. Select the key at frame 50, hold down the Shift key, and drag a copy of the key to frame 90, as shown in Figure 13.5. Use the readout at the bottom of the 3ds Max window to drag the key with precision. Copying the key will cause your biped to hold that neck pose for 40 frames, or about 1 ⅓ seconds. Scrub the time slider to review the animation.

FIGURE 13.5
Drag to copy the key.

10. Select the biped's left upper arm.

11. In the track bar, select and delete all keys between frames 50 and 100. The animation keys for the arms define their swing motion. If you scrub the time slider or play the animation, the biped will hold its arm unnaturally stiffly for 60 frames because you deleted the animation keys between two points where it holds its hand forward. That's okay; we're just making room for some new keys.

12. Move the time slider to frame 60. This is the location for the first new animation key.

Moving the Arms

Now it's time to animate the arms, which are essential components in any walk cycle. To do so, follow these steps:

1. Rotate the upper arm upward, so that it points to the same location at which the head is looking.

2. Continue adjusting the biped's left arm, hand, and finger until they appear to be pointing at something, as shown in Figure 13.6.

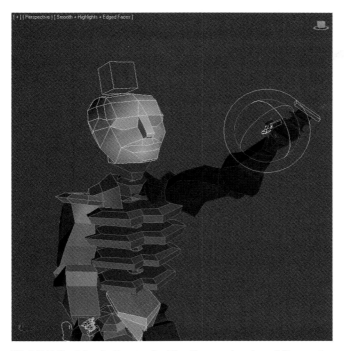

FIGURE 13.6 Rotate the biped's arm, hand, and fingers to assume a pointing posture.

3. Double-click on the left upper arm to select it and all of the components below it in the hierarchy.

4. In the track bar, select the key at frame 60, hold down the Shift key, and drag it to frame 85 to create a copy of that key.

5. Drag the time slider and watch the Perspective viewport. The biped will walk for a bit, notice something off-screen, point at it, and drop its arm while looking forward again before breaking into a run and then a jump.

6. Click the Auto Key button to turn it off.

Completing the Motion Sequence

The CSSoldierComplete02.max file in the Biped Scene Files folder on the book's web page contains the completed scene to this point.

For additional practice, add keys to the animation of the biped's arms when it jogs through the run cycle. For example, when the left foot is fully extended and the heel plants on the ground, the right arm should be bent at the elbow and swung forward and slightly in front of the biped's body. As the right foot swings forward during the next step, the right arm should swing backward and assume a nearly straight posture. Bend each of the spine links and swing both arms backward to prepare the biped for each of the jumps. Use the Body Vertical button in the Track Selection rollout to lower the pelvis into a prelaunch position, as shown in Figure 13.7, before the biped launches into its upward motion. Remember to make sure the Auto Key button is turned on to record all the changes that you make as animation keys.

FIGURE 13.7 Use the Body Vertical button to position the biped for a jump.

Modifying Animation in the Dope Sheet

To change the animation that is generated with Character Studio, you will edit the keyframes of the biped once you are happy with the base animation cycle. For this, you need to use the Track View–Dope Sheet. The Track View–Curve Editor, as you have already seen in Chapter 5, "Animating a Bouncing Ball," is used to edit the function curves between animation keys; however, the Track View–Dope Sheet interface is cleaner and is used to edit the specific value and position of the keys. It is not a different set of keyframes or animation; it's just a different way of editing them. Furthermore, access to editing the footstep keys is available only in the Dope Sheet. In the next exercise, you will add individual footsteps and modify the footstep timing in the Dope Sheet to make the biped dance and jump.

Adding Footsteps Manually

In the following steps, you will manually add footsteps to your biped character. First, create a new scene with a biped or open CSSoldierComplete03.max from the Biped Scene Files folder on the book's web page. This is the soldier biped with no footsteps applied.

1. Select a biped component and enter the Footstep mode.

2. In the Footstep Creation rollout, click the Walk button and then the Create Footsteps (At Current Frame) icon (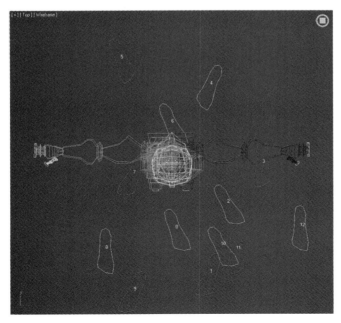).

3. In the Top viewport, click in several locations around the biped to place alternating left and right footsteps to your liking.

4. Change the gait to a jump, and then click the Create Footsteps (Append) icon ( ) to create additional footsteps. Create about 12 footsteps in all.

5. When you are done, use the Move and Rotate transforms to adjust the footstep locations and orientations as desired. Your Top viewport should look similar to Figure 13.8.

FIGURE 13.8 Manually place the footsteps in the Top viewport.

6. In the Footstep Operations rollout, click the Create Keys For Inactive Footsteps icon and then play the animation.

7. Character Studio doesn't have a collision detection feature, so it is very possible that limbs will pass through one another, which is quite uncomfortable in real life. If this happens, the footsteps must be modified to eliminate these conditions. If necessary, move any footsteps that cause collisions or other unwanted conditions during the playback.

Using the Dope Sheet

In Chapter 5, you experimented with the Track View–Curve Editor and learned how to adjust the values of animation keyframes. When the Track View is in Dope Sheet mode, frames are displayed as individual blocks of time that may or may not contain keys. Although you cannot see the flow from key to key that the Curve Editor displays with its curves, the Dope Sheet mode has its advantages. For one, the Dope Sheet has the ability to add Visibility tracks to control the display of an object, as well as Note tracks for adding text information regarding the keys as reminders to yourself.

Using the Track View–Dope Sheet, you can adjust the point in time when a foot plants on or lifts off the ground, how long the foot is on the ground, and how long the foot is airborne. Rather than appearing as single-frame blocks in the Dope Sheet like other keys do, footstep keys appear as multiframe rectangles that identify each foot's impact time with the footstep. Let's try the Dope Sheet on for size here:

1. Exit the Footstep mode.

2. In the Main toolbar, choose Graph Editors ➢ Track View - Dope Sheet. The Dope Sheet will open.

3. In the Navigation pane on the left, scroll down until you find the Bip001 entry. Expand the Bip001 and Bip001 Footsteps entries. The footstep keys appear as rectangles in the Key pane. As expected, the left keys are colored blue and the right keys are colored green. If necessary, click the Zoom Region icon ( ) in the lower-right corner of the Dope Sheet window and drag a zoom window around the footstep keys, as shown in Figure 13.9. The region will expand to fit the Key pane.

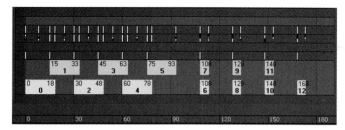

FIGURE 13.9 Zoom to the Footstep keys.

4. Select a few Footstep keys in the panel on the right.

   The white dot on the left side of a selected key identifies the frame when the heel of the biped's foot first impacts the footstep. The white dot on the right side of a selected key identifies when the biped's foot lifts off a footstep, as shown in Figure 13.10. A blue key overlapping a green key indicates that both feet are on the ground. A vertical gray area with no footstep indicates that the biped is airborne and neither foot is on the ground.

FIGURE 13.10 The dots indicate when contact begins and ends. You can drag a dot to change the duration of contact.

5. Select the first key (numbered 0), place the cursor over the right edge of the key, then drag the dot to the right to extend the length of time that the biped's foot is on the ground.

6. The double vertical line in the Dope Sheet's Key pane is another time slider that allows you to scrub through the animation. Drag the Dope Sheet's time slider to a point in time when the biped is airborne.

   Increasing the airborne time by increasing the gap between footsteps will also boost the height to which the biped rises, acting against the gravitational force pushing it downward.

7. Select the last four jump keys and drag them to the right to create a gap approximately 30 frames wide, as shown in Figure 13.11. Doing so will cause the biped to be airborne for about one second.

You can't move the end of one footstep key beyond the beginning of another one, and you must maintain a one-frame gap between same-side footsteps.

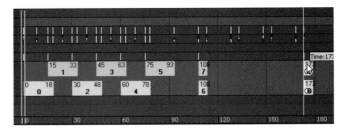

FIGURE 13.11 Create a key gap to get your biped airborne.

It is possible to move a footstep beyond the limits of the active time segment in the Dope Sheet. Use the Alt+R key combination to extend the active time segment to include all existing keys.

8. Move the time slider to the frame when both feet are planted before the jump starts. Turn on the Auto Key button.

9. Deselect any keys by clicking a blank area in the Key pane.

10. To prepare the biped to leap, turn on Auto Key and then select the Bip001 object and move it downward, causing the biped to bend its knees more. Rotate the spine links, neck, and head to bend the torso forward and tuck the chin. Rotate both arms backward into a pre-jump posture, as shown in Figure 13.12. Be sure to choose Local as the reference coordinate system for the Rotate transform.

FIGURE 13.12 Prepare your biped to jump.

11. Move the time slider forward until the biped is at the apex of the jump. Rotate the biped's components into positions you like, such as the split shown in Figure 13.13. Delete any animation keys that may interfere with your desired motion, and turn off Auto Key.

FIGURE 13.13 Position your biped in mid-jump.

The CSSoldierComplete04.max file in the Biped Scene Files folder on the book's web page contains the completed exercise so you can check your work. This file has the soldier model unhidden and the biped hidden. Play the animation and see how it looks; modify where needed.

As you saw in this section, there are several ways to animate a biped, including the footstep-driven method, the freeform method, and a combination of techniques. You can also modify the animation in the track bar, with the Auto Key button, and with Track View–Dope Sheet.

THE ESSENTIALS AND BEYOND

This chapter introduced you to animating characters with Character Studio. Using the Biped system, you can quickly create and adjust the substructure that controls a 3D model. Once the Physique modifier associates or skins the model to the biped, character animation can be added using footstep-driven or freeform animation.

ADDITIONAL EXERCISES

► Add different head or arm movements to the current footsteps on your soldier.

► Animate the soldier character running and dodging enemy fire.

CHAPTER 14

Introduction to Lighting: Red Rocket

Light reveals the world around us and defines shape, color, and texture. Lighting is the most important aspect of CG, and it simply cannot be mastered at a snap of the fingers. The trick to correctly lighting a CG scene is understanding how light works and seeing the visual nuances it has to offer.

In this chapter, you will study the various tools used to light in 3ds Max. This chapter will serve as a primer to this important aspect of CG. It will start you on the path by showing you the tools available and giving you opportunities to begin using them.

Topics in this chapter include the following:

▶ **Three-point lighting**

▶ **3ds Max lights**

▶ **Default lights**

▶ **Standard lights**

▶ **Lighting the Red Rocket**

▶ **Selecting a shadow type**

▶ **Atmospheres and effects**

▶ **Light Lister**

Three-Point Lighting

Three-point lighting is a traditional approach to lighting a television shot. After all these years, the concepts still carry over to CG lighting. In this setup, three distinct roles are used to light the subject of a shot. The scene should, in effect, seem to have only one primary or *key* light to define lighting direction and create primary shadows, a softer light to fill the scene and soften the shadows a bit, and a back light to make the subject pop out from the background.

This does not mean there are only three lights in the scene. Three-point lighting suggests that there are three primary angles of light for your shot, dependent on where the camera is located.

Three-point lighting ensures that your scene's main subject for a particular shot is well lit and has highlights and a sense of lighting direction using shadow and tone. Figure 14.1 shows a plan view of the three-point lighting layout. The subject is in the middle of the image.

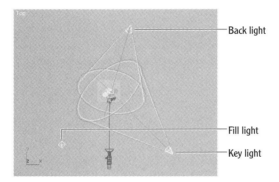

FIGURE 14.1 A three-point lighting schematic

3ds Max Lights

3ds Max has two types of light objects: photometric and standard. *Photometric lights* are lights that possess specific features to enable a more accurate definition of lighting, as you would see in the real world. Photometric lights have physically based intensity values that closely mimic the behavior of real light. *Standard lights* are extremely powerful and capable of realism, but they are more straightforward to use than photometric lights and less taxing on the system at render time. In this book, we will only discuss standard lights.

Default Lights

In the absence of lights, a 3ds Max scene is automatically lit by *default lighting* so you can easily view an object in shaded mode and test render without creating a light first. Default lighting is replaced by any lights added to the scene.

Standard Lights

The lights in 3ds Max attempt to mimic the way real lights work. For example, a lightbulb that emits light all around itself would be an omni light in 3ds Max. A desk lamp that shines light in a specific direction in a cone shape would be a spotlight. Each of the different standard lights casts light differently. We will look at the most commonly used lights.

3ds Max has a total of eight light types in its Standard Light collection. The following lights are in the collection:

> Target spotlight
>
> Target direct light
>
> Free spotlight
>
> Free direct light
>
> Omni light
>
> Skylight
>
> mr area omni light
>
> mr area spotlight

The last two on this list have the prefix "mr" to signify that they are mental ray–specific lights (see Chapter 16, "mental ray and HDRI," for more about mental ray). An advanced renderer, mental ray is commonly used in production today. It offers many sophisticated and frequently complex methods of lighting that enhance the realism of a rendered scene. In this chapter, we will cover only the first five standard lights.

Target Spotlight

A *target spotlight,* as shown in Figure 14.2, is one of the most commonly used lights because it is extremely versatile. A spotlight casts light in a focused beam, similar to a flashlight. This type of lighting allows you to light specific areas of a scene without casting any unwanted light on areas that may not need that light. You can control the size of the *hotspot,* which is the size of the cast beam.

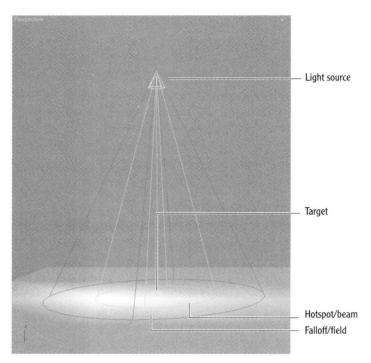

Light source

Target

Hotspot/beam
Falloff/field

FIGURE 14.2 A target spotlight

The light is created with two nodes, the light itself (*light source*) and the target node, at which the light points at all times. This way, you are able to animate the light following the subject of the scene easily, as a spotlight would follow a singer on stage. Select the target and move it as you would any other object in 3ds Max. The target spot rotates to follow the target.

Similarly, you can animate the light source, and it will orient itself accordingly to aim at the stationary target. Select the box at the end (the target) to point the light. Move (and animate) the entire light by selecting the line that connects the light source and the target. To access the parameters of the light, you have to select the top of the light (tip of the cone).

Create a target spot by going to the Create panel and clicking the Lights icon ( ) to access the light creation tools.

In any scene, click the Target Spot button, and in the top viewport, click and drag to create a target spotlight.

To create a *falloff,* select the light source of the target spot. Go to the Modify panel and open the Spotlight Parameters rollout, shown in Figure 14.3.

FIGURE 14.3
Spotlight Parameters
rollout

The falloff, which pertains to standard lights in 3ds Max, is represented in the viewport by the area between the inner, lighter yellow cone and the outer, darker yellow cone. The light diminishes to 0 by the outer region, creating a soft area around the hotspot circle (where the light is the brightest), as shown in Figure 14.4.

FIGURE 14.4 The falloff of a hotspot

Target Direct Light

A *target direct light* has target and light nodes to help you control the direction and animation of the light. It also has a hotspot and beam, as well as a falloff, much like the target spot. However, where the target spot emits light rays from a single point (the light source) outward in a cone shape, the target direct light casts parallel rays of light within its beam area. This helps simulate the lighting effect of the sun, because its light rays (for all practical purposes on Earth) are parallel. Figure 14.5 shows a target direct light in a viewport.

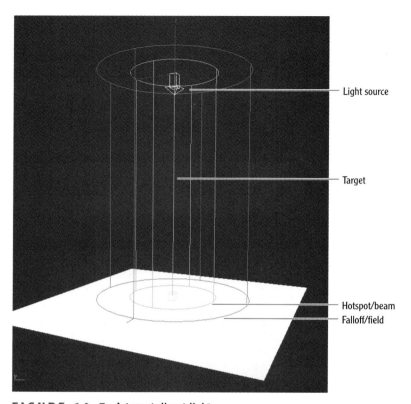

— Light source

— Target

— Hotspot/beam
— Falloff/field

FIGURE 14.5 A target direct light

Because the directional rays are parallel, the target direct lights have a beam in a straight cylindrical or rectangular box shape instead of a cone.

You can create and select/move parts of a target direct light in much the same way as a target spot. In the Directional Parameters rollout, you'll find the similar parameters for the target direct light. Although the spotlight and the directional light don't seem to be very different, the way they light is strikingly different, as you can see in Figure 14.6. The spotlight rays cast an entirely different hotspot and shadow than the directional light, despite having the same values for those parameters.

Free Spot or Free Direct Light

A *free spotlight* or *free direct light* is virtually identical to a target spot, except that this light has no target object. You can move and rotate the free spot however you want, relying on rotation instead of a target to aim it in any direction, as shown in Figure 14.7.

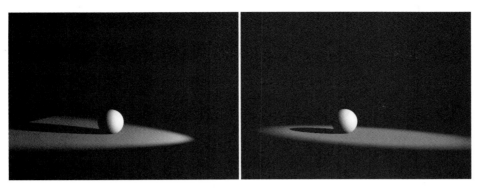

FIGURE 14.6 A target spot (left) and a target direct spot (right)

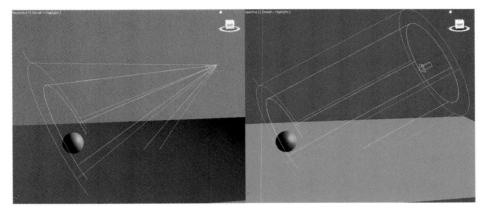

FIGURE 14.7 Free spot (left) and free direct (right) lights

To create a free spot or direct light, choose Free Spot or Direct and in the Create panel, select Lights. Click in a viewport. Then move and rotate the free spot however you want. Another difference between a free spot or direct light and a target spot or direct light is that whereas the length of the target spotlight is controlled by its target, a free spot or direct light instead has, in the General Parameters rollout, a parameter called Targ. Dist. The default is 240 units.

Adjusting the length of a spot or direct light will not matter when the light is rendered; however, seeing a longer light in the viewports can help you line up the light with objects in the scene.

Spot and direct (including target spot and direct) are great for key lighting because they are very easy to control and give a fantastic sense of direction.

Omni Light

The *omni light* in 3ds Max is a point light that emanates light from a single point in all directions around it. Figure 14.8 shows an omni light. Unlike the spot and directional lights, the omni light does not have a special rollout, and its General Parameters rollout is much simpler.

FIGURE 14.8 An omni light is a single-point-source light.

Omni lights are not as good for simulating sunlight as directional lights are. In Figure 14.9, the omni light in the image on the left creates different shadow and lighting directions for all the objects in the scene, and the directional light in the image on the right creates a uniform direction for the light and shadow, as would the sun here on Earth.

Omni lights are good for fill lights as well as for simulating certain practical light sources.

FIGURE 14.9 Omni light (left) and directional light (right)

Lighting the Red Rocket

Now that you have an overview of how lights work in 3ds Max, let's put them to good use and light the Red Rocket textured model from Chapter 10, "Introduction to Materials: Red Rocket," and create the three-point system. You will work with the lighting and settings in Chapter 15, "3ds Max Rendering."

Set your current project to the Red Rocket project you've copied to your hard drive from this book's web page, **www.sybex.com/go/3dsmax2012essentials**. Open rocket_light_start.max from the Scenes folder of the Red Rocket project.

To begin lighting the rocket, follow along here:

1. Go to the Create panel and select the Lights icon (⬛) to bring up the selection of lights you can create. Click the Photometric drop-down menu and choose Standard, as shown in Figure 14.10.

FIGURE 14.10
Choose Standard from
the Lights drop-down menu.

2. Click the Target Spot button to create a target spot. Go to the Top viewport, and click and drag from the right side of the viewport toward the middle. The click will create the light; the drag places the target.

3. Move to the Front viewport, select the light, and move it up. If your front view is not visible, simply select one of the viewports and press F for the Front viewport. The light's position should resemble Figure 14.11.

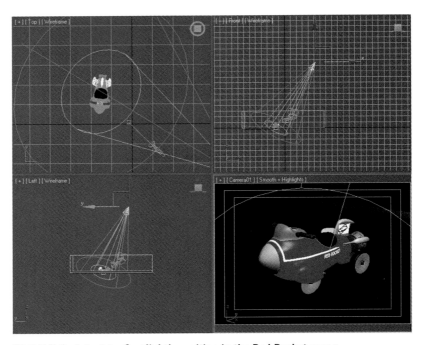

FIGURE 14.11 Spotlight's position in the Red Rocket scene

4. Name the light **Key Light**. This light will have shadows and give the scene its main source of light and direction.

5. Go to the Modify panel, select General Parameters, check the On box under Shadows, and set Shadow Type to Shadow Map. This is the default shadow type.

6. Open the Intensity/Color/Attenuation rollout, and set the Multiplier value to 0.8. The Multiplier setting acts like a dimmer switch and controls the light's brightness.

7. In the Spotlight Parameters rollout, change the Hotspot/Beam parameter to 18 and the Falloff/Field value to 38. Both these parameters affect the width of the cone of light. The closer the two values are, the sharper the edge of the light will be; the farther they are from each other, the softer the light will be.

8. Now you can try a render. Select the Camera viewport. Then, on the far left of the main toolbar, click the Render Production icon (), and you will see the rocket as shown in Figure 14.12.

FIGURE 14.12 Rendering the rocket with the first light in place

You will need to add an omni light as a fill light to make the shadows look better:

1. Select the key light (the target spot), and in the Shadow Map Params rollout, change the Bias parameter to 0.1. Bias moves the shadow toward or away from the object. The shadow is too far away from the rocket, and that is why, in Figure 14.12, it appears to be floating.

2. In that same rollout, change the Size parameter to 1500. Size specifies the amount of resolution in the shadow; the more pixels, the crisper the edge of the shadow will appear.

3. Go back to the Create panel and select Lights to create another light. Click to create an omni light. In the Top viewport, click in the bottom-left corner of the room to place the omni.

4. In the Front viewport, move the light up about half the height of the backdrop.

    The omni is just a fill light in this scene, so you don't want any shadows from it. Furthermore, you will turn off specular highlights on the rocket from this light to make sure the render looks as if there is only one light in the room. By default, shadows are always off, but you must turn off specular highlights manually.

5. With the omni light selected, go to the Modify panel and, under the Advanced Effects rollout, uncheck Specular.

6. Go to the Intensity/Color/Attenuation rollout for the omni light, and change Multiplier to 0.3.

7. Render again (press F9), and you'll see the render looks better but the rocket's shadow is still dark, as shown in Figure 14.13.

FIGURE 14.13 The rocket with a key and fill light

To fix the darkness of the shadow, you will adjust the density of the shadow.

8. Select the key light, go to the Modify panel, and in the Shadow Parameters rollout, change the Object Shadows Dens parameter to 0.8.

9. You can press F9 for another render or press the teapot icon in the main toolbar, and you will see that the rocket's shadow looks much better, as shown in Figure 14.14.

FIGURE 14.14 The rocket is lit!

Using shadows intelligently is important in lighting your scenes. Without the shadows in the rocket scene, the rocket would float in the scene and have no contact with its environment.

You can create the following types of shadows in 3ds Max:

- ▶ Advanced raytraced
- ▶ mental ray shadow map
- ▶ Area shadows
- ▶ Shadow map
- ▶ Raytraced shadows

Each type of shadow has its benefits and its drawbacks. The two most common types used are shadow maps (which you've already seen) and raytraced shadows.

Selecting a Shadow Type

To get shadows to respond to transparencies, you will need to use raytraced shadows instead of shadow maps. Additionally, if you need to soften your shadows the farther they are cast from the object, you will need to use area shadows.

Shadow Maps

The shadow map is often the fastest way to cast a shadow. However, shadow map shadows do not show the color cast through transparent or translucent objects.

When you are close to a shadow, in order to avoid jagged edges around the shadow, use the Size parameter to make the resolution higher for the cast shadow.

The following parameters are useful for creating shadow maps:

Bias   The shadow is moved, according to the value set, closer to or farther away from the object casting the shadow.

Size   Detailed shadows will need detailed shadow maps. Increase the Size value, and 3ds Max will increase the number of subdivisions for the map, which, in turn, increases the detail of the shadow cast. Figure 14.15 compares using a low Shadow Map Size setting to using one four times larger. Notice how the shadows on the left (Size = 1024) are somewhat mushy and less noticeable, and the shadows on the right (Size = 4096) are crisp and clean. Setting the shadow map size too high, though, will increase render time for little to no effect. A size around 2048 is good for most cases. Scenes like this chessboard that have a large scale to them will require higher size values, such as the 4096 we used. The rule of thumb is to use the lowest size value that will get you the best result for your scene.

FIGURE 14.15   The Shadow Map Size setting affects the shadow detail.

Sample Range   This option creates and controls the softness of the edge of shadow-mapped shadows. The higher the value is, the softer the edges of the shadow will be.

Raytraced Shadows

Raytracing involves tracing a ray of light from every light source in all directions and tracing the reflection to the camera lens. You can create more accurate shadows with raytracing than with other methods, at the cost of longer render times. Raytraced shadows are realistic for transparent and translucent objects. Figure 14.16 shows a pair of chess pieces rendered with a plane casting a shadow over them. The plane has a checker mapped to its opacity, so it has alternating transparent and opaque squares defining the checkerboard. On the left side of the image in Figure 14.16, the light is casting shadow map shadows, and on the right, the light is casting raytraced shadows.

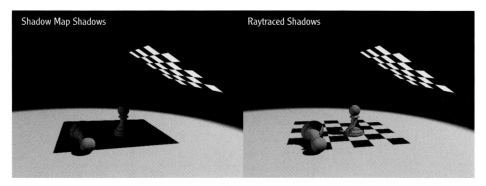

FIGURE 14.16 Raytraced shadows react to transparencies, and shadow maps do not.

Use raytraced shadows when you need highly accurate shadows or when shadow map resolutions are just not high enough to get you the crisp edges you need. You can also use raytraced shadows to cast shadows from wireframe rendered objects.

The Ray Traced Shadow Params rollout controls the shadow. The Ray Bias parameter is the same as the Shadow Map Bias parameter in that it controls how far from the casting object the shadow is cast.

Atmospheres and Effects

Creating atmospheric effects with lights, such as fog or volume lights, is accomplished through the Atmospheres & Effects rollout in the Modify panel for the selected light.

Using this rollout, you can assign and manage atmospheric effects and other rendering effects that are associated with lights.

Creating a Volumetric Light

Let's create a fog light now:

1. Open the rocket_atmosphere_start.max scene file in the Lighting Scenes folder on the book's web page. Go to the Create panel, select Lights, and click the Target Direct light. Move your mouse to the Top viewport, and click and drag from the top of the viewport down toward the rocket.

   This scene is already equipped with two omni lights that are hidden, to act as fill lights in the room.

2. Move to the Front viewport and move the light up along the *Y* axis, and then move the target so it is centered to point the light directly on the rocket, as shown in Figure 14.17. Make sure the light is shining into the room from outside through the window. Name the light Key Light.

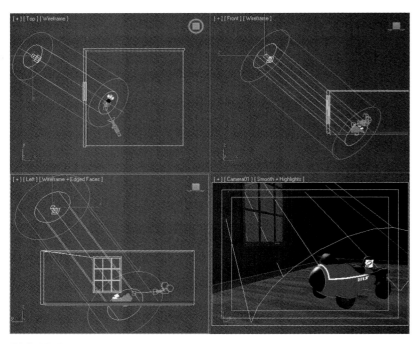

FIGURE 14.17 Move the light up and move the target.

3. Activate the Camera viewport and do a render (press F9); you will see that the scene is being lit from the direction of the light, as shown in Figure 14.18.

FIGURE 14.18 A test render of the rocket

The rocket and floor have reflections on them, so they show up even if there is no light in the scene at all. That is the way reflections work.

Adding Shadows

Now you need some shadows in the scene:

1. Select the Key Light, and from the Modify panel, open the General Parameters rollout; in the Shadows section, check the box to enable shadows. Select Shadow Map from the drop-down menu. Doing so turns on shadow map shadows for this light.

2. Go to the Shadow Map Params rollout and set the size to 2048; this will add some sharpness to the shadow's edge and make it more like a daylight shadow. Also change the Bias setting to 0.1, which will move the shadow so it is under the rocket. If you perform a Render Last operation, you won't see any shadows.

   This is because the window is blocking the light. The window glass object has a material that has its Opacity value turned down to 0. However, shadow map shadows don't recognize transparency in materials. To solve this problem, you need to exclude the window glass object from the light.

Excluding an Object from a Light

1. In the General Parameters rollout, just below Shadows is the Exclude button. Click the Exclude button to open the Exclude/Include window shown in Figure 14.19.

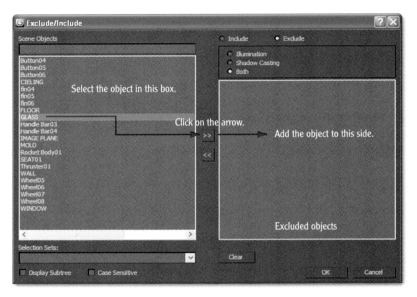

FIGURE 14.19 The Exclude/Include window allows you to exclude certain objects from being lit by the light in the scene.

2. Click on the Glass object and click the right arrows in the middle of the window, as shown in Figure 14.19, to add the Glass object to the other side, excluding the object from receiving light and casting shadows. Click OK.

3. Render your scene to take a look. Now you can see shadows. We didn't exclude the whole window with its frame because the inside frame is a nice detail to cast shadows. Figure 14.20 shows the render with the shadows.

FIGURE 14.20 Shadows!

Adding a Volumetric Effect

The whole point of this exercise is to add volume to the light. This will give our scene some much needed atmosphere.

1. Go to the Atmospheres & Effects rollout for the light. Select Add from the rollout to open the Add Atmosphere Or Effect window, select Volume Light, and click OK to add the effect to the light. Volume Light will be added to the rollout.

2. Render the scene. You should see a render similar to Figure 14.21.

FIGURE 14.21 Volume light!

To adjust the volume light, select the Volume Light entry in the rollout and click the Setup button. This will bring up the Environment And Effects dialog box. Scroll down to the Volume Light Parameters section to access the settings for the volume light, shown in Figure 14.22. Experiment with various settings to see how the volume light renders.

FIGURE 14.22 The Environment And Effects window displays the Volume Light parameters.

You can use Rocket_Atmosphere_Final.max in the Scenes folder of the Lighting scene Files project from the book's web page to see the results of this work and to adjust as you wish.

Volume Light Parameters

The default parameters for a volume light will give you some nice volume in the light for most scenes, right off the bat. If you want to adjust the volume settings, you can edit the following parameters:

Exponential   The density of the volume light will increase exponentially with distance. By default (Exponential is off), density will increase linearly with distance. You will want to enable Exponential only when you need to render transparent objects in volume fog.

Density This value sets the fog's density. The denser the fog is, the more light will reflect off the fog inside the volume. The most realistic fogs can be rendered with about 2 to 6 percent density value.

Most of the parameters are for troubleshooting volume problems in your scene if it is not rendering very well. Sometimes you just don't know what that problem is and you have to experiment with switches and buttons. The Noise settings are another cool feature to add some randomness to your volume:

Noise On This toggles the noise on and off. Render times will increase slightly with noise enabled for the volume.

Amount This is the amount of noise that is applied to the fog. A value of 0 creates no noise. If the amount is set to 1, the fog renders with pure noise.

Size, Uniformity, and Phase These settings determine the look of the noise and let you set a noise type (Regular, Fractal, or Turbulence).

Adding atmosphere to a scene can heighten the sense of realism and mood. Creating a little bit of a volume for some lights can go a long way to improving the look of your renders. However, adding volume to lights can also slow your renders, so use it with care.

Light Lister

If several lights are in your scene and you need to adjust all of them, selecting each light and making one adjustment at a time can become tedious. This is where 3ds Max's Light Lister comes in handy. Accessed through the Main menu bar by choosing Tools ➤ Light Lister, this floating palette gives you control over all of your scene lights, as shown in Figure 14.23.

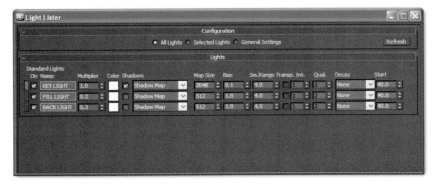

FIGURE 14.23 The Light Lister window

You can choose to view or edit all the lights in your scene or just the ones that are selected. When you adjust the values for any parameter in the Light Lister window, the changes are reflected in the appropriate place in the Modify panel for that changed light.

THE ESSENTIALS AND BEYOND

This chapter reviewed key concepts in CG lighting, including three-point lighting. You learned about the various types of lights that 3ds Max has to offer, from default lights to target spots, and how to use them. We explored the common light parameters to gauge how best to control the lights in your scene before moving on to creating various types of shadows. We ran through a set of short exercises in which you created a volumetric light for a fog effect, and we finished with a tour of the Light Lister window.

ADDITIONAL EXERCISES

▶ Try lighting the Red Rocket scene to evoke different moods: somber, jubilant, scary, and so forth.

▶ Light the soldier character from Chapter 13, "Character Studio: Animating," standing beside the rocket.

CHAPTER 15

3ds Max Rendering

Rendering is the last step in creating your CG work, but it is the first step to consider when you start to build a scene. During rendering, the computer calculates the scene's surface properties, lighting, shadows, and object movement, and then saves a sequence of images. To get to the point where the computer takes over, you'll need to set up your camera and render settings so that you'll get exactly what you need from your scene.

This chapter will show you how to render your scene using 3ds Max's scanline renderer and how to create reflections and refractions using raytracing.

Topics in this chapter include the following:

▶ **Rendering setup**

▶ **Cameras**

▶ **Safe frame**

▶ **Raytraced reflections and refractions**

▶ **Rendering the rocket**

Rendering Setup

Your render settings and what final decisions you make about your 3ds Max scene ultimately determine how your work will look. If you create models and textures with the final image in mind and gear the lighting toward elegantly showing off the scene, the final touches will be relatively easy to set up.

The Render Setup dialog box is where you define your render output for 3ds Max. You can open this dialog box by clicking the Render Setup icon (▧) in the Main toolbar, by selecting Rendering ➤ Render Setup, or by pressing F10. You've already seen how to render (▧) a frame in your scene to check your work. The settings in the Render Setup dialog box are used even when the Render button is invoked, so it's important to understand how this dialog box works. Figure 15.1 shows the Common tab in the Render Setup dialog box.

FIGURE 15.1 The Common tab
in the Render Setup dialog box

Common Tab

The Render Setup dialog box is divided into five tabs; each tab has settings
grouped by function. The Common tab stores the settings for the overall needs
of the render—for example, image size, frame range to render, and type of renderer to use. Some of the most necessary render settings are described here.

Time Output   In this section, you can set the frame range of your render output by selecting one of the following options:

> **Single Frame**   Renders the current frame only
>
> **Active Time Segment**   Renders the current range of frames
>
> **Range**   Renders the frames specified

Output Size   The image size of your render, which is set in the Output Size section, will depend on your output format—that is, how you want to show your render.

> **Resolution**   By default, the dialog box is set to render images at a resolution of 640×480 pixels, defined by the Width and Height parameters, respectively.
>
> **Image Aspect Ratio**   Changing the Image Aspect value will adjust the size of your image along the Height parameter to correspond with the existing Width parameter. For example, regular television is 1.33:1 (simply called 1.33) and a high-definition (HD) television is a widescreen with a ratio of 1.78:1 (simply called 1.78). The resolution of your output will define the screen ratio.
>
> In the Output Size section of the Render Setup dialog box, there is a drop-down menu for choosing presets from different film and video resolutions. The image quality and resolution of a render affect how long a render will take. In addition to turning down the resolution for a test render, you can use a lower-quality render or turn off certain effects, such as atmospherics.

Options   The Options section lets you access several global toggles. You can toggle the rendering of specific elements in your scene. For example, if you are using atmospherics (volume light) or effects (lens flare) and don't want them to render, you can clear the appropriate boxes.

Render Output   Use the Render Output section to indicate that the file should be saved. The image format can be selected to be a single image file or sequence of image files (such as Targa or TIFF files) that form a sequence, or it can be a movie file such as a QuickTime.

Choosing a Filename

To specify a location and file type to render to, click the Files button to open the Render Output File dialog box shown in Figure 15.2. Select the folder to which you want to render, and set the filename. You can set the file type using the Save As Type drop-down menu.

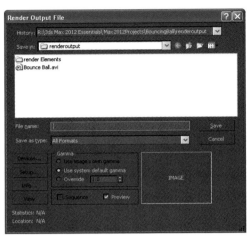

Name your rendered images according to the scene's filename. This way, you can always know from which scene file a rendered image was produced.

FIGURE 15.2 The Render Output File dialog box defines how the render saves to disk.

Rendered Frame Window

When you click the Render button in the Render Setup dialog box, the Rendered Frame window opens, as shown in Figure 15.3.

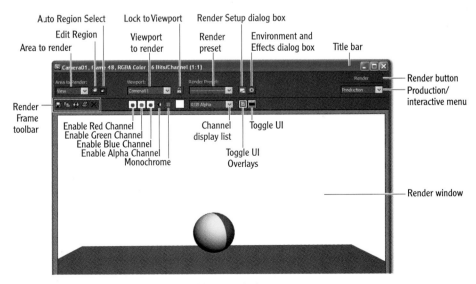

FIGURE 15.3 Rendered Frame window

The Rendered Frame window shows you how the frames look as the renderer processes through the sequence of frames. There is a collection of quick access buttons on the frame that are also available in the Render Setup dialog box.

Render Processing

When you click the Render button in the Render Setup dialog box, the Rendering dialog box shown in Figure 15.4 appears. This dialog box shows the parameters being used, and it displays a progress bar indicating the render's progress. You can pause or cancel the render by clicking the appropriate button.

FIGURE 15.4 The Rendering dialog box shows you everything you want to know about your current render.

Assign Renderer

Five types of renderers are available in 3ds Max 2012 by default (without any additional plug-ins installed), as shown in Figure 15.5. The Scanline Renderer is the default renderer, and mental ray rendering is covered in Chapter 16, "mental ray and HDRI." To access the Choose Renderer dialog box, click the ellipsis button to the right of Production ( ).

FIGURE 15.5 Choose Renderer dialog box

Rendering the Bouncing Ball

Seeing is believing, but doing is understanding. In this exercise, you will render the Bouncing Ball animation from Chapter 5, "Animating a Bouncing Ball," to get a feel for rendering an animation in 3ds Max. Just follow these steps:

1. Set your Project folder to the Bouncing Ball project that you downloaded to your hard drive from the companion web page at www.sybex .com/go/3dsmax2012essentials. Open the Animation_Ball_02.max file in the Scenes folder. Let's render a movie to see the animation.

2. Open the Render Setup dialog box. In the Time Output section, select Active Time Segment: 0 to 100.

3. In the Output Size section, select the 320×240 preset button and leave Image/Pixel Aspect as is.

By default, 3ds Max renders your files to the RenderOutput folder in the current project directory.

4. Leave the Options group at the default, and skip down to the Render Output section. Click the Files button to open a Render Output File dialog box. Navigate to where you want to save the output file, preferably into the RenderOutput folder in your Bouncing Ball project. Name the file Bounce Ball, and click the drop-down menu next to Save As Type to choose MOV QuickTime File (*.mov) for your render file type. Normally, we would render to a sequence of images rather than a movie file like this; however, for short renders and to check animation, a QuickTime file works out fine.

Apple's QuickTime movie file format gives you a multitude of options for compression and quality. The quality settings for the QuickTime file are not the same as the render quality settings.

5. After you select MOV QuickTime File and click the Save button, the Compression Settings dialog box, shown in Figure 15.6, opens. Set the parameters for the QuickTime file as indicated:

> Compression Type: Photo–JPEG
>
> Frames Per Second: 30
>
> Compressor Depth: Color
>
> Quality: High

Click OK.

◄

QuickTime is not supported on 64-bit machines, so if you don't have QuickTime installed or if you are on a 64-bit machine, you will have to output an AVI movie file instead.

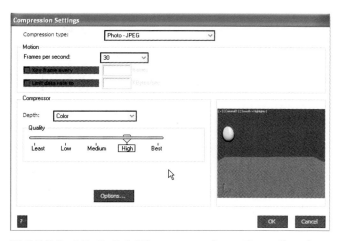

FIGURE 15.6 QuickTime compression settings affect the quality of the rendered QuickTime video file.

6. Skip down to the bottom of the Render Setup dialog box, and verify that Production is selected. Select the viewport you want to render in the View drop-down menu. You need to render Camera01.

7. Click Render.

After the render is complete, navigate to your render location (by default, it is set to the RenderOutput folder for the Bouncing Ball project). Double-click the QuickTime file to see your movie, and enjoy a latte.

Cameras

Cameras in 3ds Max, as shown in the Perspective viewport in Figure 15.7, capture and output all the fun in your scene. In theory, the cameras in 3ds Max work as much like real cameras as possible.

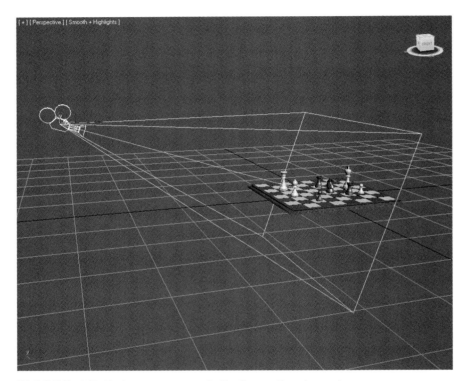

FIGURE 15.7 A camera as seen in the Perspective viewport

The *camera* creates a perspective through which you can see and render your scene. You can have as many cameras in the scene as you want. You can use the Perspective viewport to move around your scene as you work, leaving the render camera alone.

Creating a Camera

There are two types of cameras in 3ds Max: target and free. A *target camera*, much like a target spotlight, has a target node that allows it to look at a spot defined by where the target is placed (or animated). A target camera is easier to aim than a free camera because once you position the target object at the center of interest, the camera will always aim there.

On the other hand, *free cameras* have only one node, so they must be rotated to aim at the subject, much like a free spotlight. If your scene requires the camera to follow an action, you will be better off with a target camera.

You can create a camera by clicking the Cameras icon (■) in the Create panel and selecting either of the two camera types. To create a free camera, click in a viewport to place it. To create a target camera, click in a viewport to lay down the camera node, and then drag to pull out and place the target node.

Using Cameras

A camera's main feature is the *lens,* which sets the *focal length* in millimeters and also sets the *field of view* (FOV), which determines how wide an area the camera sees, in degrees. By default, a 3ds Max camera lens is 43.456mm long with an FOV of 45 degrees. To change a lens, you can change the Lens or FOV parameters, or you can pick from the stock lenses available for a camera in its Modify panel parameters, as shown in Figure 15.8.

FIGURE 15.8
Stock lenses make it easy to pick the right lens for a scene.

The most interactive way to adjust a camera is to use the viewport navigation tools. The Camera viewport must be selected for the viewport camera tools to be available to you in the lower-right corner of the UI. You can move the camera or change the lens or FOV. You can also change a camera by selecting the camera object and moving and rotating it just as you would any other object.

Talk Is Cheap!

The best way to explain how to use a camera is to create one, as in the following steps:

1. Set your project to the Rendering Scene Files project you have downloaded to your hard drive from this book's web page. Open the Camera Create.max scene file in the Rendering Scene Files

folder downloaded from the web page. This is the chessboard from the lighting chapter, but without a camera. Creating a camera is the same as creating a light. It's easier to create a camera in the Top viewport, so you can easily orient it in reference to your scene objects. Figure 15.9 shows the intended position of a camera for this scene.

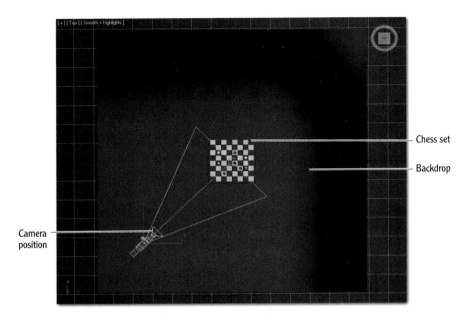

Chess set

Backdrop

Camera position

FIGURE 15.9 The camera would go here.

2. In the Create panel, click the Cameras icon. Select the target camera and go to the Top viewport. Click from the bottom of the viewport and drag to the chessboard. The first click creates the camera object. The mouse drag and release sets the location of the target, just like creating a target light. You may need to zoom out your view to accommodate placing the camera.

3. The camera was created along the ground plane. You need to move the entire camera up using the Front viewport. Select both the camera and target to move them as a unit by clicking on the line that connects the camera and target in the viewport. Use the Move tool to relocate the camera higher in the scene to place it at the level of the chess pieces.

4. To see the Camera viewport, select a viewport and press the C key. This changes the viewport to whatever camera is currently selected.

If there are multiple cameras in your scene and none are selected, when you press C, you will get a dialog box that gives a list of the cameras from which you can choose.

5. Now render the scene (press F9 or click the teapot icon in the main toolbar) through the camera you just created and positioned. Find a good framing for the chessboard and set your camera.

When the camera is set up, take some time to move it around and see the changes in the viewport. Moving a camera from side to side is known as a *truck*. Moving a camera in and out is called a *dolly*. Rotating a camera is called a *roll*. Also change the Lens and FOV settings to see the results.

Animating a Camera

Camera animation is done in the same way as animating any object. You can animate the camera or the target or both. You can also animate camera parameters such as Lens or FOV.

1. In the scene you just worked in, select the camera.

2. Move the time slider to frame 30.

3. Press the N key to activate Auto Key, or click its icon.

4. Use the Move tool to move the camera farther away from the still life. The idea is to create a dolly out of the still life.

5. Scrub through the animation and make any edits you desire.

◀

Zooming a lens (changing the Lens parameter) is not the same as a dolly in or dolly out. The field of view changes when you zoom, and it stays constant when you dolly. They will yield different framings.

Clipping Planes

In a huge scene, you can exclude or *clip* the geometry that is beyond a certain distance by using *clipping planes*. This helps minimize the amount of geometry that needs to be calculated. Each camera has a clipping plane for distance (far range), as shown in Figure 15.10 (right image), and foreground (near range), as shown in Figure 15.10 (left image), respectively. The near clipping plane clips geometry within the distance designated from the camera lens.

If you find that a model or scene you have imported looks odd or is cut off, check to make sure your clipping planes are adjusted to fit the extent of the scene, especially with imported models.

To enable clipping planes, click the Clip Manually check box and set the distances needed. Once you turn on manual clipping planes, the camera displays the near and far extents in the viewports with a red plane marker.

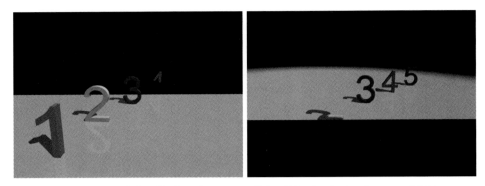

FIGURE 15.10 A far clipping plane cuts off the distant extents of a scene (right image). A near clipping plane cuts off the extents directly in front of a camera.

Safe Frame

To help make sure the action of your scene is contained within a safe area on standard-definition TV screens, you can enable the Safe Frame view in any viewport. This will, as shown in Figure 15.11, show you a set of three boundaries in your viewport.

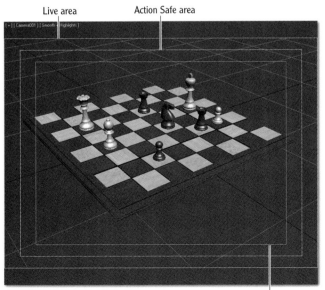

FIGURE 15.11 Safe Frame gives you a suggested boundary for the action of your framing.

The *live* area is the extent of what will be rendered. The *action safe* area is the boundary where you should be assured that the action in the scene will display on most if not all TV screens. Finally, the *title safe* boundary is where you can feel comfortable rendering text in your frame.

To view the safe frame areas in the chosen viewport, click on the viewport's name in the upper-left corner of the viewport to access the context menu, and then choose Safe Frame from the list.

Raytraced Reflections and Refractions

As you saw in Chapter 10, "Introduction to Materials: Red Rocket," you can apply an image map to a material's Reflection parameter to add a fake reflection to the object. To get a true reflection of the other objects in the scene, you will need to use the raytracing methodology. There are essentially two ways to create raytraced reflections in a scene: by using a raytrace map or by using a raytrace material.

In many cases, the raytrace map looks great and saves tons of rendering time instead of using the raytrace material. Keep in mind, though, the amount of control you will have with a raytrace map is significantly less than with the raytrace material.

Raytrace Material

In the following steps, you will learn how to use the raytrace material to create reflections in a scene with a fruit still life arrangement.

1. Set your project to the Rendering Scene Files project you downloaded from the web page. Open the Still_Life_raytrace.max file found in the Scenes folder of the Rendering Scene Files project on the web page. Change the camera view to Camera01 in one of the viewports if it isn't already.

2. Open the Compact Material Editor and select a sample slot. Click the Get Material button (▣) and select the raytrace material from the Material/Map browser.

3. The parameters to create reflections are available through the Raytrace Basic Parameters rollout. Leave most of these parameters at their default

values, but change the Reflect color swatch to white from black. This sets the reflection of the material all the way to the maximum reflectivity.

4. Change the Diffuse color swatch to black to turn the column that the fruit is sitting on black. This makes the column appear as a reflective black glass material in the render.

5. Apply the raytrace material to the column in the scene. Render the Camera viewport. Figure 15.12 shows the result.

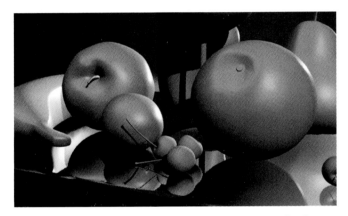

FIGURE 15.12 The raytrace material renders reflections.

Tweaking the Render

The render shows the raytrace material on the column reflecting like a flat mirror, but you may notice the jagged edges or artifacts around the reflected objects. What you're seeing is aliasing in the reflections. Clone this rendered image by pressing the Clone Rendered Frame Window icon (▓), which is found in the Rendered Frame Window toolbar.

SuperSampling is an extra pass of antialiasing. By default, 3ds Max applies a single SuperSample pass over all the materials in the scene.

In the current still life scene, select the material slot for the column's raytrace material. Go to the SuperSampling rollout and uncheck Use Global Settings. Check Enable Local Supersampler. In the drop-down menu, choose Adaptive Halton, as shown in Figure 15.13.

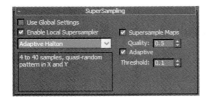

FIGURE 15.13 The SuperSampling rollout

The Adaptive Halton method performs well in this case. However, always try the regular patterns first; they tend to render faster. Render the scene, and you will notice a marked improvement in the quality of the reflections, as shown in Figure 15.14.

FIGURE 15.14 Reflections with the raytrace material with Local SuperSampling enabled

Raytrace Mapping

You can apply raytracing only to a specific map; you can't apply it to the entire material. In this case, you will assign a raytrace map to the reflection map channel of a material to get true reflections in the scene, at a faster render time than using the material as you just did. Follow these steps:

1. In the scene you just worked in, open the Material Editor and select an unassigned sample slot. Keep the material set to Standard.

2. In the Maps rollout, click the mapping bar labeled None next to Reflection. Choose the raytrace map in the Material/Map browser. Leave the raytrace map parameters at the default.

3. In the Material Editor's tool bar, click the Go To Parent button (🖼️).

4. In the Blinn Basic Parameters rollout, change the diffuse color to black to match the black column from the previous render.

5. In the Specular Highlights section, change the Specular Level to 98 and Glossiness to 90, as shown in Figure 15.15.

FIGURE 15.15 The Specular Highlights parameters

6. Apply the material to the column object in the scene and render the Camera viewport.

7. You will notice the same aliasing in the reflections as in the previous example. Set the SuperSampling as you did with the prior example, and render again.

Take a look at both the images created with reflections using the raytrace material, and those created using the standard material with the raytrace map applied to reflection. They look almost the same. However, you will notice slightly better detail in the reflections created with the raytrace material, but with longer render times.

Refractions Using the Raytrace Material

Creating raytraced refractions in glass can be accomplished using the same two workflows as raytraced for reflections. The raytrace material renders better, but it takes longer than using a raytrace map for the refraction map in a material.

Keep in mind that render times are much slower with refractions, especially if you add SuperSampling to the mix—so don't freak out. Now you will create refractions using the raytrace material:

1. In the same scene, change the Camera01 viewport to Camera02. This gives you a better view of the wineglass through which we will refract, as shown in Figure 15.16.

2. In the Compact Material Editor, select an unassigned sample slot and click the Get Material button. This material will be for the wineglass.

3. Choose the raytrace material from the Material/Map browser.

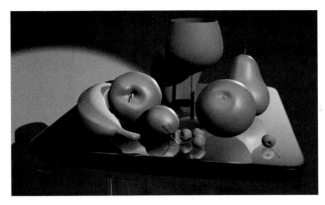

FIGURE 15.16 Changing Camera01 to Camera02

4. Go to the Raytrace Basic Parameters rollout, and change the color swatch for Transparency from black to white. (Black is opaque and white is fully transparent.)

5. Uncheck the box next to Reflect and change that spinner to 20. This sets a slight reflection for the material.

6. Take a look at the Index Of Refr parameter. This value sets the *index of refraction* (IOR) value that determines how much the material should refract its background. The value is already set to 1.55. Leave it at that value.

7. Go to the Extended Parameters rollout, as shown in Figure 15.17. The Reflections section of the parameters is at the bottom. Select Additive and change Gain to 0.7. This gives a bit of reflection brightness for the clear wineglass.

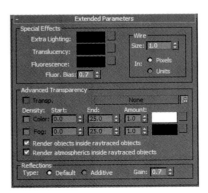

FIGURE 15.17 The Extended Parameters rollout for the raytrace material

8. Go to the SuperSampling rollout and uncheck Use Global Setting. Check Enable Local SuperSampler and keep it set to Max 2.5 Star.

9. In the Specular Highlights group, change the Specular Level to 98 and Glossiness to 90, as shown in Figure 15.18.

FIGURE 15.18 The Specular Highlights group parameters

10. Apply the material to the wineglass. The glass will turn transparent in the viewport. Render. Figure 15.19 shows the result.

FIGURE 15.19 The wineglass refraction is rendered with the raytrace material.

You will notice a very nice wineglass render, with the bell pepper refracting through it slightly. Change the Index Of Refr parameter on the material to 8.0, and you will see a much greater refraction, as shown in Figure 15.20. That may work better for a nice heavy bottle, but it is too much for the glass. An Index Of Refr parameter between 1.5 and 2.5 works pretty well for the wineglass, particularly at the bottom of the glass where it rounds down to meet the stem.

FIGURE 15.20 A much more pronounced refraction is rendered with an IOR of 8.0.

Refractions Using Raytrace Mapping

Just as you did with the reflections, you will now use a raytrace map on the Refraction parameter for the wineglass material. In the following steps, you will create another refraction material for the wineglass:

1. While still in the same scene, open the Compact Material Editor and select an unassigned sample slot. You are going to keep the material set to Standard.

2. Go to the Maps rollout and click the bar labeled None, which is next to Refraction. Choose the raytrace map from the Material/Map browser. The material in the sample slot turns transparent.

3. Click the Go To Parent button to return to the material's parameters.

4. Go to the Maps rollout and click the bar labeled None next to Reflection. Choose the raytrace map from the Material/Map browser. Be warned that this setting will take a long time to render the image. If you have a slower computer or perhaps are in a rush, uncheck the Reflection Map box in the material's parameters to turn off the reflection entirely.

5. Click the Go To Parent button to return to the material's parameters.

6. Go to the Maps rollout and change the Reflection amount to 6. This will reduce the amount of reflection.

7. Go to the Blinn Basic Parameters rollout and change the Opacity value to 0.

8. Go to the SuperSampling rollout and uncheck Use Global Settings. Check Enable Local SuperSampler and keep it as Max 2.5 Star.

9. In the Specular Highlights group, change Specular Level to 98 and Glossiness to 90.

10. Apply the material to the wineglass object in the scene and render as shown in Figure 15.21. Save the scene if you wish to keep it.

FIGURE 15.21 Use the raytrace map on the Refraction parameter to create refraction in the wineglass.

You can control the IOR through the material's parameters in the Extended Parameters rollout, in the Advanced Transparency section, shown in Figure 15.22. Set the IOR to different numbers to see how the render compares to the raytrace material renders.

The raytracing reflections and refractions slow down the render quite a bit. You can leave out the reflections if you'd like, but that will reduce the believability of the wineglass.

FIGURE 15.22 The Advanced Transparency section in the Extended Parameters rollout

Rendering the Rocket

Let's take a quick look at rendering a short 45-frame sequence of the rocket. You will essentially take the rocket scene laid out in the previous chapter (with the atmospheric fog light through the window we set up). You'll need to tweak a few of the scene settings, such as setting the rocket's and environment's materials to have raytraced reflections for maximum impact. You'll also animate a camera move so you can render out a sequence you can stick to your refrigerator door. Let's go!

Creating the Camera Move

We'll begin by animating the camera.

1. Set your project to the Red Rocket project from the web page. Start by opening rocket_raytrace_start.max.

   This file is the same one we used at the end of Chapter 14, "Introduction to Lighting: Red Rocket," but all the reflection maps have been taken out because we will be raytracing almost everything.

2. To begin animating, click the Auto Key button while at frame 0 (Auto Key) to activate it. Go to the timeline at the bottom of the interface and move the time slider to 45. Now when changes are made, keyframes will be created for any selected objects.

3. Select the Camera viewport because we are going to create a simple camera animation. When the Camera viewport is selected, the

viewport navigation tools change, as shown in Figure 15.23. These navigation tools make animating the camera easier.

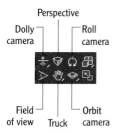

FIGURE 15.23
Camera viewport navigation tools

4. Select the Dolly Camera tool to move the camera closer to the rocket. Click and drag the Dolly Camera tool in the Camera viewport until you see only the front of the rocket, as shown in Figure 15.24.

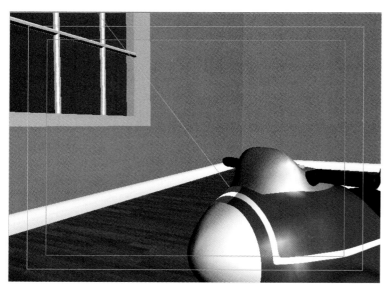

FIGURE 15.24 Dolly the camera closer to the rocket.

5. Select the Truck Camera tool, which allows you to pan the camera. Click and drag up and to the left in the Camera viewport to center the rocket in the viewport.

6. Back to the Camera Navigation tools, select the Orbit Camera tool. Center the tool in the middle of the viewport, and click and drag to the left until you get a better view of the side of the rocket.

7. Use the Truck Camera tool again to move the camera more to the left and to center the rocket in the viewport. Figure 15.25 should be the final position of the rocket in the camera view. Your camera move will end at this position at frame 45 of the animation.

FIGURE 15.25 The final framing for your rocket at frame 45

8. Go to the animation controls shown in Figure 15.26, and play the animation you created. Make any adjustments you would like to personalize the camera move. Turn off the Auto Key button and save your file. Remember to version up your file so you don't overwrite your current work.

FIGURE 15.26
Use the animation controls
to play the animation.

Adding Raytraced Reflections

In Chapter 10, we used reflection bitmaps to fake the reflections on the rocket by using a bitmap to create the illusion of reflection. The raytrace map calculates reflections as they work in the real world, reflecting the object's environment. Of course, in order for raytraced reflections to work, there has to be something around the object to reflect. To demonstrate this, we are going to add raytracing to the rocket and the room.

To add raytraced reflections to the rocket, begin here:

1. Open the Compact Material Editor and you will see all the materials that were created earlier for the rocket.

2. In the Compact Material Editor, select the first sample sphere at the top left; this is the texture for the left side of the rocket body. This is the only side of the rocket that will be visible in our renders, so that is the only side we will change.

3. Go to the Maps rollout, and you will see that the bitmap reflection from Chapter 10 has already been removed. If you are continuing with your own scene file, simply remove the current bitmap before continuing. To do so, right-click on the map bar and choose Clear from the context menu.

4. Change the Amount value for Reflection to 20, and click None to add a map. In the Material/Map browser, choose Raytrace.

5. Render a frame, and you should see some reflections of the room. If you want the rocket to have a higher amount of reflection, go back to the Maps rollout and make the Reflection value higher than 20.

6. Go through the materials in the Material Editor for the rocket's remaining parts to add raytrace to their reflections as well. For those materials in the rocket_raytrace_start.max scene, you will notice that the reflection bitmaps have already been removed from the following parts of the body to make them ready for the raytrace map:

    ▶ Both sides of the rocket's body (although you only see one side of the body in these renders, you may opt to put raytrace on both)

    ▶ Nose

    ▶ Fins

    ▶ Hubcaps (white part of the wheels)

> ► Tires (black part of the wheels)

> ► Seat

7. Go through the Material Editor and add raytracing to those materials. If you are continuing with your own scene, replace the reflection bitmap on the list of materials with the raytrace map.

We aren't adding raytracing to everything on the rocket, because raytrace reflections take a lot more time to render. Figure 15.27 shows a render of the rocket with the raytrace map applied to the aforementioned materials.

FIGURE 15.27 The rocket with raytraced reflections

In the room, the floors and the glass on the window should also have raytraced reflections, since reflections would look very good raytraced on these objects, especially with the camera move. Let's start with the hardwood floor.

The grooves between the wood panels should not have reflections; only the panels should reflect. We need to apply a mask to the reflections to block the raytrace from the grooves in the floor. The floor already has a bump map to mark out the grooves, so that is what we will use as the mask as well.

If the textures we are talking about do not display in the viewports, select the material in the Material Editor and click the Show Standard Map In Viewport icon in the Material Editor. If the bitmap files' paths are not connected when you open the scene file, 3ds Max opens an error dialog box, allowing you to browse for the missing images. This can occur when sharing projects and scenes between computers, as is a common occurrence. In this case, navigate to that project's SceneAssets\Images folder to find the disconnected bitmap images.

1. Go to the Compact Material Editor and select the sample Sphere material for the floor (the material is called FLOORS).

2. Go to the Maps rollout, change the Reflection Amount to 50, and click None to add a map. Instead of selecting Raytrace, select Mask.

3. Click the None button next to Map, and select Bitmap from the Material/Map browser. Navigate to the SceneAssets\Images folder of the Red Rocket project and choose Beachwood_honey_MASK.tif.

4. When the bitmap is applied, you will be in the Bitmap Parameters rollout. Go to the Coordinates rollout and change from Environ to Texture. Whenever you apply a bitmap to reflections by default, 3ds Max changes the bitmap to Environ because it is trying to behave like a real reflection. We need the mask bitmap to behave like a normal bitmap and look to the UVW Map modifier applied to the floor for its coordinates, as shown in Figure 15.28.

FIGURE 15.28 Change the bitmap back to Texture instead of Environ.

5. Now click the Go To Parent button in the Material Editor toolbar to get back to the Mask Parameters rollout. Select the None bar next to Mask and then click Raytrace from the Material/Map browser.

6. Render the frame, and you'll notice the reflections are pretty high. But you can also see how the grooves have no reflection, so the mask works! For a better reflection, turn the Reflection Amount setting in the Maps rollout down to 10 for the floor. Figure 15.29 shows a render of the rocket.

Turning On the Environment Effects

If you are just trying to check an animation with a render, it is wise to deactivate raytrace while you do your test renders. To do so, open the Render Setup dialog box (press F10 or click its icon in the Main toolbar) and select the Raytracer tab, then go to the Global Raytracer Engine Options group, as shown in Figure 15.30. Just remember to turn it back on when your test renders are finished.

FIGURE 15.29 The reflections on the floor look great!

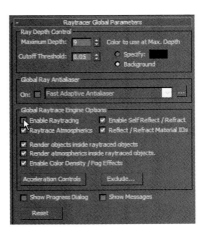

FIGURE 15.30 The Raytracer
Global Parameters rollout

To round out the scene, we need atmosphere: Volume light was already added to the key light in the previous chapter, so we just need to turn it on. The Render Setup dialog box has a Deactivate button for atmospherics, so you can easily turn them on and off as you test render. To reenable atmospherics in the render, go to the Common tab of the Render Setup dialog box and, under the Options section, check the Atmospherics box.

Render the frame shown in Figure 15.31.

FIGURE 15.31 The rocket is rendered with the volume light shining through the window.

Outputting the Render

We need to render out the entire 45 frames of the camera move. As you saw with the Bouncing Ball render earlier in the chapter, rendering out a sequence of images is done through the Common tab of the Render Setup dialog box.

In the Time Output section, click to select Active Time Segment: 0 to 45. The scene file you started with from the Red Rocket project will have its time segment set properly to 0 to 45. If you are working from your own scene file, however, you can either set the Active Time Segment in your scene to 0 to 45, or set the Range value in the Render Setup dialog box manually to render from frame 0 to frame 45.

The resolution of the render is set in Output Size. The default resolution is 640×480. On a good computer, this scene with atmospherics turned on will take just over one hour to render. Half the default size is 320×240 and will cost you one-fourth of the higher resolution's time (15 to 20 minutes or so) to render.

Go to the Render Output section of the Render Setup dialog box and click Files to open the Render Output File dialog box. Typically, animations are rendered out as a sequence of images, but for simplicity's sake, we will render out to a QuickTime movie (or to AVI if QuickTime is not available to you).

In the Render Output File dialog box, select where you want to store the rendered file, and pick a name for the QuickTime movie (Rocket_Raytrace.mov, for example). Then, in the Save As Type drop-down menu, choose MOV QuickTime File (.mov) and click Save. The Compression Settings dialog box will appear. Again, it is generally preferable to render to a sequence of images rather than a movie file; however, in this case, a QuickTime movie file will be best.

In the Compression Settings dialog box, select Photo–JPEG for the compression type, set Frames Per Second to 30, and set Quality to Best. This Quality setting applies only to the compression of the QuickTime file and not to the render itself. Click OK to return to the Render Output File dialog box, and click Save to return to the Render Setup dialog box.

Save your scene file, and you are ready to render! Just click Render in the Render Setup dialog box, and go outside to play catch with your kids or hassle your spouse or sibling into a needless argument for a little while. Then run back inside and play the QuickTime file saved in the location you chose earlier. Then take a huge magnet and stick your monitor to your fridge door. Voilà! You are now ready to enter the world of rendering with mental ray.

THE ESSENTIALS AND BEYOND

Rendering is the way you get to show your finished scene to the world, or whoever will stop and look. Nothing is more fulfilling than seeing your creation come to life, and that's what rendering is all about. And in this chapter, you learned how to set up and render your scenes out to files. In addition, you took a tour of raytracing and cameras.

Rendering may be the last step of the process, but you should travel the entire journey with rendering in mind, from design to models to animation to lighting.

ADDITIONAL EXERCISES

▶ Try rendering different resolutions and qualities for your scene, and make note of the times each frame took so you can better evaluate what settings work best versus time involved in processing the render.

mental ray and HDRI

This chapter will show you how to render your scene using 3ds Max's scan-line renderer and how to create reflections and refractions using raytracing. In addition, this chapter will introduce you to the popular mental ray Renderer and HDRI lighting workflow.

Topics in this chapter include the following:

▶ **mental ray Renderer**

▶ **Final Gather with mental ray**

▶ **HDRI**

mental ray Renderer

mental ray is a popular general-purpose renderer that has fantastic capabilities. One of mental ray's strengths is its ability to generate physically accurate lighting simulations based on *indirect lighting* principles. Indirect lighting is when light bounces from one object in a scene onto another object. In addition, incandescence or self-illumination from one object can light other objects in the scene. A direct light, such as from an omni light, is not necessarily required. Another thing to consider is that mental ray's reflections and refractions take on very real qualities when set up and lighted well.

Enabling the mental ray Renderer

To enable mental ray, in the main menu, choose Rendering ➤ Render Setup to open the Render Setup dialog box. On the Common tab, scroll down to the Assign Renderer rollout, and then click the ellipsis button for the Production entry shown in Figure 16.1. This opens the Choose Renderer dialog box shown in Figure 16.2.

FIGURE 16.1 The Assign
Renderer rollout

FIGURE 16.2 Select
mental ray Renderer in the
Choose Renderer dialog box.

In the Choose Renderer dialog box, highlight mental ray Renderer and then click OK. Once the mental ray Renderer is assigned, you can make it the default renderer by clicking the Save As Defaults button on the Assign Renderer rollout. Now the Render Setup dialog box opens with the mental ray controls in tabs.

mental ray Sampling Quality

Once the mental ray Renderer is enabled, click the Renderer tab in the Render Setup dialog box. The following is a brief explanation of the render settings most useful for you in your work.

Under the Sampling Quality rollout, shown in Figure 16.3, are the settings that let you control the overall image quality of your renders.

The Minimum and Maximum Samples Per Pixel values specify the number of times mental ray samples a pixel to determine how best to anti-alias the result to avoid jagged lines. Spatial Contrast values for Red, Green, Blue, and Alpha determine the exact sample level within that range. The lower the values set for Spatial Contrast, the higher the sample rate, leading to a smoother render at a higher render time.

The image shown in Figure 16.4 was rendered with a Minimum Samples Per Pixel value of 1/16 and a Maximum Samples Per Pixel value of 1 using a Spatial Contrast setting of 0.1 for all four RGBA values. With the Minimum Samples Per Pixel value at 4, the Maximum Samples Per Pixel value at 16, and the Spatial Contrast value at 0.04 for RGBA, the render becomes much cleaner, with an acceptable increase in render times, as shown in Figure 16.5.

FIGURE 16.3 The Renderer tab shows mental ray's common settings.

FIGURE 16.4 A jagged render

FIGURE 16.5 A clean render

Final Gather with mental ray

A popular feature in mental ray is indirect illumination—the simulation of bounced light (explained in the next section). In the tabs at the top of the Render Setup dialog box, click the Indirect Illumination tab. There are three rollouts, the first of which we will explore further:

- ▶ Final Gather
- ▶ Caustic And Global Illumination (GI)
- ▶ Reuse (FG And GI Disk Caching)

Final Gather

Final Gather is a method of mental ray rendering for estimating global illumination (GI). In short, GI is a way of calculating indirect lighting. This way, objects do not need to be in the direct path of a light (such as a spotlight) to be lit in the scene. In short, mental ray accomplishes this by casting points throughout a scene. These light points are allowed to bounce from object to object, contributing light as they go, effectively simulating how real light photons work in the physical world.

This type of rendering can introduce artifacts or noise in the render. Finding the right settings to balance a clean render and acceptable render times is an art form all its own and is rather difficult to master. Figure 16.6 shows the Final Gather rollout. Some of Final Gather's options, including how to deal with quality and noise, are explained next.

Basic Group

These are the most important parameters in the Basic section of the Final Gather rollout; they set the accuracy and precision of the light bounces, therefore controlling noise.

FG Precision Presets Slider   Sets the accuracy level of the Final Gather simulation by adjusting settings for the renderer such as Point Density, Rays Per Point, and Interpolation. Use this slider first in setting how good your render's lighting looks. In Figure 16.7 (left image), three spheres are rendered with a Draft setting for Final Gather, while Figure 16.7 (right image) is set to High. Notice the right image is a cleaner render, and also shows more of the background and the spheres than does the Draft quality in the left image. This slider will adjust the settings for several of the values covered in the following list.

FIGURE 16.6 The Final Gather rollout in the Indirect Illumination section of the Render Setup dialog box

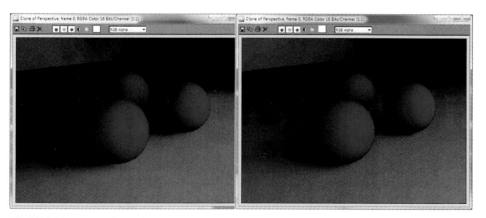

FIGURE 16.7 In the left image, a Draft setting produces a test render of the spheres. In the right image, a High setting produces a better-quality render of the spheres.

Initial FG Point Density   This multiplier is one of the settings adjusted by the FG Precision Presets slider but may also be set manually. This value sets the quantity and density of FG *points* that are cast into the scene. The higher the density of these points, the more accurate the bounced light appears, at a cost of render time.

Rays Per FG Point   This value is controlled by the Precision slider but may also be manually set. The higher the number of rays used to compute the indirect illumination in a scene, the less noise and the more accuracy you gain, but at the cost of longer render times.

Interpolate Over Num. FG Points   Interpolation is controlled by the FG Precision Presets slider as well as manual input. This value is useful for getting rid of noise in your renders for smoother results. Increasing the interpolation will increase render times, but not as much as increasing the Point Density or Rays values.

Diffuse Bounces   The number of bounces governs how many times a ray of light can bounce and affect objects in a scene before stopping calculation. If you set the bounces higher, the light simulation will be more accurate but the render times will be costly. A Diffuse Bounces setting of 1 or 2 is adequate for many applications. Figure 16.8 shows the same render of the spheres as Figure 16.7, but with a Diffuse Bounces value of 5. This render is brighter and also shows color spill from the purple spheres onto the gray floor.

FIGURE 16.8   More diffuse bounces mean more bounced light.

Advanced Group

The Advanced group of settings gives you access to additional ways of controlling the quality of your Final Gather renders. Some are described next in brief. You should experiment with different settings as you gain more experience with Final Gather to see what settings work best for your scenes.

Noise Filtering (Speckle Reduction)   This value essentially averages the brightness of the light rays in the scene to give you smoother Final Gather results.

The higher the filtering, the dimmer your Final Gather simulation, and the longer your render times. However, the noise in your lighting will diminish.

Draft Mode (No Precalculations)   This setting allows you turn off a good number of calculations that mental ray completes prior to rendering the scene. Enabling this setting results in a faster render for preview and draft purposes.

Max. Reflections   This value controls how many times a light ray can be reflected in the scene. A value of 0 turns off reflections entirely. The higher this value, the more times you can see a reflection. For example, a value of 2 allows you to see a reflection of a reflection.

Max. Refractions   Similar to Max. Reflections, this value sets the number of times a light ray can be refracted through a surface. A value of 0 turns off all refraction.

The mental ray Rendered Frame Window

When you render a frame in 3ds Max, the Rendered Frame Window opens, displaying the image you just rendered. When you render with mental ray, an additional control panel is displayed under the Rendered Frame Window, as shown in Figure 16.9.

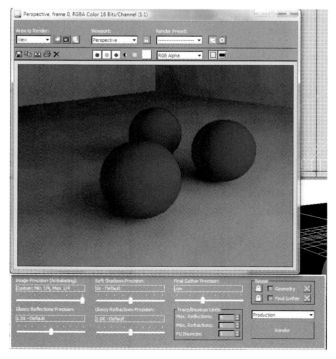

FIGURE 16.9 The Rendered Frame Window now shows several mental ray controls.

This control panel gives you access to many of the most useful settings in the Render Settings dialog box so you can adjust render settings easily and quickly.

mental ray Materials

For the most part, mental ray treats regular 3ds Max maps and materials the same way the Default Scanline Renderer does. However, a set of mental ray–specific materials exists to take further advantage of mental ray's power.

The mental ray Arch & Design material works great for most hard surfaces, such as metal, wood, glass, and ceramic. It is especially useful for surfaces that are glossy and reflective, such as metal and ceramic.

To showcase these materials, we will re-texture a few parts of the red rocket from Chapter 10, "Introduction to Materials: Red Rocket." Figure 16.10 shows the main material parameters for the Arch & Design material. We will look at the features that we need for the rocket next.

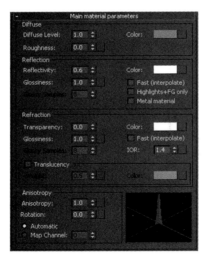

FIGURE 16.10 Main material
parameters for the Arch & Design material

1. Set your project to the mental ray project that you downloaded from the web page. Open the `rocket_mental ray_start.max` file from the Scenes folder of the mental ray Scene Files project on the book's web page. This file has mental ray already assigned as the renderer. The scene has the room, the rocket body, and the thruster already textured. There are no lights in the scene but because Final Gather is enabled, it utilizes the default lights to generate a lighted scene, as shown rendered in Figure 16.11.

FIGURE 16.11 The rocket file rendered

2. Open the Slate Material Editor; at the top of the view area, you will see the two tabs for the room and rocket. Right-click in the blank area next to the tabs, as shown in Figure 16.12, and create a new view area. Name it **More Rocket**.

FIGURE 16.12 Create a new view area.

3. Drag an Arch & Design material to the new view area from the mental ray material section of the Material/Map Browser.

4. Double-click on the thumbnail picture of the sample sphere to enlarge in the view area. This will also display the Arch & Design material in the Material Parameter Editor.

5. Name the material **Rocket Seat** and, in the Diffuse group of the main material parameters, click on the color swatch. Change the color to R: 0.0, G: 0.0, B: 0.0 for a pure black color.

6. Leave the Reflection values at their defaults. This will give the seat a slight reflection.

   By default, Arch & Design materials have reflection enabled. The area below the Diffuse group in the parameter section of the Slate is the Reflection group of parameters. Reflections for this material are calculated using the Reflectivity and Glossiness values. The higher the Reflectivity value is, the clearer the reflections are. The Glossiness value controls the blurriness of the reflections from sharp (a value of 1) to completely blurred (a value of 0). When you blur your reflections, the blurrier they are, the noisier they will be in the render. You can use the Glossy Samples value to increase the quality of the blurred reflections once you set Glossiness to anything less than 1.

7. Drag a wire from the material's output socket to the seat of the rocket in the viewport, as shown in Figure 16.13.

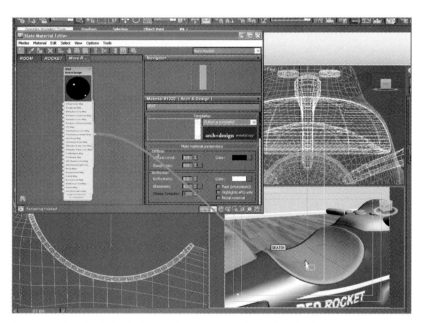

FIGURE 16.13 Seat material applied to the object in the scene

Render the Camera viewport to see the new material on the seat. Next move on to the fins. There are three fins: two with a white shiny material and one with the decal already applied from Chapter 10. The rocket body and the fin with the decal are already textured in this scene. To get acquainted with the Arch & Design material, you will texture just a few parts of the rocket.

   8. Drag another Arch & Design material into the new view area and name it **Fin**.

   9. In the Diffuse group of parameters, click on the color swatch and change the color to white, using these values: R: 1.0, G: 1.0, B: 1.0.

   10. Drag a wire from the material output socket to the objects fin04 and fin05 in the viewports. Those are the two white fins on the sides of the rocket.

The wheels will be done in the same way as in Chapter 10: by using the Multi/Sub-Object material and dragging the individually created materials to the selected polygons. The difference now is you will use the Arch & Design material instead. The wheel is divided into three materials: shiny red for the bolt, shiny white for the face, and bumpy black for the tire.

   1. Select one of the wheels, and go into Polygon mode. Select all the polygons for the bolt on the wheel, referencing Chapter 10 for selecting techniques.

   2. In the Slate Material Editor, you'll next create a shiny red material. Drag an Arch & Design material to the view area. Change the Diffuse color to R: 0.8, G: 0.0, B: 0.0 and rename it **Wheel_Bolt**. Then drag it onto the selected polygons of the bolt.

   3. Select the white parts of the wheel. Then in the Slate, instead of creating a new material, you'll use the Fin material you've already created. Drag a wire from the existing white fin material's output socket to the selected polygons.

   4. Repeat step 3, but select the polygons for the black part of the wheel. Then in the Slate, go to the tabs at the top of the view area and click the Rocket tab. This tab has a few materials already set up for you. Choose the Arch & Design material node called HANDLE BAR and drag it onto the selected polygons of the wheel.

   5. Repeat the same process (steps 1–4) on the remaining three wheels, or just delete them and clone the one that is finished.

   6. Render the Camera01 viewport. If it isn't loaded into a viewport, just select a viewport and press the C key; this will bring up the Select Camera list. Choose Camera002. The render is shown in Figure 16.14.

FIGURE 16.14 The textured rocket

3ds Max Photometric Lights in mental ray Renderings

Many of the parameters for photometric lights are the same as or very similar to the standard lights we looked at in Chapter 14, "Introduction to Lighting: Red Rocket." Here, we will show you the parameters that are specific to photometric lights. Photometric lights simulate real lighting by using physically based energy values and color temperatures.

1. Either continue with the file you are working with or open the rocket_mental ray_light.max file from the Scenes folder of the Mental Ray Scene Files project from the book's web page.

2. In the Main Menu bar, choose Create ➢ Lights ➢ Photometric Lights ➢ Target Light to create a photometric target light.

3. When you click on the photometric target light, you will get a pop-up recommending that you use the mr (mental ray) Photographic Exposure Control. Click OK.

4. In the Top viewport, drag to create the light from below the rocket and up.

5. Switch to the Right viewport and move the light up. Make sure the light stays within the room.

6. With the light still selected, go to the Modify panel. The first rollout under the modifier stack is Templates.

This rollout gives you access to several light type presets to save you time in creating a light. Feel free to play around with the different presets and render the rocket frame a few times to see the differences before continuing with the exercise and the next step.

7. In the Select A Template drop-down menu, select Recessed 75W Lamp (Web).

   A photometric light with a "web" distribution essentially defines the light's behavior and the light it casts. Lighting manufacturers provide web files that model the kinds of lights they make, so using these distribution patterns as templates gives you a lot of options in simulating real-world lights, like this 75-watt recessed lamp. Figure 16.15 shows the distribution pattern for this light as seen in the Command panel.

FIGURE 16.15
Distribution (Photometric Web) rollout

8. You need to take care of some basic stuff now, so with the light still selected, open the General Parameters rollout and check the Targeted box. You originally created a targeted light but when you used the template, it took away the target. Having a target on a light makes it easier to edit the light's position. Checking this box turns the target back on for the light.

9. Click the Shadows On box to turn it on. From the drop-down menu, choose Ray Traced Shadows.

10. Make the Camera001 viewport active and on the Main Menu bar, choose Rendering ➤ Environment. On the Exposure Control rollout, click the Render Preview button, as shown in Figure 16.16. You may notice the preview will show as either very bright or very dark at first. If so, the preview function will work perfectly once you render a frame for the first time.

FIGURE 16.16 Exposure Control and mr Photographic Exposure Control rollout in the Environment And Effects dialog box

Exposure controls adjust output levels and the range of colors of a rendering. These controls are similar to real-world film exposure settings on a physical camera.

11. Under the mr Photographic Exposure Control rollout, select Exposure Value (EV), if it isn't already selected. Set some different values for the EV and see what happens in the Render Preview dialog box. The higher the EV number, the darker the scene will be. Set the EV value to 7 or so and render, as shown in Figure 16.17. You can continue to work with the EV value to experiment with the luminance level. Be sure to set the EV back to 7 and close the Environment And Effects dialog box.

Photometric Light Parameters

Now let's look in the Command panel at the photometric light's Intensity/Color/Attenuation rollout for our 75W light, as shown in Figure 16.18.

FIGURE 16.17 The rocket so far

FIGURE 16.18
Photometric light's
Intensity/Color/
Attenuation rollout
in the Command
panel

The Color group of parameters controls the color temperature of the light, which you can set either with a color or in Kelvin degree values just as with real-world photographic lights. In the drop-down menu, there are different color/temp settings. The default is D65 Illuminant (Reference White).

The Intensity group of parameters controls the strength or brightness of the lights measured in lm, cd, or lx at:

lm (lumen)   This value is the overall output power of the light. A 100-watt general purpose lightbulb measures about 1750 lm.

cd (candela)   This value shows the maximum luminous intensity of the light. A 100-watt general-purpose lightbulb measures about 139 cd.

lx at (lux)   This value shows the amount of luminance created by the light shining on a surface at a certain distance.

The Dimming group of parameters is another place to control the intensity of the light. When the Resulting Intensity box is checked, the value specifies a multiplier that dims the existing intensity of the light and takes over control of the intensity. Picking up from the last step in the previous exercise, let's start to experiment with these values in the following steps:

1. With the 75W light still selected, go to the Command panel and, in the Color group under the Intensity/Color/Attenuation rollout, click the button next to Kelvin and change the value to 4000. This will give the light a bit more warmth by adding in more yellow/red.

2. In the Dimming group, uncheck the box next to the 100% spinner under Resulting Intensity to enable the Intensity parameter.

3. In the Intensity group, select cd and set the cd amount to 2500. This will brighten things up a bit.

4. Render, as shown in Figure 16.19.
   The scene still looks a bit dark and the shadows are very dark; they look like black holes. You will use Final Gather to brighten up the overall render. So far, you have used Final Gather's default settings. The one thing you need is for the rays that are generated by the light to bounce. The more bounces the light makes, the more luminance in the room. But more bounces slow down the render. It is good to balance bounces with exposure control and the intensity of the light for the best and most efficient result.

5. In the Rendered Frame Window, when you are already rendering with mental ray, the mini Final Gather panel is available for quick changes. Most of these controls also have a home in the Render Setup dialog box, and changing the value in one dialog box updates the corresponding value in the other. In the mini panel below the Rendered Frame Window, as shown in Figure 16.20, change FG

Bounces to 7. Render and compare the resulting render shown in Figure 16.20 to Figure 16.19. Figure 16.21 is the final rocket.

FIGURE 16.19 The rocket render with color and intensity changes

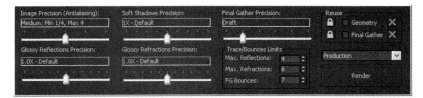

FIGURE 16.20 This mini panel gives you access to Final Gather controls to adjust your render easily.

FIGURE 16.21 The final mental ray render of the red rocket

3ds Max Daylight System in mental ray Renderings

The Sunlight and Daylight systems simulate sunlight by following the geographically correct angle and movement of the sun over the earth. You can choose location, date, time, and compass orientation to set the orientation of the sun and its lighting conditions. You can also animate the date and time to achieve very cool time-lapse looks and shadow studies. In essence, this type of light works really well with mental ray and Final Gather. In this exercise, you will use it in the most basic way, using all of its defaults:

1. Open the rocket_mental ray_final.max file from the Scenes folder of the Mental Ray Scene Files project on the book's web page. This is the file you ended with after applying the Arch & Design textures earlier in the chapter.

2. In the Main Menu bar, choose Create ➢ Lights ➢ Daylight System, as shown in Figure 16.22.

    A Daylight System Creation warning will come up, as shown in Figure 16.23, asking if you want to change the exposure controls to suit the Daylight system. Click Yes.

FIGURE 16.22 Daylight system

FIGURE 16.23 Daylight System Creation warning

3. In a Top viewport, click and drag at the center of the scene. This will create a compass that is attached to the Daylight system. Make it the size of the room.

4. When you release the mouse button, move the mouse so the light is placed outside the walls of the room. The Daylight system is supposed to simulate the sun and sky, so it needs to be outside the room.

5. With the light still selected, open the Modify panel and in the Daylight Parameters rollout, change the drop-down menus under both the Sunlight and Skylight parameters to mr Sun and mr Sky, respectively. When you change the Skylight parameter, a mental ray warning will appear asking if you want to place an mr Physical Sky environment map in your scene. Click Yes, as shown in Figure 16.24.

FIGURE 16.24 Add the mr Physical Sky environment map into the scene.

6. Also in Daylight Parameters, under Position, select Manual. This will allow you to use the Move tool to move the light to where you want it. The default position represents noon. The lower the light is to the horizon in your scene, the more it will simulate darker skies at sunset. We will leave the light in the default position.

7. Select the Camera01 viewport and render. As you can see, it is too dark. You are trying to simulate a sunny day, and beyond the direct light coming through the window, it's pretty dark, as shown in Figure 16.25. A good tool to use in this situation is mr Sky Portal. It gives you an efficient way of using a scene's existing sky lighting within interior scenes that do not require costly Final Gather or GI resulting in very long render times. A portal acts just like a mental ray area light. This light gets its brightness and color from the environment already in your scene.

8. In the Main Menu bar, choose Create ≻ Lights ≻ Photometric Lights ≻ mr Sky Portal.

9. In the Front viewport, drag an mr Sky Portal so it fits the window size in the wall. Then in a Top viewport, move the mr Sky Portal back so it is aligned with the opening of the window inside the room,

as shown in Figure 16.26. Make sure the arrow is pointing into the room. Render the Camera viewport again. That helps but is not enough; it is still too dark. So it's time to play with exposure controls.

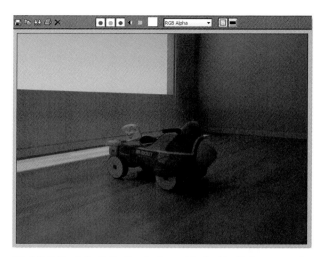

FIGURE 16.25 Rendering with the Daylight system is too dark.

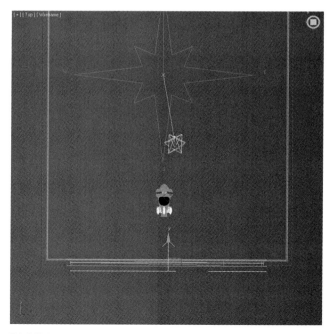

FIGURE 16.26 Move the mr Sky Portal to the window in the wall in the Top viewport.

10. In the Main Menu bar, choose Rendering ➤ Exposure Control. Click Render Preview.

11. In the mr Photographic Exposure Control rollout, change Exposure Value (EV) from 15 (the default) to 12, as shown in Figure 16.27. You should see the rendered preview change to show the update. Render the Camera viewport again to see the difference. It looks good but is still a bit dark, so it's time to add Final Gather bounces.

FIGURE 16.27 The mr Photographic Exposure Control rollout

12. In the Rendered Frame Window mini mental ray controls, change FG Bounces to 5. Render the image again; it should look like Figure 16.28.

FIGURE 16.28 Render with Final Gather Bounces set to 5

That's it! If you want to play around some more, we recommend moving the light for a more dramatic shadow on the floor. Moving the light can have a dramatic effect on the luminance levels too, so be prepared to edit FG Bounces and Exposure Controls. The last render is shown in Figure 16.29.

FIGURE 16.29 The final render

HDRI

The high-dynamic-range image (HDRI) is used in CG to create more realistic scenes than the more simplistic lighting models used.

An HDRI is created when several photos at varying exposures are taken of the same subject, ranging from very dark (underexposure) to highlight only the brightest parts of the scene, to very bright (overexposure) to capture the absolute darkest parts of the scene. When these images (typically five or seven images) are compiled into an HDR image, you get a fantastic range of bright to dark for that one subject or environment.

mental ray can create an environment map in your scene to which you assign an image, usually an HDRI. That environment map uses the brightness of its image to cast light in your scene.

The best type of image to capture for an HDRI is sometimes called a light probe. This is a picture of an environment, such as the office reflected in a chrome ball shown in Figure 16.30. You can also take a light probe using a fish-eye camera lens capable of capturing a field of view of close to 180 degrees.

Figure 16.31 shows the range of photos from underexposed (dark) to overexposed (bright) that were used to compile this sample HDRI.

FIGURE 16.30 A light probe photo of the author's desk, taken with a chrome ball

FIGURE 16.31 The five exposures that make up a sample HDRI of a desk

In the next exercise, you will use an HDRI that is from the 3ds Max default HDRI library installed with the program. See Figure 16.32.

FIGURE 16.32 HDR image from the 3ds Max default library

Open the soldier_mental ray_start.max file from the Scenes folder of the Mental Ray Scene Files project on the book's web page. This scene has the final textured soldier and a tank modeled by Federico Esparza, a student of one of the authors, who was inspired by a tank design from the popular video game *Warhammer 40,000: Dawn of War* from THQ. There is a flat plane with some cracked dirt texture on it, and the file is set up with mental ray as the renderer. Nothing too fancy, but it'll get the job done.

1. When the scene is open, in the Main Menu bar, choose Create ➤ Lights ➤ Standard Lights ➤ Skylight. Just click anywhere in your scene to create the skylight.

2. Next, load the HDRI file into the environment. Choose Rendering ➤ Environment. In the Common Parameters rollout in the Environment tab, click the None button under Environment Map, as shown in Figure 16.33. This will bring up the Material/Map Browser.

FIGURE 16.33 Add the HDR image in the Environment map.

3. Choose Bitmap from the Standard Maps rollout. Navigate to 3ds Max's free library in the Maps folder that is installed when you install the 3ds Max 2012 application (typically here: `C:\Program Files\Autodesk\3ds Max 2012\maps\HDRs`) and select `KC_outside_hi.hdr`. The HDRI Load Settings dialog box appears; click OK, as shown in Figure 16.34.

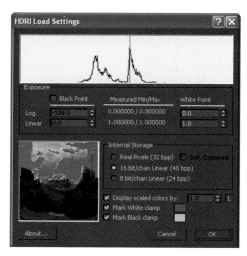

FIGURE 16.34 HDRI Load Settings box

4. The mapping of the HDRI that is loaded in the environment needs to be edited. With the Environment And Effects dialog box still open, open the Slate Material Editor, and place the windows side by side. Drag the Environment Map button in the Environment tab to the view area of the Slate Material Editor. This will open an Instance (Copy) dialog box. Click Instance and then OK to load the HDRI map into the Material Editor. Double-click on the HDRI map node to load the parameters. In the Coordinates rollout, select Environ and change the Mapping drop-down menu to Spherical Environment, as shown in Figure 16.35.

FIGURE 16.35 The Mapping parameter set to Spherical Environment

5. Select the skylight and in the parameters, under Sky Color, select Use Scene Environment. This will tell the light to refer to the HDRI loaded into the environment for the lighting.

6. Render the Camera viewport, as shown in Figure 16.36. As you can see, all the chrome parts on the tank look good but, overall, the scene appears fairly dull. It certainly doesn't look like it is outdoors in the daytime on a dry lake bed, as shown in Figure 16.36.

FIGURE 16.36 A dry lake bed as an example for the lighting of the soldier and tank

We need more light—specifically, sunlight! The skylight's job is to create the indirect illumination. Now, for the sun. With the Daylight system, the scene had both direct and indirect illumination, but the Daylight system doesn't work with HDRI, so we will need another way of creating sunlight for this scene. For the sun, we can use almost any light that can be directed. We will use the mr Area Spot. These lights work well with mental ray and have parameters very similar to any standard lights. Shadows are turned on and set to Raytraced by default.

7. In the Main Menu bar, select Create ➤ Lights ➤ Standard Lights ➤ mr Area Spot. To create the light in the viewport, start in the Top viewport and drag from below the soldier and tank and go up; then switch to the Left viewport and move the light up and away from the scene, as shown in Figure 16.37.

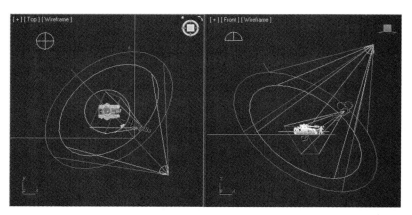

FIGURE 16.37 Place the mr Area spotlight.

8. With the light selected, open the Spotlight Parameters rollout in the Command panel and check Overshoot. This causes a spotlight to flood beyond its falloff area and cast light in all directions. Set the Falloff amount to 90, as shown in Figure 16.38.

FIGURE 16.38
mr Area Spotlight
Parameters rollout

9. In the Intensity/Color/Attenuation rollout, change the Multiplier setting to 0.5. Render the frame and compare it to Figure 16.39. Bam!

With the tank example, the HDRI environment map created an overall fill light for the scene, but also acted as a great reflection environment for the chrome accents on the tank. Adding the extra mr Area Spotlight allowed you to create a sunlight for a key light that gave the scene highlights as well as defined directional shadows. HDRI environment maps are very good ways to insert complex lighting scenarios, but are often augmented with standard or photometric lights to bring out the subject of the scene.

FIGURE 16.39 The final tank and soldier render

THE ESSENTIALS AND BEYOND

In this chapter, you learned the basics of rendering with mental ray in 3ds Max 2012. You saw the quality settings and how they could help you with better renders. Finding the right balance of settings for a clean render is an art all to itself. You also started lighting with Final Gather and then learning how HDRI can be useful for lighting.

ADDITIONAL EXERCISES

▶ Try out some of the other HDRI maps that come with the 3ds Max installation to see how they affect the scene and the reflections in the metal in the tank example.

▶ Experiment with different Final Gather settings to get the best look for the least render time in the red rocket example.

INDEX

Note to the Reader: Throughout this index **boldfaced** page numbers indicate primary discussions of a topic. *Italicized* page numbers indicate illustrations.

A

acceleration in animation, 116, *116–117*
accuracy of light bounces, 344
action safe areas, 323
Active Time Segment setting
  Dope Sheet, 286
  red rocket, 338
  time output, 313
Adaptive Halton option, 324–325
Add Atmosphere Or Effect window, 307
Adjust Pivot rollout, 112, 166
Advanced Effects rollout, 300
Advanced settings for Final
  Gather, 346–347
Affect Pivot Only option, 95, 112, 166
Align Selection dialog box, 95
alignment
  lathes, 89
  red rocket
    body, 219–220, *220*
    thruster, 95
  UVW mapping, 214, *214*
ambient color for materials, 202
Amount of noise setting, 309
animation
  biped footsteps, 266–270, *266–269*
  bouncing ball. *See* Bouncing Ball
    project
  cameras, 321, 331–333, *332–333*
  keying controls, 3
  knife throwing. *See* knife throwing
    animation
  soldier. *See* soldier character
animation curves. *See* curves and Curve
  editor
animation cycles, 113–115, *114–115*
Animation Playback controls, 16
Ankle Attach parameter, 261
ankles
  biped, 261
  soldier, 161–162, *161*
antialiasing, 324
anticipation in animation,
  135–136, *135–136*
Application button, 2, *2*
Application menu, 1
Apply And Continue option, 8
Arch & Design material, 348–351, *348*
armhole for soldier, 149–154, *150–154*
armpit area for soldier, 172–173, *172–173*
arms
  biped, **263–264**, *263–264*
  soldier
    animating, 280–281, *281*
    creating, 154–157, *155–157*

  pelting, 233–235, *234–236*
  UV unwrapping, 228, *228*
Arrange Elements rollout, 245, *245*
aspect ratio, **313**
Assign Renderer rollout, 341–342, *342*
associating biped with soldier
  creating, **258–263**, *259–263*
  default, 256–257
  defined, 256
  neck and head, **264–265**, *265*
  Physique modifier,
    265–268, *266–268*
  testing, **266–268**, *266–268*
  torso and arms, **263–264**, *263–264*
  tweaking, **270–273**, *270–272*
  view, **268–270**, *268–269*
atmosphere in red rocket rendering, 338
Atmospheres & Effects rollout, 303, 307
Attach List dialog box, 199
Auto Key option, 112, *113*, 120, 123
Auto tangent, 118
axes in viewport, 9
axle assembly in red rocket,
  76–78, *76–79*

B

back lights, 290, *290*
back of soldier head, 196, *196–197*
back wheel axle assembly, 76–78, *76–79*
ball. *See* Bouncing Ball project
base color for materials, 205–206
base materials for red rocket fins,
  212–213, *212*
Basic settings in Final Gather,
  344–346, *345–346*
beams
  target direct lights, 293–294, *294*
  target spotlights, 291, *292*, 299
belt for soldier, 169–170, *170*
bevels and Bevel caddy
  dresser
    drawers, 29, *29*
    top, 23–24, *23–25*
  red rocket
    body, 82
    model wheels, 98
    wheel wells, 68
  soldier
    armpit area, 173
    hands, 182
Bias setting
  omni lights, 299
  shadow maps, 302
binding character models to
  skeletons, 255

Biped rollout, 268
Biped system, 255
bipeds
  animating. *See* soldier character
  associating. *See* associating biped
    with soldier
Bitmap Fit button
  red rocket body, 219
  UVW mapping, 214
Bitmap Parameters rollout, 213
Black Wheel material, 207
Blinn Basic Parameters rollout, 202,
  205, 326
Blinn shaders, 204
blocking, 112
body
  red rocket
    creating, **55–59**, *56–60*
    details, **62–64**, *63–64*
    materials, **216–220**, *217, 219–221*
    smoothing, **61**, *62*
    touching up, **79–82**, *79–82*
  soldier
    seams, 240, *241*
    unfolding, 241–248, *242–248*
Body Vertical button, 282, *282*
bolts for red rocket
  material, 205, *206*, 351
  wheel, 210
Bones system, 257
Boolean operations
  dresser bottom, 36, 40–41, *40*
  red rocket
    seat, 83–84
    thruster, 94–95
boots
  biped, 261–262, *262*
  soldier, 176–179, *176–179*
borders
  red rocket body, 81, *81*
  soldier
    armhole, 151
    arms, 154
    legs, 161–162, *162*
    wrists, 156–157
bottom of dresser, 33–42, *34–42*
bounces
  Daylight System, 361, *362*
  diffuse, 346, *346*
  photometric lights, 356–357
Bouncing Ball project, 111–112
  animation curves
    editing, 118–119, *119–120*
    reading, 116–117, *116–117*
  copying keyframes, 113, *113*
  exercises, 128
  finessing, 120

moving forward, 123–124, *123–124*
refining, 118, *118*
rendering, 316–317, *317*
roll, 124, *125*
squash and stretch,
    120–121, *120–121*
summary, 128
timing, 121–122, *121*
Track View - Curve Editor,
    113–115, *114–115*
XForm modifier, 125–127, *127*
boundaries in Frame view, 322–323, *322*
bounds, envelope, 272
box modeling techniques, 48
Box Projection gizmo, 215
Box Under Mapping option, 215
boxes
    dresser top, 21–22, *22*
    red rocket, 52–55, *52–55*
    soldier torso, 144, *145*
bridges and Bridge caddy for soldier
    boots, 177, *177*
    face, 194, *194*
    head, 189–192, *190–191, 193*
    leg strap, 174, *175*
    legs, 159, *160*
    pouch, 171–172, *171–172*
brightness in HDRIs, 363
Building Envelopes rollout, 271
bump maps
    soldier, 249–252, *250–252*
    wheel object, 211

C

caddies, 8, *8*
calf of biped, 261
cameras and Camera viewport, 318, *318*
    animating, 321
    clipping planes, 321, *322*
    creating, 318–321, *320*
    HDRIs, 363
    red rocket, 331–333, *332–333*
    target spotlights, 299
    volumetric lights, 305
    working with, 319, *319*
candela (cd) metric, 356
Cap Poly tool, 82
    soldier armhole, 151
    soldier legs, 160
Capsule tool, 56
cascading menus, 7
cd (candela) metric, 356
center points, 126
CG (computer-generated)
    characters, 165
Chamfer caddy, 26
chamfer cylinders, 97, *97*
chamfers
    dresser top, 26
    red rocket thruster, 94
    soldier
        arms, 156, *157*
        belt, 169
        boots, 178

hands, 181, *181*
head, 192, *192*, 196, *196*
leg strap, 173
torso, 147
changing viewports, 9–10
characters and Character Studio, 141
    associating biped with soldier. *See*
        associating biped with soldier
    materials, 143, *143*
    planes, 142, *142*
    soldier animation. *See* soldier
        character
    workflow, 255–257, *256–257*
Checker Map settings, 232
chest of drawers. *See* Dresser project
child objects in knife animation,
    137–139, *138–139*
Child Overlap option, 272
child rocket model. *See* Red Rocket
    model
Choose Renderer dialog box, 316, *316*,
    341–342, *342*
chrome ball, 363, *363*
clavicles for biped, 263–264, *263*
clipping planes for cameras, 321, *322*
Clone Options dialog box
    dresser knobs, 47, *48*
    red rocket
        planes, 142, *142*
        thruster, 95
Collapse option for pelvis, 162
Collapse Stack option, 81
collision detection, 284
color
    base, 205–206
    dresser, 42, *42*
    footsteps, 278
    materials, 202, 206, *206*, 218
    photometric lights, 355, 357
    refraction, 327
    soldier, 248–249, *249*
    specular maps, 253
Color Selector dialog box, 202
Command panel, 13–14
    modifier stacks, 14, *15*
    object parameters and values, 14
    objects and subobjects, 15
    tabs, 3
Common Parameters rollout, 365, *365*
Common tab, 311–313, *312*, 341
Compact Material Editor, 202–203, *203*
    MSO materials, 205, 208
    shaders, 204, *204*
    standard material, 203
Compression Settings dialog box
    bouncing ball, 317, *317*
    red rocket rendering, 339
computer-generated (CG)
    characters, 165
Connect Edge Segments setting, 156
Connect Edges caddy, 30, *31*
Connect tool for dresser drawers, 30, *30*
control panel for red rocket
    creating, 69–75, *69–75*
    materials, 221–222

Controller window, 121–123
Convert To Editable Spline option, 92
Convert To Poly option
    dresser, 22, *23*
    red rocket
        body, 57, *57*
        wheel, 97
    soldier torso, 144
coordinates and Coordinates rollout
    bipeds, 260, *260*
    coordinate display area, 3
    red rocket
        body, 219, *219*
        fins mapping, 211–216,
            212, 214–216
        rendering, 336, *336*
    viewport, 9
Copy/Paste rollout, 262
Copy Posture button, 262
Copy Shape dialog box, 106
copying
    dresser knobs, 47–48, *48*
    keyframes, 113, *113*
    keys, 280, *280*
    loft shape, 106–108, *107*
Create Footsteps (Append) option, 283
Create Footsteps (At Current Frame)
    option, 283
Create Key dialog box, 16
Create Keys For Inactive Footsteps
    option, 267, *268*, 276–277
Create Multiple Footsteps dialog box,
    266–267, *266*, 276–277
Create panel, 14
Creation method rollout, 44
cross-sections for lofts, 105
crossing boxes technique, 52
Crowd system, 255
crown for dresser top, 23–24, *24–25*
curve vertices, 44
curves and Curve editor
    animation
        knife throwing,
            130–138, *131–137*
        moving ball forward,
            123–124, *123–124*
        reading, 116–117, *116–117*
        refining, 118–120, *118–120*
        roll, 124, *125*
        squash and stretch,
            120–121, *120–121*
        timing, 121–122, *121*
        trajectory, 132–133, *132*
        XForm modifier, 125–127, *127*
    profile, 44, *44–45*
Custom User Interface dialog box, 258
Cut tool for soldier
    armhole, 150, *150*
    face, 194, *195*
    head, 192, *193*
    legs, 158, *159*
cycles, animation
    curves, 113–115, *114–115*
    walk, 266–270, *267–269*

cylinders
soldier
boots, 176
neckline, 186–187, *187*
subtracting, 83–84, *84*
wheel object, 208

D

D65 Illuminant (Reference White)
setting, 355
da Vinci pose, 255, *256*
Daylight Parameters rollout, 359
Daylight System, 358–362, *358–362*
Daylight System Creation warning,
358, *358*
decal for red rocket fins, 215, *215*
adding, 213
flipping, **218–219**
defaults
biped, **256–257**, *257*
lighting, **290**
delta wings, 78, *78*
Density setting for volume lights, 309
dents, lighting, 250
details for red rocket
body, **62–64**, *63–64*
handlebars, **105–109**, *106–109*
thruster, **91–95**, *92–96*
Diffuse Bounces setting, 346, *346*
diffuse color
materials, 202, 206
red rocket, 349, 351
reflections, 324
Diffuse Color input socket, 231, *231*
Dimming setting, 356
Direct3D driver mode, 8
Directional Parameters rollout, 294
Display panel, 14
displaying objects, 8–10, *9*
Distribution (Photometric Web) rollout,
353, *353*
dollies, 321
Dolly Camera tool, 332, *332*
Dope Sheet, 114, **282–287**, *285–287*
Draft setting for Final Gather, 344, *345*
Draft Mode (No Precalculations)
setting, 347
drawers for dresser, 28–33, *28–33*
Dresser project, 16, **19**
bottom, 33–42, *34–42*
drawers, **28–33**, *28–33*
exercises, 49
knobs, 42–48, *43–48*
reference photos, 20, *20*
summary, 49
top, 21–27, *21–27*

E

ease-in and ease-out in animation,
116, *116–117*
Edge Bridge tool, 171, *171*
Edge Chamfer setting, 156

Edged Faces mode, 21
edges and edge loops, 63, *63*
dresser
drawers, 30, *30–31*
top, 26–27, *26–27*
red rocket
body, 62–63, *63*, 81, *81*
control panel, 69, *70*
soldier
armhole, 150–154, *151*, *153–154*
arms, 155–157, *155–157*
belt, 169
body, 166–168, *167*
boots, 176–178, *176–178*
face, 194, *194*
groin area, 163, *163*
hands, 180–182, *181*
head, 188–193, *188*, *190–193*,
196, *196–197*
leg strap, 173
legs, 158–161, *158–161*
neckline, 187
pelvis, 163
pouch, 171, *171*
torso, 144, 146–149, *146–150*
waist, 163
wrists, *157*, 158
UV unwrapping, 226–228
Edit UVs rollout, 242
Edit UVWs dialog box for soldier
arm pelt, 234–235, *234*
body, 242, 244–246, *244–245*
editable-poly modeling, 19
editable splines
conversions to, 92, *93*
dresser bottom, 38, *39*
editing
animation curves, **118–119**, *119–120*
profiles, 46–47, *46–47*
elbows of soldier, 156
enabling mental ray renderer,
341–342, *342*
envelopes, biped, **270–272**, *271*
Environment And Effects dialog box
exposure control, 354, *354*, 361, *361*
HDRIs, 366
volume lights, 308, *308*
environment effects in rendering,
337–338, *337–338*
environment maps, 363, 365, 368
Esparza, Federico, 365
Exclude/Include window, 306, *306*
excluding objects from lights,
306, *306–307*
Exit Isolation Mode icon, 63
Expand Face Selection To Seams icon,
233, 242
Exponential setting, 308
Exposure Value (EV)
Daylight System, 361
photometric lights, 354
exposures and Exposure Controls
Daylight System, 362, *362*
HDRIs, 363, *364*
photometric lights, 353, *354*

Extended Parameters rollout, 327, *327*,
330, *331*
Extrude Polygons caddy, 8, *8*
dresser bottom, 35, *35*
red rocket wheel wells, 65, *65*
extrusions
dresser
bottom, 35–36, *35–36*
drawers, 33, *33*
red rocket
back wheel axle assembly,
76–77, *77–78*
control panel, 71
thruster, 94–95
wheel wells, 65–66, *65*
soldier
arms, 154
belt, 169–170, *170*
body, 167
boots, 176–177, *176*
face, 194, *195*
hands, 182
head, 188–191, *188–191*
leg strap, 173
legs, 158–160, *162*
neckline, 187, *187*

F

face for soldier, **194**, *194–195*
face mask for soldier
merging, 198
seams, 238, *238*
falloff
red rocket body, 58, *58*
target direct lights, 293, *294*
target spotlights, 293, 299
feet for biped, 261, 270–271, *270–271*
FG (Final Gather), 344
Advanced settings, **346–347**
Basic settings, **344–346**, *345–346*
bounces, 361–362, *362*
lighting, 356
field of view (FOV), 319
Figure mode, 259, *259*
file management, 16
projects, 16–17, *17*
versions, 17–18
filenames in rendering, **313–314**, *314*
fill lights, 290, *290*, 299–300, *300*
fillets
dresser bottom, 38, *39*
red rocket handlebars, 101
Final Gather (FG), 344
Advanced settings, **346–347**
Basic settings, **344–346**, *345–346*
bounces, 361–362, *362*
lighting, 356
Final Gather rollout, 344, *345*
fingers
biped, 264, *264*
soldier, 280, *281*
fins for red rocket, **211–216**,
212, *214–216*
fish-eye camera lens, 363

flat objects, 208–209, *208–209*
flipping red rocket
    body, 61
    decal, **218–219**
floors, 335–336
Flow Connect option, 149, *149–150*
focal length, cameras, 319
fog light
    adding, **307–308**, *307–308*
    creating, **304–305**, *304–305*
    parameters, **308–309**
    in red rocket rendering, 338, *338*
folders, 16
follow-through in knife animation,
    136–137, *137*
Footstep Creation rollout, 266, *266*,
    276, 283
Footstep mode, 266
Footstep Operations rollout, 276, 284
footsteps
    biped, **266–270**, *266–269*
    Dope Sheet, **284–286**, *285–286*
    footstep-driven animation, 275–276
    numbering and color-coding, 278
    soldier, **283–284**, *283*
forearms
    biped, 264
    soldier, **228**, *229*
four-viewport layout, 4–5, *4*
FOV (field of view), 319
frames in time slider, 112
free cameras, 318–319
free direct lights, **294–295**, *295*
free spotlights, **294–295**, *295*
freeform animation, 276
    motion sequence, **281–282**, *282*
    soldier
        adding, **277–278**
        arms, **280–281**, *281*
        head, **278–280**, *278–280*
front view, 4, 53, *54*
frozen objects, 258

G

General Parameters rollout
    excluding objects, 306
    freespot and direct lights, 295
    omni lights, 296
    photometric lights, 353
    shadows, 305
Generate Mapping Coords option, 211
Geometry (All) tab, 82
Geometry rollout, 38, 41
GeoPoly tool for soldier
    armhole, **151**, *151*
    legs, 160
GI (global illumination), 344
gizmos, **11–12**, *12*
Glass object, 306
global illumination (GI), 344
Glossiness setting
    MSO materials, 206
    red rocket, 350

Glossy Samples setting, 350
gloves for soldier
    creating, **180–183**, *180–183*
    UV unwrapping, 230, *230*
goggles for soldier
    merging, 198
    seams, 238, *238*
Graphite Modeling Tools ribbon, 2, *2*,
    13, *13*
gravity in animation, 118
green keys on timeline, 113
groin area for soldier, 159, *160*, 162, *163*
grooves for handlebars, 108, *108*
gross animation, 112
gun holster leg strap, **173–174**, *174–175*

H

handlebars for red rocket, **100–101**, *100*
    detail, **105–109**, *106–109*
    paths for, 101, *102*
    shapes for, 102, *103–104*
handles for keyframes, 118, *118*
hands
    biped, 264
    soldier
        animating, 280, *281*
        creating, **180–183**, *180–183*
hardwood floors, 335
HDRI Load Settings box, 366, *366*
HDRIs (high-dynamic range images),
    363–368, *363–369*
head
    biped, **264–265**, *265*
    soldier, 185
        accessories, **198–200**, *199–200*
        animating, **278–280**, *278–280*
        back of, **196**, *196–197*
        creating, **185–187**, *186–187*
        face rounding out, **194**, *194–195*
        mirroring, 198
        outlining, **188–193**, *188–193*
        pelting, **236–240**, *237–240*
        seams, 238, *238*
height of bipeds, 259, *259*
helmet for soldier
    merging, 198
    seams, 237–238, *237*
    straps, 238, *239*
Hide Attached Nodes option, 270
Hide Selection option, 91
Hide Unselected option, 237–239
Hierarchy panel, 14
high-dynamic range images (HDRIs),
    363–368, *363–369*
high-poly modeling, 141
highlight color in specular maps, 253
holster leg strap, **173–174**, *174–175*
Home Grid, 9
hotspots
    target direct lights, 293, *294*
    target spotlights, 291, *292*, 299

I

Ignore Backfacing option
    red rocket body, 217, *217*
    soldier armhole, 152
Image Aspect Ratio setting, **313**
image-plane boxes, **52–55**, *52–55*
In Place Mode button, **268–269**, *268*
indents for red rocket thruster,
    94–95, *96*
index of refraction (IOR) setting,
    327–330, *329*
indirect lighting, 341, 344
InfoCenter, 3
Initial FG Point Density setting, 345
inner bounds for envelopes, 272
Input Sockets, **231**, *231*
Insert Keys icon, 122
insets and Inset caddy for dresser
    bottom, **35–36**, *36*
    drawers, 29, *29*, **31–32**, *31–32*
Instance (Copy) dialog box, 366
instances
    dresser knobs, 48
    mirroring, 166, 168, *168*
Intensity/Color/Attenuation rollout
    HDRIs, 368
    omni lights, 300
    photometric lights, **354–356**, *355*
    spotlights, 298
intensity of photometric lights,
    356–357, *357*
intent in animation, 120
interface. *See* user interface
Interpolate Over Num. FG Points
    setting, 346
interpolation
    FG points, 346
    step, 117, *117*
IOR (index of refraction) setting,
    327–330, *329*
Isolate Selection option, 63

J

jumps for soldier
    Dope Sheet, **284–287**, *285–287*
    run-and-jump sequence,
        276–277, *277*

K

Key Editing window, 119
Key Entry tools, 121
key lights, **289–290**, *290*, 295
Key pane in Dope Sheet, 285
Keyboard Entry rollout, 21, *21*, 53, *53*
keyboard shortcuts, 9–10
keyframes and keyframing, 16, **111–112**
    copying, **113**, *113*
    handles, 118, *118*

keys, animation
  copying, 280, *280*
  creating, 276–277
  deleting, 279, *279*
  editing, 277–278, *278*
knee of soldier, 160
knife throwing animation, **129**
  anticipation, **135–136**, *135–136*
  blocking out, **129–131**, *130–131*
  follow-through, **136–137**, *137*
  momentum, **137**
  parent and child objects,
    137–139, *138–139*
  rotation, **133–135**, *133–134*, 137
  trajectories, **132–133**, *132*
knobs, dresser, 42–48, *43–48*
knuckles for soldier, 182

L

lathes
  knobs, 42, 46–47, *47*
  red rocket thruster, 87–91, *88–90*
layering animation, 123
left view, 4
leg strap for soldier, 173–174, *174–175*
legs
  biped, 260–262, 270
  dresser bottom, 36
  soldier, 158–162, *158–162*
lenses
  camera, 319, *319*
  HDRIs, 363
  zooming, 321
Light Lister, 309–310, *309*
light probes, 363
lighting, **289**
  bumps and dents, 250
  default, **290**
  photometric, **290**, 351–357,
    353–355, *357*
  red rocket. *See* Red Rocket model
  standard. *See* standard lights
  three-point, 289–290, *290*
line segments, 46
Line tool
  dresser knobs, 43–45
  red rocket thruster, 88
lips
  dresser
    bottom, 36, *37*
    top, 23, *23*
  red rocket body, 81, *81*
live areas, 323
lm (lumen) metric, 356
loading MSO materials, 207–208
lofts for red rocket handlebars
  cross-sections for, 105
  detail, 105–109, *106–109*
  paths for, **101**, *102*
  shapes for, 102, *103–104*
  splines for, 105

loops
  animation, 113–115, *114–115*
  edges. *See* edges and edge loops
Loops tab, 30, *30*
low-poly modeling, 141
lumen (lm) metric, 356
lux (lx at) metric, 356

M

Main toolbar, 2, *2*
Make New Folder option, 17
Make Unique icon, 168
Map Parameters rollout, 227
Map Seams option, 226, *226*
maps and mapping
  bump
    soldier, 249–252, *250–252*
    wheel object, **211**
  color, 248–249, *249*
  coordinates, 211–216, *212*, *214–216*
  environment, 363, 365, 368
  HDRIs, 366, *366*
  pelt, 234–235, *234*, 240
  raytrace, 325–326, *326*,
    329–330, *330–331*
  red rocket. *See* materials and
    Material Editor
  shadows, 302
  specular, 253, *253–254*
Maps rollout
  bump maps, 211
  materials, 218
  reflections, 209, *209*
Mask Parameters rollout, 336
Material/Map Browser, 232, *232*
Material Parameter Editor, 349
materials and Material Editor, 202
  character modeling, 143, *143*
  Compact Material Editor,
    202–208, *203–204*
  creating, 218
  fine-tuning, 208–210, *208–210*
  mental ray, 348–351, *348–350*, *352*
  MSO. *See* Multi/Sub-Object (MSO)
    materials
  overview, 201–202
  red rocket, 204
    body, 216–220, *217*, *219–221*
    control panel, 221–222
    fins, 211–216, *212*, *214–216*
    nose, 222–223, *223*
    raytrace. *See* raytrace material
    seat, 223
    wheels, 205–211, *205–210*
  textures. *See* textures
Max. Reflections setting, 347
Max. Refractions setting, 347
Maximize Viewport Toggle icon, 10
maximizing viewports, 9–10
Maximum Samples Per Pixel
  setting, 342–343

mental ray renderer
  Daylight System, 358–362, *358–362*
  enabling, 341–342, *342*
  Final Gather. *See* Final Gather (FG)
  materials, 348–351, *348–350*, *352*
  photometric lights, 351–357,
    353–355, *357*
  Rendered Frame Window,
    347–348, *347*
  sampling quality, 342–343, *343*
Menu bar, 3
menus, quad, 5–7, *7*
merging and Merge dialog box
  red rocket into scene, 85, 223
  soldier head accessories,
    198–199, *199*
Mini Curve Editor, 119–121
Minimum Samples Per Pixel
  setting, 342–343
Mirror dialog box, 166, *167*
Mirror tool, 165–166
mirroring
  red rocket body, 61
  soldier
    body, 166–168, *167–168*
    head, **198**
    neckline, 186
  mitten hands for soldier,
    180–183, *180–183*
Modes And Display rollout, 268
modifier stacks, 14, *15*
Modify panel, 14
Modify tab for dresser bottom, 38
momentum in knife animation, **137**
Motion panel, 14
mouse buttons, 6, *6*
MOV QuickTime files
  bouncing ball, 316–317
  red rocket rendering, 339
Move gizmo, 11, *12*
Move tool
  red rocket wheel wells, 66, *66*
  UVW mapping, 215
Move Keys tool, 135
Move Keys Horizontal tool, 121,
  131, 133–134
Move Keys Vertical tool, 138
moving. *See also* animation
  clavicles, 264
  pivot points, 165, *166*
mr Area Spot option, 367–368, *368*
mr Photographic Exposure Control,
  352–354, 361, *361*
mr Physical Sky map, 359, *359–360*
mr Sky Portal menu, 359, *360*
Multi/Sub-Object (MSO) materials, 351
  creating, 205–206, *206*
  loading, 207–208
  polygons for, 206–207, *207*
Multiplier setting for target
  spotlights, 298

N

names
   dresser, 42, *42*
   in rendering, 313–314, *314*
navigating viewports, 10–11
neck
   biped, 264–265, *265*
   soldier, 167–168, *167*,
      185–187, *186–187*
New Scene dialog box, 21
NGons, 151, *152*
noise
   coordinates, 211
   Final Gather, 346–347
   red rocket control panel, 221
   volume lights, 309
Noise Filtering (Speckle Reduction)
   setting, 346–347
Noise Parameters rollout, 221
nonuniform rational mesh smooth
   (NURMS) surfaces for red rocket
   back wheel axle assembly, 76, 78
   body, 61, *62*, 80
   control panel, 74–75, *74–75*
   wheel wells, 66, *67*, 69
normal maps, 250–252, *251–252*
nose material for red rocket,
   222–223, *223*
numbering footsteps, 278

O

objects
   Command panel, 14–15
   displaying, 8–10, *9*
   excluding from lights, 306, *306–307*
   frozen, 258
   selecting, 9
omni lights
   characteristics, 296, *296–297*
   red rocket, 299–300, *300*
Open Mini Curve Editor option, 119, *119*
Options settings in rendering, 313
Orbit tool
   red rocket, 55
   soldier, 162–163
   viewports, 11
Orbit Camera tool, 333
organic modeling, 141
Out-of-Range Types option, 114
outer bounds of envelopes, 272
outlining soldier head,
   188–193, *188–193*
Output Size settings, 313, 338
outputting red rocket render, 338–339

P

panning viewports, 11
Parameter Curve Out-of-Range Types,
   114, *115*, 121, 124
Parameter Editor, 232, *232*

parameters and Parameters rollout
   bump maps, 251
   Command panel, 14
   materials and maps, 232, *232*
   red rocket seat, 83, *83*
parent objects, 137–139, *138–139*
Parent Overlap option, 272
Path Steps setting, 106, *106*
paths for red rocket handlebars, 101, *102*
Peel rollout, 233, 237
Pelt Map dialog box, 234–235, *234*
pelting soldier
   arm UVs, 233–235, *234–236*
   head, 236–240, *237–240*
pelvis
   biped, 260, *261*
   soldier, 162, *163*
Perspective viewport, 4
   cameras in, 318, *318*
   red rocket
      body, 56, *56*
      thruster, 90
   soldier torso, 144
Phase setting for volume lights, 309
photometric lights
   description, 290
   mental ray renderings, 351–357,
      353–355, 357
Physique Initialization dialog box, 266
Physique Level Of Detail
   rollout, 270–271
Physique modifier, 255–256, 265–268,
   266–268, 271
Pick Boolean rollout
   dresser bottom, 41
   red rocket thruster, 95
Pick Object dialog box, 266
pivot points
   description, 126
   moving, 165, *166*
planes in character modeling, 142, *142*
Play Animation button, 267–269, 276
Point To Point Seam tool for soldier
   body, 240
   helmet, 237
   UV unwrapping, 227–230, *227*
points in Final Gather, 345
Polygon Modeling tab, 13, 22, 57–58
Polygon subobject mode, 65–67, *65*
polygons
   extruded. *See* extrusions
   for MSO materials, 206–207, *207*
Position keyframes, 113
postures for biped, 262–263, *263*
pouch for soldier, 170–172, *171–172*
precision in Final Gather, 344
ProBoolean operations
   dresser bottom, 36, 40–41, *40*
   red rocket
      seat, 83–84
      thruster, 94–95
profiles
   curves, 44, *44–45*
   editing, 46–47, *46–47*

red rocket
   handlebars, 102, *103–104*
   thruster, 88–89, *89*
projects, setting, 16–17, *17*
prompt line, 3

Q

quad menus, 5–7, *7*
quality setting in rendering, 339,
   342–343, *343*
Quick Access toolbar, 1–3
QuickTime files
   bouncing ball, 316–317
   red rocket rendering, 339

R

radial scale for bipeds, 271–272
Range setting in rendering, 313
Ray Bias setting, 303
Ray Traced Shadow Params rollout, 303
Rays Per FG Point setting, 346
Raytrace Basic Parameters rollout,
   323, 327
raytrace material, 323–324
   mapping, 325–326, *326*
   reflections, 334–336, *335–336*
   refractions, 326–330, *327–331*
   tweaking, 324–325, *325*
raytraced shadows, 303, *303*
Raytracer Global Parameters rollout,
   337, *337*
Realistic mode, 9
Recessed 75W Lamp (Web) option, 353
Rectangle tool, 37–38, *37*
Red Bolt material, 207, 209
red boxes on timeline, 113
Red Rocket model, 51
   body
      creating, 55–59, *56–60*
      details, 62–64, *63–64*
      materials, 216–220, *217, 219–221*
      smoothing, 61, *62*
      touching up, 79–82, *79–82*
   control panel
      creating, 69–75, *69–75*
      materials, 221–222
   exercises, 85–86, 110
   handlebars, 100–101, *100*
      detail, 105–109, *106–109*
      paths for, 101, *102*
      shapes for, 102, *103–104*
   image-plane boxes, 52–55, *52–55*
   lighting, 297–301, *297–301*
      excluding objects from,
         306, *306–307*
      Light Lister, 309–310, *309*
      photometric lights, 351–357,
         353–355, 357
      shadows, adding, 305–306
      shadows, types,
         301–303, *302–303*

volumetric lights,
304–305, *304–305*,
307–309, *307–308*
mental ray materials, 348–351,
348–350, *352*
merging into scene, 85, 223
rendering, 331
camera moves,
331–333, *332–333*
environment effects,
337–338, *337–338*
output, 338–339
raytraced reflections,
334–336, *335–336*
seat
creating, 83–84, *83–84*
materials, 223, 350, *350*
summary, 85, 110
thruster, 82, *82*, 87–88, *88*
3D object for, 91–95, *92–96*
lathes for, 88–91, *88–90*
wheels. *See* wheels for red rocket
reference materials, 143, *143*
reference photos, 20, *20*
refining animation, 118–120, *118–120*
reflections
Final Gather, 347
raytrace material, 324–325, *325*
red rocket, 349–350
fins, 213
rendering, 334–336, *335–336*
wheel, 208–210, *209–210*
specular maps, 253
Reflectivity setting, 350
refractions
Final Gather, 347
raytrace mapping,
329–330, *330–331*
raytrace materials,
326–328, *327–329*
Relax By Face Angles option, 235
Relax Tool dialog box, 235, *235*, 242–243
Render Map dialog box, 246
Render Output File dialog box,
313–314, *314*
bouncing ball, 316
red rocket, 339
Render Output folder, 16
Render Output settings, 313
Render Preview dialog box, 354
Rendered Frame window
Daylight System, 361
photometric lights, 356
settings, 314–315, *314*, 347–348, *347*
rendering and Render Setup dialog
box, 311
bouncing ball, 316–317, *317*
cameras, 318–321, *318–320*, *322*
Common settings, 311–313, *312*
filenames, 313–314
Final Gather, 344
mental ray renderer, 341–342
photometric lights, 356
processing, 315, *315*
raytrace material. *See* raytrace
material

red rocket, 331
camera moves,
331–333, *332–333*
environment effects,
337–338, *337–338*
output, 338–339
raytraced reflections,
334–336, *335–336*
Rendered Frame window,
314–315, *314*
renderer assignments, 315–316, *316*
Safe Frame view, 322–323, *322*
Rendering dialog box, 315, *315*
resolution in rendering, 313, 338
Resulting Intensity setting, 356
RGB channels for normal maps, 250
ride-on toy model. *See* Red Rocket model
rigging
associating biped with soldier. *See*
associating biped with soldier
workflow, 255–257, *256–257*
rocket model. *See* Red Rocket model
roll in animation, 124, *125*
rollout, 3
rolls, camera, 321
Rotate gizmo, 12, *12*
rotating
biped clavicles, 264
knife animation, 133–135,
133–134, 137
red rocket
decal, 215
lathe for thruster, 89, *89*
lofts for handlebars,
108–109, *109*
wheel wells, 66, *66*
soldier head, 279–280, *279*
Rotation keyframes, 113
rubber band line, 227–228, *227*
run-and-jump sequence, 276–277, *277*

S

Safe Frame view, 322–323, *322*
Sample Range setting, 302
Sampling Quality rollout, 342–343, *343*
Save As dialog box, 18
Scale gizmo, 12, *12*
Scale keyframes, 113, 121–122
scaling
bipeds
boots, 271–272
clavicles, 264
head, 265, *265*
pelvis, 260, *261*
dresser knobs, 47
red rocket
body, 59, *60*
decal, 215
handlebars, 108
wrist borders, 156
Scanline Renderer, 315
Scenes folder, 16
scrubbing time slider, 112
seams

red rocket
back wheel axle assembly, 77
body, 79–80, *79–80*
soldier
body, 240, *241*
face mask, 238, *238*
goggles, 238, *238*
head, 238, *238*
helmet, 237–238, *237*
helmet straps, 238, *239*
UV unwrapping,
226–231, *227–230*
seat for red rocket
creating, 83–84, *83–84*
materials, 223, 350, *350*
see-through
frozen objects, 258
red rocket body, 56
soldier
pouch, 171, *171*
torso, 144
segments, line, 46
Select And Move tool, 55, 57, 123
Select and Rotate tool, 133
Select Bitmap Image File dialog box,
249, 252
Select From Scene dialog box, 265
Select Image dialog box, 214
selecting
objects, **9**
polygons, 206–207, *207*
Set Project Folder option, 16–17, *17*
Set Tangents To Fast icon, 119
Set Tangents To Linear icon, 124
shaders, 204, *204*
Shadow Map Params rollout, 299, 305
shadows
adding, 305–306
maps, 302
omni lights, 296, **299–301**, *300*
raytraced, **303**, *303*
target spotlights, 298
types, **301–303**, *302–303*
Shape Steps setting, 106
Shape subobject mode, 105
shapes for red rocket handlebars,
102, *103–104*
shininess in specular maps, 253
shoes for soldier, 176–179, *176–179*
shortcuts, keyboard, 9–10
shoulders
biped, 264
soldier
extruding, 167, *167*
UV unwrapping, 227, *227*
Show End Result option, 61, *62*
Show Frozen As Gray option, 258
Show Standard Map In Viewport option,
213, 218, 335
Single Frame setting, 313
size
bipeds, 259, *259*
renders, 313, 338
shadow maps, **302**
volume lights, 309
Skin modifier, 255, 257

Skin Parameters rollout, 106, *106*
skinning, 255, 257, 265–268, *266–268*
Sky Color settings, 367
Skylight parameter, 359
skylights in HDRIs, 367
Slate Material Editor, 202
    HDRIs, 366
    overview, 231–232, *232*
    shaders, 204
    UV unwrapping, 231
Smooth + Highlights mode, 9
smoothing
    red rocket body, 61, *62*
    soldier boots, 178, *179*
Soft Selection, 58–59
Soft tab, 58, *58*
soldier character
    accessories
        belt, 169–170, *170*
        boots, 176–179, *176–179*
        leg strap, 173–174, *174–175*
        pouch, 170–172, *171–172*
        vest, 172
    animating, 275–276
        arms, 280–281, *281*
        Dope Sheet, 282–287
        footsteps, 283–284, *283*
        freeform animation, 277–278
        head, 278–280, *278–280*
        jumps, 284–287, *285–287*
        motion sequence, 281–282, *282*
        run-and-jump sequence,
            276–277, *277*
    armpit area, 172–173, *172–173*
    arms
        animating, 280–281, *281*
        creating, 154–157, *155–157*
        pelting, 233–235, *234–236*
        UV unwrapping, 228, *228*
    biped for
        creating, 258–263, *259–263*
        neck and head, 264–265, *265*
        torso and arms,
            263–264, *263–264*
        tweaking, 270–273, *270–272*
        view, 268–270, *268–269*
    body
        seams, 240, *241*
        unfolding, 241–248, *242–248*
        fixing up, 162–164, *163–164*
        hands, 180–183, *180–183*
        head, 185
            accessories, 198–200, *199–200*
            animating, 278–280, *278–280*
            back of, 196, *196–197*
            creating, 185–187, *186–187*
            face rounding out, 194, *194–195*
            mirroring, 198
            outlining, 188–193, *188–193*
            pelting, 236–240, *237–240*
            seams, 238, *238*
        legs, 158–162, *158–162*
        main body, 165–169, *166–168*
        skinning with Physique modifier,
            265–268, *266–268*

textures
    bump map, 249–252, *250–252*
    color map, 248–249, *249*
    head seams, 240, *241*
    pelting arm UVs,
        233–235, *234–236*
    pelting head, 236–240, *237–240*
    specular map, 253, *253–254*
    unfolding body,
        241–248, *242–248*
    UV unwrapping,
        226–233, *226–233*
    torso, 144–154, *145–154*
sources
    target direct lights, 293, *294*
    target spotlights, 292
Spatial Contrast setting, 342, *343*
specular color, 202
specular highlights, 208, 326, *326*, 328
specular level of materials, 206
specular maps, 253, *253–254*
Sphere material, 336
Spherical Environment setting, 366, *366*
splines
    conversions to, 92, *93*
    dresser knobs, 43–46, *44–45*
    for lofts, 105
Spotlight Parameters rollout, 293, *293*,
    299, 368
spotlights
    characteristics, 291–293, *292–293*
    HDRIs, 368
    red rocket, 298, *298*
squash and stretch animation,
    120–121, *120–121*
standard lights, 290–291
    free spotlights, 294–295, *295*
    omni lights, 296, *296–297*
    target direct lights, 293–294, *294*
    target spotlights, 291–293, *292–293*
Standard Maps rollout, 366
standard material, 203
Start Picking feature, 41, *41*, 95
status bar, 3
step interpolation, 117, *117*
Subdivision Surfaces cage, 74–75, *74*
submenus, 7
suboojects in Command panel, 15
subtraction
    cylinder shape, 83–84, *84*
    dresser bottom, 41
sunlight
    Area Spot lights, 368
    omni lights, 296
    skylights, 367
    Sunlight system, 358–359
SuperSampling rollout, 324–328,
    325, *328*
SwiftLoop tool
    red rocket
        body, 62–63, *63*
        control panel, 69, *70*
    soldier
        arms, 155
        boots, 178, *178*
        hands, 180–181, *181*

leg strap, 173
legs, 161
    torso, 144, 146–149, *146–149*
symmetry and Symmetry modifier for
    red rocket
        body, 61, 79–80
        control panel, 71

T

tangents for curves, 117–119, *117*, *120*,
    124, 127, *127*, 135–138
target cameras, 318
target direct lights, 293–294, *294*
target spotlights
    characteristics, 291–293, *292–293*
    red rocket, 298, *298*
Target Weld for soldier
    face, 194, *195*
    head, 189–191, *190–191*
targets in knife animation,
    137–139, *138–139*
Templates rollout, 352, *353*
testing biped model, 266–268, *266–268*
textures
    red rocket control panel, 221–222
    soldier, 225
        bump map, 249–252, *250–252*
        color map, 248–249, *249*
        head seams, 240, *241*
        pelting arm UVs,
            233–235, *234–236*
        pelting head, 236–240, *237–240*
        specular map, 253, *253–254*
        unfolding body,
            241–248, *242–248*
        UV unwrapping,
            226–233, *226–233*
thighs of soldier, 159–160, *160*
3D object for red rocket thruster,
    91–95, *92–96*
three-point lighting, 289–290, *290*
thruster for red rocket, 82, *82*
    3D object for, 91–95, *92–96*
    creating, 87–88, *88*
    lathes for, 88–91, *88–90*
thumbs for soldier, 182, *182*
Tiling settings, 232, *233*
Time Configuration dialog box, 130, *131*
Time Output settings, 313, 338
Time slider
    description, 3
    knife animation, 130, 135
    scrubbing, 112, *112*
    working with, 15–16
timing in animation, 121–122, *121*
tip of red rocket, 57, *58*
tires for red rocket, 205–211,
    205–210, 351
title safe boundaries, 323
toes for biped, 261–262, *262*, 271, *271*
top of dresser, 21–27, *21–27*
top view
    in four-viewport layout, 4
    red rocket, 53–55

topology dependency warning,
    236–237, *237*
torso
    biped, 263–264, *263–264*
    soldier, 144–154, *145–154*
toy model. *See* Red Rocket model
Track bar, 3, **15–16**
Track Selection rollout, 259, *260*, 282
Track View - Curve Editor. *See* curves
    and Curve editor
Track View - Dope Sheet,
    282–287, *285–287*
trajectories for knife animation,
    132–133, *132*
transforming objects with gizmos,
    11–12, *12*
transparency in refraction, 330, *331*
Truck Camera tool, 332–333
trucks, 321
TV screens safe areas, 322, *322*

U

U Tiling setting, 232, *233*
underarms for soldier, 228, *228*
Undo option, 135
Undo Scene Operation icon, 2
unfolding soldier body,
    241–248, *242–248*
Unhide By Name option, 91
Unhide Objects dialog box, 91, *92*, 270
Uniformity setting, 309
unwrapping
    soldier
        arm, 233–235, *234–236*
        head, 236–240, *237–240*
    UV, 226–233, *226–233*
Use NURMS icon, 61
Use Scene Environment option, 367
Use Scene Material, 199
Use Soft Selection icon, 58–59, *58*
user interface
    caddies, 8, *8*
    Command panel, 13–15, *15*
    elements, 1–4, *2*
    exercises, 18
    file management, 16–18
    Graphite Modeling Tools ribbon,
        13, *13*
    mouse buttons, 6, *6*
    quad menus, 6–7, *7*
    summary, 18
    time slider and track bar, **15–16**
    ViewCube, 5–6, *5*
    viewports, 4–5, *4*
        gizmos, 11–12, *12*
        navigating, 10–11
        object display in, 8–10
Utilities panel, 14
UV workflow, **225**
UVs. *See also* textures
    soldier
        arm, 233–235, *234–236*
        head, 236–240, *237–240*
        unwrapping, 226–233, *226–233*

UVW Mapping modifier
    red rocket
        body, 219–220, *220*
        control panel, 222
        fins, 213–216, *214–216*
        rendering, 336
    soldier head accessories, 199

V

V Tiling setting, 232, *233*
values in Command panel, 14
versions, file, 17–18
vertical fins for red rocket, 211–216,
    212, *214–216*
vertices and Vertex mode
    dresser
        bottom, 38, *39*
        knobs, 43–46, *45*
    red rocket
        back wheel axle assembly, 77
        body, 59, *60*, 80, *80*
        control panel, 70–72, *71–74*
        detail, 64, *64*
        handlebars, 101–102
        thruster, 94, *94*
        tip, 57, *58*
        wheel wells, 66
        wheels, 97–99, *98*
    soldier
        armhole, 150–151, *150*, *153–154*
        armpit area, 173
        arms, 155, 157
        body, 166–169, *167*
        boots, 178
        face, 194, *195*
        hands, 180, *180*
        head, 189, 193, 196–198, *197*
        legs, 159–161, *162*
        pelvis, 162
        torso, 144, *145*, 147, *148*
        wrists, 157
    splines, 43
vest for soldier, 172
ViewCube control, 5–6, *5*
Viewport Configuration dialog box, 4
viewports, 3–5, *4*
    bipeds, 268–270, *268–269*
    navigating, 3, 10–11
    object display in, 8–10, *9*
volumetric lights
    adding, 307–308, *307–308*
    creating, 304–305, *304–305*
    parameters, 308–309
    in rendering, 338, *338*

W

waist edges for soldier, 163
walk cycle, 266–270, *266–269*
weight in animation
    bouncing ball, 120
    knife animation, 135–137, *137*, 139
Weld Core option, 46

Weld Vertices caddy, 157, *157*, 169
welds for soldier
    body, 169
    boots, 177–178, *177*
    face, 194, *195*
    head, 189–191, *190–191*, 193, 198
    legs, 162
    wrists, 157, *157*
Wheel Black material, 211
Wheel White material, 207
wheels for red rocket, 96, *96*
    back wheel axle assembly,
        76–78, *76–79*
    bump maps, 211
    creating, 97–99, *97–99*
    materials, 205–211, *205–210*
    mental ray, 351
    placing, 99, *100*
    reflections, 208–210, *209–210*
    wheel wells, 64–69, *64–69*
wineglass, 328–330, *328–330*
Wireframe mode, 9, *9*
wobble in knife animation, 138
workflow in Character Studio,
    255–257, *256–257*
workspace, **1**
    Command panel, 13–15, *15*
    file management, 16–18, *17*
    Graphite Modeling Tools ribbon,
        13, *13*
    interface. *See* user interface
    time slider an track bar, **15–16**
wrists for soldier
    borders, 156–157
    hands, 181, *181*, 183
    UV unwrapping, 228–230, *229*

X

X Position in animation, 123–124, *124*,
    126, 134
X-Ray mode, 168, *168*
X Rotation track, 137
XForm modifier, 125–127, *127*
XY-axis, 59, *59*

Y

Y Position in animation, 123–124,
    126, 134
Y Rotation track, 138

Z

Z Position in animation, 126, 134
Z Position track, 119
zooming
    footsteps, 267, *267*, 284, *285*
    Key Editing window, 119
    lenses, 321
    for selections, 91
    viewports, 11
    wheel for, *6*

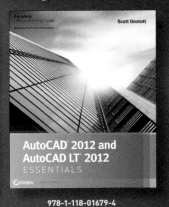